IDIOTS Revisited

IAN BROWNE

Foreword by
David Ortiz

Memere,
Enjoy. Go 'Sox!.
Ian Browne

TILBURY HOUSE
PUBLISHERS

THOMASTON, MAINE

Tilbury House, Publishers
12 Starr St.
Thomaston, ME 04861
800-582-1899 · www.tilburyhouse.com

Design by Lynda Chilton
www.booksdesigned.com

ISBN: 978-0-88448-384-7
First edition: May 2014
10 9 8 7 6 5 4 3 2 1

eBook: ISBN 978-0-88448-385-4

Library of Congress Cataloging-in-Publication Data

Browne, Ian, 1971-
  Idiots revisited : catching up with the players who changed Red Sox history / by Ian Browne. -- First edition.
      p. cm.
    ISBN 978-0-88448-384-7 (pbk. : alk. paper) -- ISBN 978-0-88448-385-4 (ebook) -- ISBN 978-0-88448-386-1 (enhanced ebook)
    1. Boston Red Sox (Baseball team)--History. 2. Boston Red Sox (Baseball team)--Biography. 3. Baseball players--Massachusetts--Boston--Biography. I. Title.
  GV875.B62B75 2014
  796.357'640974461--dc23
                                              2014001429

To my wife Amy, the best
person I know. I could
not ask for a better
friend or wife.
And our three boys
could not have a better
mother. Thanks for
being you.

CONTENTS

Foreword

by David Ortiz

Y ou know what I remember most when we went down three games to none against the Yankees in 2004? The sad faces. I was in my second year with Boston then, but I had already fallen in love with that city. Those were my people and I hated to see them hurt.We might have called ourselves "idiots," but you can never forget the character of that team, and that had a lot to do with us winning. Every night, someone had something to bring to the table. What a team to play for. What a bunch of winning players. And we had the perfect manager. Tito was unbelievable. I guarantee you that every single guy wanted to be part of his ballclub.

But even with all that, we were one game—and then one inning— from being swept by the Yankees. We were working on eighty-six years without a World Series and the reputation that we couldn't beat the Yankees when it counted. But everyone on that team felt like we could beat them—we felt it was just a matter of time.

Game Four set everything up. Dave Roberts stole the base. Billy Mueller drove him in by getting a game-tying hit off the great Mariano Rivera. In the twelfth inning, we were still playing and I got the chance to win it. What a good feeling. I remember that I faced Paul Quantrill for that at-bat. He had a good front-door, two-seam fastball that would ride in on me and would switch directions, and he had gotten me out on it before. I was ready. I was saying to myself, "Here we go again." Even a decade later, I remember the whole thing so well.

Once I hit that ball and saw it going over the fence, I was so happy because I knew we were going to get another opportunity. Nobody was crying anymore; the crowd was going crazy. We were still down three games to one, but everything felt different.

Sure enough, the next day—this time in the fourteenth inning—here I was again, with another chance to win the game. This time I could send the series back to New York, which was the last thing the Yankees wanted. I was facing Esteban Loaiza. Once I got to two strikes, I didn't try to do anything crazy, and that's how I got that knock that kept us going to the next day. Johnny Damon raced around from second, and we got to play another day.

Once we got to New York, we couldn't be stopped and took the last two games there and got to the World Series. To be the first team to come back from three to nothing was just unbelievable.

We didn't let up after that. In the Cardinals, we faced another monster team. But after we beat the Yankees, everybody got locked in. Everybody did something in that World Series. Even in the first game when the Cardinals scored nine runs, we still beat them. That's crazy.

It just shows you how free we all felt after finally beating the Yankees. It wasn't as if someone had to be a superhero for that World Series, because everybody came through. It was the whole group.

I've been lucky enough to win two more World Series since then, but the first one helped to set everything up. Everything with this organization is different now. The winning has changed the whole culture and it all started in 2004.

This is a fun story to re-live and I'm glad that Ian Browne is telling it. He has covered my entire career in Boston and knows the ins and outs of our ballclub as well as anyone.

Introduction

t was a couple of hours before Game 2 of the 2013 World Series when some old friends reunited in an interview room at Fenway Park. Pedro Martinez, wearing a leather coat and an impish grin, was flanked by Derek Lowe and Trot Nixon. It had been nine years since those three men had won a World Series together, but the excitement and camaraderie never seems to subside. Put any combination of 2004 "Idiots" together and they are bound to create a sense of electricity in the room. Martinez couldn't seem to contain his enthusiasm, nor did he try. The man regarded by many as the greatest pitcher in Red Sox history announced theatrically to the seated reporters, "It's gonna get interesting. You guys ready for this?" For the next 15 minutes or so, they swapped remembrances and stories and perspective, and it could have gone on all night if only for the fact there was a more current event on the docket—a World Series game between the Red Sox and Cardinals.

The reason for their return to Boston on this occasion was to participate in a first-pitch ceremony. As part of their opening remarks, Lowe and Nixon both reiterated that they weren't there to steal thunder. "I know this is the current team's moment," Lowe said before completing the rest of his thought. "These guys, it's their moment, like Derek said," said Nixon.

Why did they have to keep reminding everyone? Well, the answer to that is easy. No matter how self-effacing they try to be, it will be hard—if not impossible—for any subsequent baseball champion from Boston to top what the Red Sox did in 2004. Combine the unprecedented and still unmatched accomplishment (coming back from a 3-0 deficit in a postseason series) with the time between championships (eighty-six years) and the characters who pulled off the feat and it's hard to imagine what it will take. For some, the historical achievements take a while to soak in. But Curt Schilling, the man who lit up everybody's Thanksgiving weekend in New England back in 2003 by agreeing to a trade to the Red Sox, grasped it immediately.

"I made these T-shirts, I made twenty-five T-shirts after the World Series," Schilling said from his home in Medfield, Massachusetts, in November 2013. "And on the front, it said 'I am' and on the back, it said 'one of the twenty-five.' And they had our names on them, and the only twenty-five people in the world that got them were the twenty-five players."

Yes, only twenty-five players, one manager, one coaching staff, one front office, and one ownership group can ever say they were on the ground floor when the Red Sox finally won it all again. And when the players from the history-making team got off their duck boats at the end of the most joyous championship parade in the history of Boston sports, there was a tinge of sadness. That team would never play a game together again, at least not all twenty-five of them.

"Some guys, I still haven't seen to this day," said Lowe in June 2013. "You go from such a close-knit group to getting off the float, and you shake hands and off you go." But when paths crossed during the ensuing years, the bittersweet aspect of the equation became sweet again. Martinez was the first to realize that the parade actually didn't end on October 30, 2004, even if he thought it had at the time.

"The parade never goes away from my mind," Martinez said. "In fact, it has continued on. Every time I come in to Boston, people receive me like it's just another day for the parade. Everybody goes back to parade mode and it's like 'Yeahhhhhh.' "

The 2013 Red Sox would have their own parade, just nine days after the players from the 2004 team held court prior to Game 2 of the World Series. And, much like the '04 team, the 2013 squad captured the heart of the city with their personalities and their perseverance. But before the bearded wonders came along in 2013 and recaptured the collective baseball heart of New England, there was a transcendent group of self-proclaimed "Idiots" who gained a magnitude and stature that might never be equaled in a baseball-crazed region.

For all the similarities between the 2004 Red Sox and their scrappy successors of 2013, there are considerable differences. Back in 2004, angst was the buzzword in the Boston baseball scene. The beloved Old Towne Team hadn't won a World Series in eighty-six years! Not only that, but they came up with every type of way to come close to and fall short of the ultimate prize. When the 2013 Red Sox showed up for Spring Training, they too, were surrounded by negativity, but they were simply trying to answer for a last-place finish the season before and a collapse of epic proportions in September 2011. The Red Sox had won a World Series in 2007, so it wasn't as though the city had been deprived of a fairly recent celebration.

The vibe in 2004 was much different, and more intense. That year, they were not only answering for the collapse that took place in Game 7 of 2003 at Yankee Stadium, but also for eight-and-a-half decades of the Red Sox failing to bring home a World Series winner. There was an edginess that came with playing for the Red Sox back in those days. Or at least there should have been.

Perhaps more recent Red Sox editions cared too much about the pratfalls of history. In 2003, as a pennant slipped away in Game 7 at Yankee Stadium, manager Grady Little would later admit that he heard players in the dugout mentioning that they didn't want to become the next "Bill Buckner." The 2003 team was a pretty carefree bunch in its own right, with their Cowboy Up mantra, but they ultimately succumbed in the biggest moment, and Little—fairly or not—was the one portrayed as "the next Bill Buckner" for leaving future Hall of Fame ace Pedro Martinez in past his boiling point.

By 2004, clubhouse ringleaders like Kevin Millar and Johnny Damon finally got their wish. They had a team that acted oblivious on the subject of history. Maybe they could tell you about the Boston Tea Party or the Battle of Bunker Hill or the Revolutionary War, but Bill Buckner or Bucky Dent or Mike Torrez or even Aaron Boone the year before? The '04 Sox tuned all that stuff out. Not only that, but they'd mock anyone who asked about it. Because it's been a decade, perhaps a refresher is needed on why this legendary team was referred to as, yes, the Idiots.

"Everyone calls themselves an idiot every now and then but the whole ['Idiot'] thing was just saying that we didn't care what happened to these teams of the past," said Damon, who coined the Idiot moniker that spread like wildfire.

As a short-haired, mostly clean-shaven Damon sat on the patio of a nearly empty golf club near Orlando, Florida, in the fall of 2013, he realized that the Idiot mantra on that team was actually pure genius, and the perfect way to diffuse all the pressure they should have felt.

"We were our own team," said Damon. "We had our own identity. People kept talking about the Curse of the Bambino. Well, shit, we weren't even around. Why do we feel this pressure? That's why I was like, 'We're a bunch of idiots, we don't care about any of the stuff that's happened before.' We knew then that our job was to go out and win right now. But yeah, it caught on."

The inspiration for this book is clear, and had been rumbling around in my mind for several years. As the "Idiots" of 2004 celebrate their 10-year anniversary, it is important to recall not so much what they did, but why they were the group that could snap eighty-six years of franchise heartache with one galvanizing summer and fall. There are other iconic seasons in Red Sox history. The pure joy of the Impossible Dream Season of 1967 is still felt today (in fact, that generation spawned much of the mania that has presided over the team in the past few decades). Many Sox fans still light up when they think about 1975, and the Gold Dust Twins, Fred Lynn and Jim Rice. And perhaps 2013, in all of its crazy unexpectedness, will have the same impact years and generations from now.

But to find one team that can produce an accomplishment that meant as much to a region as what the Red Sox did in 2004? That might be as difficult as overcoming a 3–0 deficit in a best-of-seven series against your forever rivals, the ones who had tortured them for so long with such glee. Just by the merit of their accomplishments, the Sox of 2004 are one for the history books. Entering the 2014 baseball season, 34 teams have trailed a best-of-seven postseason series, 3-0. The 2004 Red Sox remain the only one to survive that scenario.

"It's the toughest thing to do in all of sports," Millar said. "Especially to beat the mighty Yankees in four straight games. It will happen again. It will probably be a while. To beat someone four straight games in a seven-game series, that's a very hard thing to do, no matter who you're playing. We were a group that just believed and overpowered the odds."

They didn't just overcome the odds, but they did so with characters who were endearing and, in quite a few cases, a little rebellious. Damon had his flowing long hair and beard that would have made him a kindred spirit to all the players on the 2013 team. Millar had the Texas twang and the boyish enthusiasm for the game that never left him as a player, and still hollers all things baseball on a daily basis for those fans who tune into the MLB Network. Martinez? Not only was he one of the most dominant players in history, but he had a charisma that was off the charts. In 2004, Martinez grew his hair into Jheri Curls in an effort to bond with the cast of characters who would form his final team in Boston.

Curt Schilling brought bravado to the equation, not to mention his previous history of dethroning the Yankees. Manny Ramirez was in a class by himself when it came to his various personality traits (giddy, petulant, spacey, aloof, hitting savant) that could show up on a given day, but the 2004 team, more than any other team Ramirez played for, found ways to keep him focused when the pressure mounted. David Ortiz spent that season becoming the best clutch hitter any Red Sox fan had seen since Carl Yastrzemski. By the time the 2013 team won it all, Ortiz—the MVP of his third World Series—was perhaps in a pantheon by himself of Boston baseball sluggers. Even general manager Theo Epstein was a cult hero in 2004, helped by his youth (30 at the time), his roots (Brookline, Massachusetts), his guitar playing, and his willingness to be bold. Manager Terry Francona created an atmosphere in which he could somehow be a leader and a friend at the same time. The mix the Red Sox had in 2004 might never quite be matched.

"The truth of the matter is that group of guys was a family—it wasn't just a team," said Millar. "It was a unit that literally hung out together and ate together and liked each other. That doesn't go on. You can't buy that. That was the one thing about that that I remember is that we all went to different teams, we all played on different teams, [Keith Foulke] went to Oakland, Pedro played with the Mets. But that one group that we had—we had so many different guys from Billy Mueller to Trot Nixon to Pedro Martinez to crazy-ass Manny Ramirez to Keith Foulke, who had every coolest car in the world and cool little gadget thing, to Fake Cowboy Millar to David Ortiz."

The personalities blended together over the spring and through the summer, and ultimately into an historic autumn. But chemistry is nothing without talent. And the 2004 Red Sox had a ton of that. Not only that, but they had a collective baseball IQ that belied their "Idiot" disguise. "I can say one thing about the Boston team: Some may consider us idiots, but we were some of the smartest players who have ever played the game, knowing just what to do in any situation," said Damon.

In the following narrative, you will relive countless situations Damon and his teammates were involved in with riveting fresh details that come from almost a decade of perspective from those who were involved. Everyone remembers the euphoria at the end. But the moments that were just as compelling were the struggles along the way, all of which would be overcome by the end. After all, success always tastes better when there is more to overcome.

Through these pages, you will read first-hand accounts of the adversity that threatened to stand in the way of a championship during that season. While the 2013 Red Sox were a remarkably consistent machine, the 2004 team was a thrill ride at an amusement park, swaying back and forth, and up and down. If you were smart, you kept your seatbelt on. The story lines were countless.

Derek Lowe was annoyed at himself for turning down a contract offer during Spring Training to the point that he admitted it impacted his performance all season. Just before the playoffs, Lowe was told he was out of the rotation and proceeded to throw a hissy fit in manager Terry Francona's office at Baltimore's Camden Yards. His teammates helped to talk him off the ledge, something Lowe remains grateful for to this day.

Trot Nixon, who had been with the organization longer than any other player of that championship squad, had a quad injury so severe his chances of playing in the postseason were in severe jeopardy. But Nixon raced against the calendar and found a way to get back. Martinez stewed early on about his contract uncertainty, but eventually got over it and reveled in the ride—first the season, and then the duck boat.

The Jason Varitek–Alex Rodriguez fight was, in the minds of most of the players, the defining moment of the regular season. But did you know Keith Foulke nearly trampled poor Johnny Pesky in his haste to get from the clubhouse to the melee? Meanwhile, Gabe Kapler feels he found a friend for life in the middle of that fight in Trot Nixon. And even if Orlando Cabrera and Dave Roberts wound up having magical three-month stints in Boston, you will learn here why they were both disappointed when they first learned they'd been traded to the Red Sox. And Cabrera would carve a special niche in his stint in Boston because he could light a fire under the mercurial Manny. Schilling had an ankle issue you might have heard about, but he kept pitching, and his former teammates are awed by it to this day. Schilling's ankle remains achy, but his 2004 ring—and that t-shirt he created—are constant reminders of why it was worth it. Foulke was heartbroken from a pending divorce as the '04 postseason started, and he pitched his heart out, in large part out due to his burning desire to keep playing and put off the return to an empty home.

Though this book was written from this keypad, its contents were shaped at field level by the roster full of characters who created their unique place in history, and by a manger who stands alone with his 8-0 record in World Series play. They also had a heavily invested, hometown general manager who loved to take a risk or two. Going down memory lane with this group was a labor of love, one that I hope readers will enjoy every bit as much as I did.

Winter to Spring Training
Woozy Damon Lets Hair Down

The long-haired, thirty-one-year-old man with the shaggy beard was sprinting out of his house on random afternoons in January 2004, trying to keep up with the cars in his residential neighborhood in an Orlando, Florida, suburb. Quite a few of the oncoming drivers must have looked at Johnny Damon, whether they knew it was him or not, and muttered, "What an idiot!" Rest assured, though, Damon had not gone crazy in his pursuit of getting ready for the 2004 season, his third in Boston. Instead, he had gone stir crazy. Ten days before the loss that had crushed New England and only reinforced the ridiculous notion that the Red Sox were some kind of jinxed outfit, Damon had been the victim of a nasty collision with teammate Damian Jackson in deciding Game 5 of the 2003 Division Series in Oakland. Damon and second baseman Jackson converged on a shallow popup that dropped, and Damon got the worst of it. While the Red Sox celebrated an epic win that night, Damon suffered a concussion and had to watch the end of the game from a nearby hospital.

Under current medical standards, there was no way Damon would have played baseball again that postseason. But 2003 was a different time, and Damon, who was the very definition of a gamer, didn't want to miss the American League Championship against the mighty Yankees—matchups like that were why he came to Boston in the first place. He was back in the lineup for Game 3, just five days after the jarring collision with Jackson. And Damon played every inning in the final five games of the series, which ended on Aaron Boone's home run against Tim Wakefield in the bottom of the eleventh inning of Game 7.

"I was definitely messed up, but I wasn't just messed up for that series, I was messed up for five or six years where I would get headaches every day," said Damon. "I would have to go see a chiropractor quite a bit."

Because of Damon's head trauma, the loss to the Yankees in Game 7 probably hit him a little differently than it did his teammates. Sure, the loss was painful. But the pain in his head was worse. Damon remembers getting back to Boston after the loss in Game 7, then getting in his car the next day and high-tailing it home to Florida.

"I just jumped in my car and just started driving back and we passed New York City that night, made it all the way past D.C., and the next day, continued home," Damon said. "I don't think it would have been great to be seen in Boston because it did hurt. Sometimes when you see teams lose, you see the players out the next day, and that's just not me. I wanted to get as far away from Boston [as I could] and get back to the old drawing board."

But when he returned home, Damon's energy and motivation were at an all-time low. His pounding head left him bedridden much of the time. "I would sit around quite a bit watching football. That wasn't all too bad. But the headaches just kept coming."

The other things that kept coming were Damon's hair and beard. Shaving and going for a haircut both required too much of him at the time. So he let it grow and grow and grow, and he took on the look of a true caveman by the end of the winter. Who knew that his look would become a fashion statement for the '04 Red Sox, one that still resonates to this day? In many ways, Johnny Damon was setting himself up to be the face of a counterculture type of team that would go down in lore.

"He was bigger than just a baseball player," Derek Lowe said of Damon. "Kevin Millar talked the most, but look at this guy [Damon]. He's got the hair, he's got the beard, he's got that swagger. He was our prototypical 'That's what the Red Sox were that year.' "

Knowing that the Red Sox were counting on him to bat leadoff and play center field in 2004, Damon had to shake away the cobwebs and do something productive. "And finally in January, I was like, I've got to get in shape for baseball and that's where the racing the cars stuff came from," Damon said. "Fortunately the street that I lived on before was just twenty-five miles per hour and I was able to do that, obviously not for quite a long distance. Sometimes I'd scare the cars because they'd see this caveman running along."

Damon would get near-daily migraines in that winter before the 2004 season, lasting anywhere from an hour to an hour and a half. By January, he needed to get some fresh air. Chasing the cars—typically a canine rather than a human activity—got Damon into passable shape for 2004. But he could take care of the rest of his conditioning at Spring Training in Fort Myers, Florida. If nothing else, his physical appearance created levity for a team that probably needed some at the time. The bone-crushing defeat at Yankee Stadium, in which they had been five outs away from the World Series and three runs ahead, wasn't easy for the players to put out of mind, particularly when the man who led them, Grady Little, was no longer the manager. He had been replaced by Terry Francona, who would also gain enormous popularity throughout the clubhouse in fairly short order. "I was a huge fan of Grady Little; he was seriously one of the best managers I ever played for," recalled Millar. "He was a good man. I was bummed out. I felt terrible for him. I felt that he was in a no-win situation if the reason he lost his job was because he left Pedro Martinez in. It was damned if you do, damned if you don't. So, yeah, that was tough for me personally because I really had a great relationship with Grady. I thought he handled people great and cared about people. But now you've got Terry Francona, who I don't think could have been any more perfect to replace a guy like Grady Little. A good man, funny, more like a player.

The doors are open, kind of similar to Grady. Very similar guys, one is a little more country, one's a little bit . . . Tito? I don't know what the hell he is. Moral of the story is, he put a smile on your face, a lot like Grady Little did, and that was big for the group of guys we have."

There would have been more smiles in that spring of 2004 if the Sox had arrived in Fort Myers as the defending champs. "Collectively, I think we thought we were better than the Yankees in '03," said outfielder Gabe Kapler. "We came into '04 with a little chip on our shoulders and with the understanding it shouldn't have happened that way. In fact, I can remember in '03, Doug Mirabelli and I—and I think Millar might have been involved in that conversation, too—we were talking about what the rings would look like in the warm-ups before Game 7 in '03. We were really believing that we were going to win that game." Then again, the loss wasn't all bad, considering it served as motivation the next year.

"I don't know about the rest of the guys, but I had some kind of resentment or anger inside about the previous season and I wanted to actually pay it back to the Yankees the best way possible," said Martinez.

The way most of the players remember it, their hearts were mostly repaired by the Spring Training, but the loss had some residual sting. And for some, it might always sting. "You know, even though we won in '04, that loss in '03 was very devastating, even to this day," said Damon. "Especially when your playing days are more than likely behind you, you look back and say, that was another opportunity where we could have won another championship. Those things never go away. That doesn't just go for the '03 team. That goes for every team I played on that made the playoffs and was eliminated. I think it still lingers."

For pure emotion in a dugout and clubhouse, it's hard to match what took place on the visitors' side at Yankee Stadium in the aftermath of Game 7 in 2003. Nixon, nicknamed the Volcano, expressed the anger most outwardly by punching an orange water cooler on his way into the clubhouse. And in that clubhouse, grown men wept at a season that had slipped away. Pedro Martinez's eyes, which had always been filled with confidence, looked glassy and vulnerable. Tim Wakefield, the most respected veteran on the team in those days, wondered if he would ever live down the one flat knuckleball that Boone put into the seats. Then there was Grady Little, who knew deep down within minutes of that loss that he would never manage the Red Sox again. All season, Little had patiently waited for the club to pick up his contract option for the following year. It never happened, which signified that it certainly wasn't going to happen after a defeat in which he ignored statistics that were so precious to owner John Henry and a large portion of the front office.

"There were tears in the clubhouse," said Kapler. "My recollection was Grady walks around, shakes everybody's hand. And there was sort of, 'Oh no, what does this mean?' as he's shaking our hands. We all sort of anticipated what might happen next. I was choked up when he shook my hand. I was choked up. That's how I felt. I think everybody is a little bit choked up at that moment. He was a good manager. He was caught up in a bad moment. It would have shocked nobody to see that turn out differently. It would have shocked nobody to see Pedro get the outs. It's a fork in the road. Managers all come to their fork in the road. I see that decision he made, the road that he chose, as one that would have worked a lot of times. I bet if you played that out a hundred times, it would have been like fifty-fifty."

While Henry, among others, fumed at Little's decision to keep Pedro in Game 7 although the numbers begged him to do the opposite, it was hard to find a player who had a problem with it. And when Little was formally dismissed two days after the Marlins beat the Yankees in the 2003 World Series (MLB prohibits teams from making major announcements during the Fall Classic), the players he left behind were leery of losing the manager they appreciated so much. "It was a tough transition, especially because Grady Little was a player favorite," said Damon. "None of us ever put the blame on him. Those teams we had in Boston, they felt like a family. Grady was a big part of it. He was a perfect manager. He went by people's heart and character and didn't really need the sheet to say what he should do. He'd say, 'I don't care if he's 0-for-5 off this guy. Maybe he was in a slump at the time.' I respected him very much and that was tough to see him go. But bringing Tito in, Tito was great, too."

As horrifically painful as the losses of Game 7 and the manager were, there was no time to wallow. In fact, it was time to regroup. And nobody set that tone better than the front office. Theo Epstein, the general manager who grew up two miles from Fenway Park before landing his dream job at the age of twenty-eight, literally spent his Thanksgiving holiday prying Curt Schilling away from the Arizona Diamondbacks. It was a move with countless implications, all of them good. Schilling had the bravado the Red Sox had needed, particularly when you consider he had teamed with Randy Johnson to dethrone the Yankees in an epic 2001 World Series. And he also had the right arm that could give the rotation the necessary boost alongside Martinez, who had dropped a tick from a few years earlier, when he was the best pitcher on the planet. Keith Foulke, the lights-out closer the Sox lacked the year before, came along a couple of weeks before Christmas. Alex Rodriguez nearly came to Boston as well as part of a historic exchange that would have sent Manny Ramirez to Texas and also shipped franchise icon Nomar Garciaparra out of town in a separate deal with the White Sox. The moves Epstein made turned to gold, and the potential A-Rod addition that was foiled by the Players Association turned out to be the best thing that could have happened for the '04 Sox. Ramirez might have been flaky and maddening at times, but most of his teammates were quite fond of him. Meanwhile, Rodriguez never had an easy time fitting in on teams, and the brilliant chemistry of the 2004 Sox likely never would have emerged if he had been on that team.

In the short term, though, when the Yankees felt compelled to pry Rodriguez free from Texas—thanks to Aaron Boone, of all people, ripping up his knee playing basketball—it sent shockwaves throughout New England. Not only did an already-loaded Yankees squad get A-Rod smack in the middle of his prime, but they also added two starters who were highly regarded at the time, Kevin Brown and Javier Vazquez. Most of the panic was on the streets, though, and not in Boston's clubhouse. After all, there was a newcomer who had helped to diffuse the mystique and aura right out of the Yankees recently enough (October 2001), that it was still fresh in everyone's mind. Considering the Yankees–Red Sox rivalry had been remarkably one-sided over the previous eight decades, it would sound silly for Boston's players to boast. But Schilling could rightfully do all the boasting he wanted, and he loved doing so, even if it put added pressure on him.

"Everybody was talking about New York and how awesome New York was going to be," said Schilling. "On paper, it was a ridiculous, ridiculous team. I think there was some semblance from us of, 'Who the fuck do they think they are?' And if you looked around the clubhouse, we had a lot of guys with that kind of mindset. I certainly felt that way. I loved it. Because in my mind, the day Alex signed there, beating them was going to be even better than it was the day before."

Although it generally isn't good business to replace a manager who had won 95 games the previous season and guided his team to within five outs of a World Series, Epstein was meticulous in his search for a successor and found the man who turned out to be perfect in Francona. Instead of resenting the fact that his holdovers had great affection for Little, even after his departure, Francona joined them in those emotions. In 1992, Francona had been a coach for manager Little in the Arizona Fall League. They even shared an apartment and Francona would chuckle at Little's obsession with going to the local convenience store for scratch tickets. Still, it was unique to find a new manager who was so secure in himself that he in no way felt threatened by fondness for his predecessor. In many ways, it was such a different situation than the normal manager switch. "Most times, when you take over, you're not taking over a ninety-five–win team," Francona said. "The one thing that I guess I had in common was I liked Grady, too. I didn't ever discourage anybody from liking him. I don't think just because they liked Grady didn't mean they had to dislike playing for me. I don't think you have to promote yourself by putting somebody else down. When I'd hear guys talking about Grady kind of fondly, shoot, man, I kind of felt the same way. I really—I guess I kind of liked it."

Little, a folksy man with a thick Southern accent, had a way of making people feel good about themselves. Francona had the same quality, but could blend analytical thinking with the human touch, where

Little was old school in his strategy, which made Francona the manager the organization wanted.

As the Red Sox got the band back together for 2004, it was strikingly similar to the group that nearly made it to the World Series. The only difference in the position player alignment was that Todd Walker, the second baseman and No. 2 hitter for the 2003 squad, had left as a free agent for the Chicago Cubs. The plan going in was that defensive whiz Pokey Reese would be the second baseman, with switch-hitter Mark Bellhorn serving as backup. Other than that, the lineup, which set team records for productivity the season before, was projected to be the same. The rotation still had Martinez, Derek Lowe, and Wakefield, and now had another ace in Schilling. Bronson Arroyo, a waiver pickup from the Pirates the previous year, would win the fifth spot out of the rotation, which was originally targeted for Byung-Hyun Kim, who nearly cost Schilling his 2001 World Series ring with the Diamondbacks with his shoddy relief pitching. An injury-plagued disaster in Boston, Kim actually flipped off the Fenway fans when they booed him during the introductions before Game 3 of the 2003 Division Series.

As for Schilling, he would become a focal part of the team before long. But he spent much of his first spring embracing his new surroundings while also getting the lay of the land. "The thing that blew me away was walking out there the first day, because I was there early. I had heard about it and I grew up a baseball fan, but I wasn't ready for Red Sox Nation, and I mean that in a good way," said Schilling. "It was amazing, these people, they ate and they slept and they breathed Red Sox baseball. I played in Philadelphia where they're hard-core sports fans, but this was different. I think that is kind of the twenty-sixth man here from an accountability perspective. You've got to have players who hold each other accountable and push each other in the locker room. But having fans that do the same is not a bad thing."

As hopeful as Schilling was that the Red Sox could join the Phillies and Diamondbacks as teams that he helped pitch to a World Series, at first he couldn't know for sure what his team was made of. All he knew was that he'd practically lie down in traffic for his manager, Francona, the man he pitched for during his final four seasons in Philadelphia.

"And so, early on, I was trying to look around and figure out what we had and who we were because I'm the new guy. I knew the guys from competing against them, but I didn't really know them," said Schilling. "I talked to Tito a lot because he was the one guy in camp I knew. As Spring Training went along, I think we felt like we were going to be good. But to me, the Yankee thing was always kind of looming there—like, we could be good but it might not matter."

Aside from the obvious stiffness of the competition, there were some issues. Trot Nixon, the hard-nosed right fielder who was a critical left-handed bat, arrived at camp with a messed-up back. "I knew I wasn't going to be on the Opening Day roster. I went for most of Spring Training over to Miami and rehabbed," said Nixon. "Didn't have surgery, and just rehabbed and got into a situation where my back was a lot stronger. I didn't have pain shooting down my leg—I had what felt like a constant knot or stiffness that went down into my glutes and into my butt."

It was the start of an entirely frustrating season for Nixon in which his body let him down repeatedly. But he would finally gain momentum just before the postseason.

Of all the Spring Trainings of Nomar Garciaparra's career, this one easily led the way in awkwardness. For so many years, he had been the face of the franchise and, in many ways, the face of the Red Sox. But by 2004, after the team's willingness to trade him and subsequent hesitancy to complete a long-term pact he once felt was a mere formality, Garciaparra wondered if he was being phased out. "Well, you know, it was definitely difficult because I thought our deal was pretty much going to be done that offseason. It was done. It was something we agreed to. Certain numbers were agreed to," Garciaparra said. "There were just other numbers we were talking about working out. I thought it was pretty much a matter of just signing papers and it never worked out that way."

And darkening his mood even more was a right Achilles tendon that started barking—would you believe it?—the very day Alex Rodriguez and the Yankees made their lone trip to Fort Myers for Spring Training. "It was really strange how I started feeling something that one day and I'm like, 'What is this?' We're thinking maybe just rest it right away and it will go away. That's how we were all thinking," Garciaparra said. "It just kept getting worse and worse. And the season started and it stunk that I had to deal with an Achilles injury. I'm like, 'Great, now I have to deal with this.' That was not fun."

The indefinite absence of Nomar loomed large at the time because he was still an All-Star performer in 2003 and a centerpiece of the lineup. There was even boundless speculation on how Garciaparra sustained the injury in the first place. He mentioned that he was hit by a ball one day during batting practice, but nobody ever saw it. Then again, there are hardly ever cameras on the field during BP in Spring Training, and players get struck by batted balls in batting practice quite often. "I got hit by something, but I don't know if that was the ultimate cause for [the injury]," Garciaparra said. "That whole thing was like, 'Nomar said he got hit.' I was like, 'Look, I know there was a time I did.' And I even said it wasn't a big thing. And then I said, 'I don't even know if that's it.' " The whole thing got uncomfortable, particularly considering some of the more far-fetched reports, one of which hit a Boston television station one night. "They wanted to say I was playing soccer," Garciaparra said. "They wanted to say all sorts of stuff."

Then there was Derek Lowe. After breaking out in 2002 with a twenty-one–win season and salvaging a decent 2003 season with some memorable playoff moments, he came to camp in 2004 consumed by contract uncertainty. Some players perform best when their future is at stake, but others, like Lowe, obsess over it and are swallowed up by the angst. As he sat on his couch at his home in Fort Myers in June 2013, shortly after his final Major League team (the Texas Rangers) had released him to end his solid career, Lowe was still annoyed that he hadn't accepted a contract extension from the Red Sox in the spring of 2004. "When I think of that year, it started in Spring Training because I was a free agent, I wanted to stay there," Lowe said. "They offered an extension in Spring Training. We didn't take it and it's funny, because their first offer was more than I got when I went to the Dodgers—by a lot."

Epstein remembers the deal he offered as something like three years at $27 million. The deal Lowe would get in Los Angeles was four years at $36 million. In other words, Lowe's recollection is a little fuzzy, but it's easy to see why he remembers it the way he does. Keep in mind that Lowe spent nearly the whole year of 2004 in a panic, envisioning dollar after dollar being flushed down the toilet while he endured one sub-par start after another.

"And I wanted to stay there so bad," Lowe said. "Every start that whole year, I felt like I had to throw a shutout. I put all this pressure on myself and every time I pitched bad, I'm like, 'I'm costing myself millions of dollars every time I go out,' and I couldn't stop it."

Foulke, the new closer, had all the financial security he could have ever hoped for. But in Spring Training, he couldn't get anybody out. This wasn't a big concern for Foulke because he knew how his body operated and it made him hardly ever a contender for the Mr. Spring Award. "I think it was more, my body, my knees were bothering me and it seemed like every year it was just a matter of trying to get it fired back up again, so I couldn't do as much early," said Foulke. "It was just kind of adjusting to what my body would allow me to do."

But even an established veteran like Foulke, who was 31 at the time, wanted some validation that he could do his job before Spring Training ended. So when the Red Sox departed Fort Myers and got to Atlanta, Foulke knew time was running out. "We played one of the exhibition games before we started the season and I remember being in the outfield with [trainer] Chris Correnti working on stuff trying to figure out what the heck is going on here," said Foulke.

In the final exhibition game, Foulke gave up a home run to Marcus Giles. Over a third of an inning, he allowed two runs, as his Grapefruit League ERA swelled to 15.00. Once he got that one out, Francona got him out of there.

The signing of Foulke was one that Francona was heavily invested in. The year before, they were together with the Athletics, where Foulke was the closer and Francona was the bench coach. Francona made it abundantly clear to Epstein that Foulke had all the traits to be a championship closer in Boston. "Oh, man, panic is not the right word," Francona said in November of 2013. "But we were definitely concerned because I had gone to bat so heavily to get him over there. I do remember, we were in Atlanta and we were trying to get him in and out of a game because we didn't want to use him up too much, but we kind of wanted him to kind of have a good feel about himself going into the season. I think he gave up a line drive, and then a line drive out and we got him out of there. And right when the season started, he started dealing. It just goes to show you that you really can't go on [preseason performance]."

Kapler, one of the indispensable role players on the team, also learned something vital during that two-day stop in Atlanta—that it was not his job to try to prevent Manny from being Manny. That was out of his domain. Others would be in charge of that. Kapler's job was to be ready whenever Francona needed him to be. And when you're Ramirez's backup, those opportunities aren't always predictable. To make a long story short, when Ramirez decided he didn't feel like playing, be it for a day or for an inning, Kapler was going to get thrust into emergency duty.

"I think my role had to be zero ego," Kapler said. "I remember, prior to 2004, we had an exhibition game in Atlanta. I think it was like the last game before the season started. Manny just out of the blue pulled himself out of the game. Nobody really understood why. He just came in, called 'hamstring' or whatever it was. And I came in—I was absolutely cold."

A man of impeccable physique, Kapler liked to have his body in perfect working order when it was his time to play. For innings before his entrance, Kapler would do all kinds of exercises; nobody had to tell him when or how to get ready.

"Because I knew when I was going to enter a game," Kapler said. "We would pinch run for [Manny] and play defense. I was ahead of [bench coach] Brad [Mills] and Tito when it came to how I was going to be used late in a game, or at least I was on par with them. I'd usually be ready from the fifth or sixth inning on.

"That was an exhibition game, and it's a little different; I was cold. He came out of the game and after the game, I walked up to him and said, 'Manny, you can't do that. It's not just you. There are other people that are affected by that decision. Just give me a heads up. Come talk to me in the sixth and be like, 'Hey Kap, I'm going to come out of this game.' Let me be ready, and I've got your back. I'm all for it.' " However, Ramirez wasn't very responsive at that particular moment.

"That day, I knew that my role was to not be pissy about shit like that," Kapler said. "It was my role to be like, no matter what happens, just be ready and have no ego attached and do whatever it takes. So I saw that as my role—no matter what somebody needed from me, that's who I was going to be."

From there, a bench leader for 2004 was born. And Kapler would be joined by another vital reserve, catcher Doug Mirabelli, who specialized in handling Tim Wakefield's knuckleball, but also knew how to keep his teammates loose. Backup first baseman David McCarty was another reserve that everybody respected and liked. For a team that was going to be tested several times in the ensuing months, it was vital for the Red Sox to know they had each other's backs. Though Ramirez could definitely be about himself on the days the stars weren't aligning just right, the 2004 team that left Fort Myers was already one that cared a lot about each other.

"There's winning players and there's losing players," Lowe said. "There's guys that just know how to win and get the best out of everybody. They're not always the most talented guys on the team, but they help you create this winning mantra. That's why role players are so important. With that team, we had so many guys who understood. The Doug Mirabellis of the world. Those guys knew when they weren't playing, they needed to keep the clubhouse loose, keep the bench loose. That was their role for that day. They weren't bitter that they weren't playing. It was just a unique and special twenty-five guys."

It was a dynamic the Red Sox were going to need. Despite how loaded they appeared on paper, there would be challenges, plenty of them, on the way to a history-making finish. And the new manager was savvy enough to know how best to lead the group. "They were good players and they liked to play, and the last thing that team needed was a manager that wanted to hit and run and bunt and get in the way," Francona said.

In that first spring, Francona spent a lot of time learning the personalities of his players. By the time the Red Sox departed Atlanta for the first series of the season in Baltimore, Francona already felt like he was part of the family that Little had departed. "I really felt like that was important and it was on me to get to know them and what they could do and maybe even in some instances, what they couldn't do," Francona said. "Just to be able to put them in a position where they could have some success. That team was built to win, man. Sometimes the best thing you can do is stay out of the way."

April
Pair of Aces

From his arrival in Boston in 1998, Pedro Martinez was viewed as the transcendent ace who could finally give the Red Sox that elusive World Series parade. By 2004, Pedro was still thirsting after that ring. From an individual standpoint, he basically had nothing left to accomplish. From the year before Pedro got to the Red Sox through 2003, he went on a seven-season run (118-36, 2.20 ERA, .198 opponents average, 0.98 WHIP) that only legends like Sandy Koufax could relate to. Koufax, the Hall of Fame lefty for the Dodgers, actually only had a six-year peak, but it was a golden one (129-47, 2.19 ERA, .197 average, 0.97 WHIP). But Martinez was doing it in hitter-friendly parks against many hitters— as history would later prove—who were taking performance-enhancers. Koufax had Don Drysdale as backup and would be part of three World Series–winning teams.

No disrespect to Derek Lowe, Tim Wakefield, or Bret Saberhagen, but Pedro could never look around the clubhouse and see a near-equal talent during his pre-2004 time in Boston, as Koufax could with Drysdale. The fact that the Red Sox still hadn't won it all was tearing at Martinez as he entered the final year of his contract. In fact, he still hadn't done what many players had done by the end of 2003—autograph the inside of the Green Monster. In his mind, Martinez could only justify putting his signature inside that wall when he was a World Series champ. That's why November 28, 2003—the day Epstein got Schilling—was a big day for Martinez, one that would ultimately help lead to the only championship of his glittering career. Martinez liked to be The Man, there's little doubt about that. But he swears that he didn't feel his turf was being threatened by Schilling's presence, despite some speculation, which continued into the summer of 2004, that maintained otherwise.

"No, no, no, I actually applauded that decision," said Martinez. "I kept asking every year—bring someone to help me out. There were three different playoff series in '98 and '99 when I was the only starter to win a game. We needed someone else. That was the last piece of the puzzle. Adding a guy that could win after me, a guy you were certain would give you a legit chance to win—especially in the playoffs! Schilling is a big-game pitcher. I'll take Schilling any time."

Even though Pedro wanted another big arm to ride shotgun, the Red Sox knew they had to be careful not to offend their ace while trying to get a new one. So as Schilling, acting as his own agent, negotiated his deal with the Red Sox, he saw the ways in which the club tried to avoid a firestorm with the great Pedro Martinez, who had one year left on his contract. "They were walking very gingerly around Pedro's contract because they didn't want that to be [a stumbling block]. That came up early. They couldn't pay me more than they were paying Pedro," said Schilling. "They made that very clear early on. My rebuttal to that was, 'I don't care what Pedro is making. I don't need to make more than him. I know what the market is.' So that kind of gave me a heads-up on how this might [play out]. I was trying to put myself in the reverse position and I wouldn't give a shit what somebody was getting paid if they came here. But that was clearly a very big thing for them."

Eventually, the deal would get done, in Schilling's Arizona home the day after Thanksgiving. On Turkey Day, the Schillings were so moved by Epstein's persistence and commitment that they invited him and assistant Jed Hoyer to their home for Thanksgiving dinner. When Theo Epstein's career in baseball ends, the job he did in trading for Schilling, and then persuading him to forego his no-trade clause, might go down as the biggest conquest of his career. "Curt was so engaged the whole time and had a real glint in his eye, like he could imagine himself in a Red Sox uniform," recalled Epstein. "I felt it was fate that we would get a deal done and that he wanted it, but we were really far apart on money and I was concerned. Once he invited Jed and I to stay for Thanksgiving dinner I got more hopeful. Once we finally agreed after three days of grinding talks, Jed and I went into Curt's home office to print out the term sheet."

And that short visit to Curt's home office led to the one final light-hearted moment Epstein and Hoyer needed after seventy hours of sweating out whether they'd be able to get a deal done with this confident player who represented himself. "There we saw a dog-eared copy of *Negotiating for Dummies* and laughed our asses off," Epstein said.

Schilling's re-worked deal would pay him $39.5 million from 2004–2006, and it had perhaps the most unique incentive clause of all time. If the Red Sox won a World Series, Schilling would have his $13 million option for 2007 automatically picked up. It was fitting, because all Schilling and the Red Sox were thinking about at that time was the ring. Within days of the trade, Schilling filmed a commercial for Ford in which he stated he was coming to Boston to break an 86-year-old curse. In the first few minutes of his introductory press conference with the Sox, Schilling proclaimed that he now "hated the Yankees." He was setting himself up to prove he was the ultimate at backing up brash talk. Either that, or he was setting himself up to fail and be reminded of it forever. Other big-name players had come to Boston hoping to bring World Series glory with them. But nobody sounded as convincing as Schilling. His swagger was exactly what the city needed at the time.

"It was different for me because I basically made a promise, so, from a personal perspective, I looked at this very differently and I tried early on to make sure everybody knew I was okay with it," Schilling said. "I didn't mind the [Dan] Shaughnessys of the world saying, 'What are you going to do if you fuck this up?' That stuff never bothered me. In all the teams

I ever played on, I tried to be that [presence]. The press never bothered me. So I always tried to be the guy that had the bulls-eye [on him]. I said quite a few things around the trade that kind of put a bulls-eye [on me], not just here, but in New York. But again, I always felt like no one was going to pressure me more than [I was] so I never worried about the things I said, quote unquote, backfiring."

Schilling was so confident in his ability to win the big games that he told the Red Sox straight out in the negotiations that he was the missing piece to their winning it all. What athlete has the confidence to say that? And Schilling even had his own prop. "It's funny because when we were in the midst of the negotiations, and the negotiations were breaking down with Theo, and Larry [Lucchino] was there for one day, and we were sitting in my den in my house, and honest to God, my hand to God, we didn't strategically place it, but the World Series trophy was sitting on a table by our fireplace," Schilling said. "And it was sitting between Theo and Jed and Larry. They were [harping] about the average annual value of the contract. And I kept going back to them, 'Listen guys, if this is what you're worried about, this is going to be a problem.' And I looked at the trophy and I said, 'The bottom line is, you're bringing me to Boston to win that. And you don't have a guy that can do that, and I've done it.' I don't know how it came across but that's one of the reasons I was brought here."

He was also brought there to provide the team with elite innings that could either match or top Martinez's elite innings. And for Schilling, that dynamic was like putting on an old shoe. For the previous three-and-a-half years, he had teamed with Randy Johnson, who was basically the lefty version of Martinez in the late 1990s and early 2000s. Schilling had never pitched better in his life than he did during his years with the Diamondbacks; the only pitcher who was better in the National League during that time was his teammate Johnson. "I certainly don't ever feel like I pitched behind Randy but Randy was clearly the Cy Young Award winner and I felt like I was the second best pitcher on the planet."

If Schilling earned a Bachelor of Arts degree in pitching while studying every nuance of Johnson, he could earn a Master's while studying

Pedro, a fellow right-hander. It was reminiscent of when Tom Seaver came to the Red Sox in 1986 and puppy dogs Roger Clemens and Bruce Hurst joked that they were going to the University of Seaver. As accomplished as he was as a pitcher by 2004, Schilling was never too proud to keep learning. In fact, he couldn't get enough. When Martinez would go to throw his bullpen sessions in Spring Training, Schilling would follow. If Martinez was pitching an exhibition game at City of Palms Park in Fort Myers, Schilling wouldn't leave early so he could golf. Instead, he would watch Martinez—the master at work.

"And I was at the point in my career where I didn't hang around for Spring Training games, but I did when he pitched, a lot of times," said Schilling. "In addition to seeing that he had the biggest hands of anybody I've ever met in my life, I wanted to see the other things that made him great. And the one thing I realized early on that I couldn't be taught, and I wasn't going to be able to learn from him, was he had a better feel for pitching than anybody I've ever met. He could see and feel. I almost equate Pedro pitching to like a Zen thing. He could see and feel and react on the fly. And I could never do that, so that wasn't something he was going to be able to teach me."

In the mind of Schilling, Martinez was that student who showed up to class naturally brilliant, almost as if his pitching brain was some sort of gift from God. Schilling was the worker bee who had to pore over his notes for hours and hours just to get a decent grade. This isn't to say Martinez didn't work also. He was obsessive about his physical training, doing everything he could to make his slight frame hold up for as many years as it could. But Martinez in Schilling's mind, was a genius.

"I had my nose in the books," Schilling said. "It was not intuitive, it was not natural for me. For me to feel confident in myself, I had to spend hours in the video room, and he didn't spend literally any time in there and he was still great. He just had a feel for it."

Schilling and Martinez had pitched against each other in the National League for a number of years, before Pedro moved to Boston.

But their interactions were limited, and the most involved one wasn't positive. In 1996, Martinez was engaged in a bench-clearing brawl with Schilling's Phillies, after Mike Williams had drilled him as retaliation for some brushbacks in the middle of the game. No Phillies player was more involved in protecting his teammate in that fight than Schilling, and all of his ire was directed at one Pedro Martinez, who was a year away from winning his first Cy Young Award and didn't have Schilling's full respect in those days. In the mid-1990s, Martinez had to work long and hard to shed the reputation that he was a headhunter.

"He was pretty vocal," Martinez remembers of Schilling during that fight. "He wanted to kind of jump on me. As a matter of fact, in the bottom of the pile, he was pulling me by a chain that I was wearing. He was kind of choking me. So I went and squeezed harder on Mike Williams, because I had his neck, so he was trying to grab my arm and I wouldn't let him. Uggie Urbina got me out of the pile."

Part of Martinez wondered if there would be any lingering awkwardness between the two when Schilling arrived in '04, but there wasn't. "I didn't expect him to later show the respect that he did. But he saw that I was getting better and by the time he got to Boston, he actually respected me," Martinez said. "When he got to the Red Sox, he showed respect. But at the same time, I had already achieved so much. He knew that pitching inside was a key for me. And so was it for him. He was always asking questions. I remember him having a hard time throwing a cutter. So I went on and spoke to him, I got him throwing it. We never had anything [negative]. He pulled for me. I pulled for him."

"He was cordial," Schilling said. "We never had an, 'Oh my God, you're my best friend' relationship. But I never, ever felt any animosity in any way toward him. I'm sure I had some words to say when he did some of the things he did to Terry. But he was one of the greatest pitchers who ever lived, so I looked at it as a chance to get educated again."

Ah, yes, things with Terry. It was a Sunday night in Baltimore when the Red Sox opened their 2004 season. And as the holdover ace, Martinez was the one who got the first game. Pedro had a night that would have been sufficient for many pitchers. But giving up three runs (two of them earned) over six innings on Opening Day? Martinez had built such high standards that it seemed like a real disappointment. The Red Sox lost the game, 7–2. And when the clubhouse opened after the game, Martinez had already left. In his first game as manager, having his star pitcher leave the clubhouse before the game had even concluded made Francona look bad. It became a firestorm, particularly after Francona met with the beat writers in his hotel suite the next day (the team's off-day) and took the blame for Martinez's early departure, saying he hadn't conveyed the rules properly. Years later, Francona still doesn't mind that he took the heat for his ace who had some diva tendencies. "That's just part of being a manager. You know what, you do what you think is right," Francona said. "I guess the biggest thing is, you do what you think is right for the players and for the organization and not for yourself. I think in the long run, if you do it like that, things will take care of themselves."

Later that day, in a nearly empty clubhouse at Camden Yards, Francona sought out Martinez and let it be known how disappointed he was. From Francona's recollection, Martinez stood there stonefaced.

"Everybody's got their own style and I didn't expect Pedro to really like it that day, to be honest with you. But I had to say [something]. I thought that doing it on an off-day when nobody else is around is a heck of a lot better than calling him into the office. Again, sometimes, being a manager, sometimes you have to tell people stuff they don't want to hear. That's just part of it," Francona said.

Interestingly, Martinez denies in retrospect that he left Camden Yards early, even though plenty of people remember seeing him leave. And back in '04, Martinez never denied the incident.

"I did not leave before the game was over," Martinez said in August 2013. "I was next door. I was next door in the family room. When you guys went in, I took off. Because I did not want to see the media to talk about this. I was watching the game on TV. I left as soon as you guys went in, because you guys would pile up there. You guys were expecting me to be at my locker, and

I wasn't there, but I saw you all go in. I just left. I didn't feel like I had anything to explain to you guys. It was a tough time, and I wasn't talking to the media."

Quite possibly, Martinez simply forgot about the incident with the passage of time being close to a decade. But as Francona points out, it certainly would have made no sense for him to make it up at the time. "The last thing I'm going to do is promote a guy leaving. I would have just as soon not even answered [the question]," said Francona.

The very beginning of 2004 was one of the most difficult points of Martinez's seven-year tenure with the Red Sox. He wanted to stay with the Red Sox long term, but was having a hard time finding common ground on a contract extension. And when the front office urged Martinez that both sides should keep quiet about the negotiations, the pitcher suspected that the team was leaking stories about his velocity dropping and his release point lowering, perhaps signs that he was on his way to losing some of the dominance he'd had for all those years.

"It was always a comment that someone in the front office leaked something," Martinez said. "I remember Gordon Edes [then of the *Boston Globe*] always coming up to me and saying, 'Pedro, they said this, or they said that.' And then I had been told by my agent, 'No, this is going to be strictly professional, no arguments. We're going to keep it secret. We're going to talk about it under the table and behind closed doors.' I followed that rule. It surprised the heck out of me when I saw that someone went out and said this and that. It bothered me. That's why I was upset."

As Pedro stewed, Schilling was in his honeymoon phase with the team, gearing up for his debut in the second game of the season. The controversy over Martinez's early exit didn't faze him at all, with the exception of the residual heat Francona took for the cover-up. Of the twenty-five Red Sox players that season, Schilling was the most fiercely loyal to Francona, and it made sense, given their history.

But Schilling wasn't about to let that bit of annoyance deter him from producing a strong performance in Baltimore in his opening act. The best way he could reward Francona was put him in the win column, which he did. The Big Schill allowed just one run over six innings, walking one and striking out seven. It was an eerily familiar feeling for Francona, considering his first win as the Phillies' manager had also come on the strength of a gem by Schilling, who outdueled Pedro's brother Ramon in a 3–0 win on April 1, 1997.

"I'd had history with Schill. I knew him and man, that's a nice feeling," Francona said. "The bigger the game, the more Schill wants to pitch. That is a really nice feeling. You could tell very quickly that in Boston, every game was like a big deal. I thought that boded well for Schill."

During their time together in Philly, Schilling and a young, emerging third baseman named Scott Rolen were really the only bright lights Francona had. There weren't many big games for Schilling to pitch in during Tito's time in Philly, but he always enjoyed the fierce competitiveness of his star righty.

"You're right, we didn't have that many big games. I remember when the Yankees came in for Interleague, we had three straight games that were sold out," Francona said. "I think he struck out sixteen. His first pitch was ninety-seven and his last pitch was ninety-seven. He logged so many innings, it wasn't even fair. When we got to Boston, it was a good feeling knowing that the bigger the game, probably the better the pitcher."

There are few regular-season games in his entire career that Schilling was so hyped up for as his Boston debut on April 6 in Baltimore.

"Oh yeah, because you have to prove yourself again. Not only was I having to prove myself to the twenty-four guys that I was suiting up with, which are really the opinions that matter most to me, but Sox Nation was tuned in," Schilling said. "This was the trade, in a lot of people's minds, that was going to help them get over the hump. And so there were expectations and I loved that. I loved the fact that they wanted me to go out and they wanted something special. That was what drove me."

Next time through the rotation, Martinez took the mound on a Saturday night at Fenway against the Blue Jays and proved that reports of his demise were greatly exaggerated. He outpitched Roy Halladay in a vintage performance and set the stage for Schilling's Fenway debut on Easter Sunday afternoon. For one of the very few times in 2004, Schilling didn't come through. Perhaps he was too hyped up. Staked to a 2–0 lead, he would record ten strikeouts on the day. But that was overshadowed by the fact that he gave up four runs, including two on a go-ahead, two-run shot by Eric Hinske.

"The only start I will tell you I was more amped up for [than the debut in Baltimore] was coming back here to Fenway, for the first start against Toronto. I'll tell you, it was one of the low points of my year," said Schilling.

David Ortiz ended the day with a walk-off homer over the Monster. And for the most part, the Red Sox had little to complain about in April. Both aces got off to strong starts. Pedro went 3-1 with a 3.03 ERA. Schilling had the same mark, posting a 3.30 ERA. In fact, those were somewhat heady days for the Sox in that they took three out of four from the Yankees at Fenway, with Schilling throwing heat en route to a Saturday matinee win. And on April 25, Martinez finished a three-game sweep in Yankee Stadium by firing seven shutout innings. Even though Garciaparra and Nixon were still on the shelf, and would remain there until June, the Sox would go 15-6 for the month. Pokey Reese electrified everybody with his defense at shortstop while Bellhorn started making a name for himself as a reliable second baseman who had a little pop in his switch-hitting bat.

There was one little storm—both literally and figuratively—when torrential rain forced two straight rainouts at Fenway on April 13 and 14. Instead of juggling his whole rotation, Francona skipped Derek Lowe for an entire start, giving the righty ten days of rest between his first and second starts of the season. Lowe was not in the mental position to be skipped at that point. He was already overanalyzing everything. So when Francona skipped over him, Lowe vented to reporters that Roy Halladay wouldn't be treated like that. Halladay was the only AL pitcher who had more wins (forty-one in 2002–03 compared to the thirty-eight by Lowe). When the rest ended, Lowe got drilled, giving up eight hits and seven runs over two and two-thirds innings. The only thing that suffered more than his ERA was his mood. "I wasn't in a very positive place. [I] took everything as a negative. I think I was so wrapped up in trying to justify the deal that I'd turned down," said Lowe. "Not that people in the industry would have known that, but I just felt like 'You're not giving me my normal starts.' Now we're in April and I've got three starts. I need more. I need my thirty-five. Again, I think it was more just my mindset at the time. There was so much added pressure I was putting on myself and then every little, small thing—[I] just took it as a big thing."

There was also a hidden storyline early in the season, one that would surface later. Nobody knew at the time that Schilling was already pitching through right ankle pain—the very same ankle that would cause his sock to be famously blood-stained by late October. And who would have believed that the infancy of injury actually developed because Schilling was trying to mimic Pedro?

"That was the thing. People don't know that I had the injury in Spring Training. I actually got it, and I need this to be worded correctly, I got it from Pedro," said Schilling. "I was out watching Pedro throw in the bullpen one day and I noticed that when he rotated his right foot on the rubber, his back foot, he kept his foot half on and half off."

To find out why the ace did this, Schilling went to trainer Chris Correnti. The bridge between Schilling and Pedro for much of that 2004 season, Correnti worked exhaustively with all the pitchers to keep them strong throughout the season; Martinez was the biggest Correnti fan imaginable, and Schilling would soon become a big believer, too. "I asked Chris about it and Chris said that Pedro, given his size, wants to create more leverage. So what he does is, he puts his foot half on and half off. He collapses and creates momentum and drive and gives him more velocity," said Schilling. "So I'm like, 'Hell, let me try that.' I tried it and I actually started throwing the ball a little harder. I was like, 'Oh damn.' so I started doing it. What happened was when my foot collapsed, it was pinching, and it created the injury."

If Schilling would prove anything in 2004—early, middle, and late—it would be that injuries weren't going to stop him.

May–Mid-July
The Lull

J ust when new manager Terry Francona was starting to like what he had after a solid opening month, his Red Sox suddenly became as unpredictable as left fielder Manny Ramirez's personality. L, L, L, L, L. That was how the Sox started May, on a road with severe potholes in Texas and Cleveland. At least a personal matter was cleared up right around midnight as the calendar shifted from April to May. After hours of waiting out a rain delay in Texas for a game that was eventually postponed, Pedro Martinez called the media over to his locker to say that in-season negotiations with the Red Sox had ended, and that he would become a free agent at the end of the season. This wasn't a case of Martinez being self-serving. It was actually a cleansing period in which he could put the stressful negotiations out of his mind and even start talking to the media again, which he hadn't done for all of April. It was smart of Martinez to put his personal problems out of his mind and simply enjoy life with a room full of characters.

"The whole team was a team that actually made me forget about everything that was going on," said Martinez. "I didn't have to really think that much about my situation."

If Martinez was suddenly at ease despite his contract uncertainty, his team started swaying in different directions. After those five losses in a row, the manic Red Sox followed with four straight wins. The streak included a Friday night game at home against the Royals when Mark Bellhorn clocked a game-tying, two-run homer in the ninth. This was the moment when Red Sox fans started seeing that Theo Epstein had come up with a low-risk find in Bellhorn, whom he acquired simply for some cash considerations from the Rockies. And this was when Bellhorn realized the worst fears he had in the offseason wouldn't be realized. "I had a good year in '02, and then in '03 I was terrible. I thought my career was over and I was going to be in the Minor Leagues forever. I got the call when I was in Mexico playing winter ball, that I had been traded to the Red Sox," said Bellhorn. "I didn't really know what my position was and I knew I had a chance to make the team. I wasn't sure. I didn't really have that good of a Spring Training. Guys got hurt and I kind of fell into the role and ended up playing well when I got a chance. It ended up pretty good."

You had to take the good and the bad with Bellhorn. He would strike out 177 times during that '04 season, a team record until Mike Napoli broke it in 2013. But much like Napoli years later, Bellhorn had the patient approach the Red Sox loved in their hitters and was an above-average second baseman, one who was extremely proficient at turning the double play. And with the Red Sox, he got to hit in the catbird seat, behind Johnny Damon, and in front of the premier big boppers in baseball—David Ortiz and Manny Ramirez.

"It doesn't get much better than that, I don't think," said Bellhorn. "Johnny's always on and then you've got those two guys behind you. You see a lot of fastballs. They want to make sure they get you out and not let you on base and that's what I always liked to hit. I always liked hitting at the top of the lineup anyway."

The quiet but unflappable type, Bellhorn, who had eyes that looked perpetually sleepy, seemed oblivious to the market he was playing in. If his strikeouts caused angst with the home crowd, Bellhorn was kind of clueless about it. "I always struck out but it didn't really bother me that much," Bellhorn said. "I always walked a lot, so I thought, you've got to get on base to score runs, so that was always my approach. Granted, I didn't want to strike out a hundred-seventy-some times. That was just part of it. I figured I did a lot of other good things to go along with it."

Though his voice could hardly be heard within that boisterous clubhouse, Bellhorn was likeable and actually fit in well with the group. His long, curly hair, which always seemed to be greasy by the third or fourth inning, helped him look the part on this team.

"I kind of messed around when I got into pro ball with the long hair and went back and forth. I had it before I had gotten there. I always kind of had, like, the five o'clock shadow so I guess I kind of fit right in," said Bellhorn. "I think [the long hair in '04] was partly because I probably was in Mexico for two and a half months and I really didn't want to get it cut down there."

The day after Bellhorn's game-tying homer set up Jason Varitek's walkoff double, Schilling was spectacular on a Saturday afternoon against the Royals, firing a complete-game five-hitter in which he walked none and struck out five and ended the day with a ninety-six mph fastball. Boston fans were in love with their new ace. They also were enamored with Pokey Reese, the defensive showstopper who had a breakout day with the bat to help set up Schilling. Reese hit an inside-the-park homer that Juan Gonzalez misplayed down the line in right. Later in the game, he hit one over the Green Monster. With a big, bushy afro and a clear love for the game, Reese was another one of the many players who just looked the part of the 2004 Red Sox. And he was creating a somewhat weird dynamic in which fans suddenly weren't sweating about when Nomar Garciaparra would be back. They couldn't get enough of watching Pokey Reese, who had won two Gold Gloves for his defensive excellence at second base for the Reds in 1999 and 2000. At that point in the season in particular, Reese was a revelation for a Boston squad that was, well, slow and unathletic. Reese's defense—which would include leaping catches in which he was probably airborne long enough to dunk a basketball—gave the team some life at that point.

But Millar got off to an almost silent start at the plate. So if Damon wasn't hitting on a given night, or Ortiz and Ramirez had the nerve to be in a slump for a day or two, Boston's offense could get quite boring to watch. And that's part of what caused the frustrating stretch of mediocrity in the middle of the season, in which Boston would go 41-41 between May 1 and August 1. The one thing they had going for them during that trying stretch was the perfect manager to handle frustration. No matter what expectations were, Terry Francona was not going to get down on his team, as long as they were giving him an honest effort every night.

"We weren't very fast," Francona said. "When we didn't hit, we'd go on the road and we'd get beat up. And we weren't hitting on all cylinders. I remember thinking, if we can just relax here a little bit and find our footing, we're gonna be okay. There's so much noise in Boston that it's hard to do that." At the time, Francona was 45 years old, young for a manager.

"Part of it, I think, was good that I was naïve because I didn't know what they were saying about me on the radio and stuff," Francona said. "But I knew Larry [Lucchino] and those guys were upset. I just think as a manager, you can't go up and down. The players do, the fans do, everybody does. But as a manager, the more you go up and down, it doesn't help anybody."

The players from 2003, though they missed Little, knew how fortunate they were to have another manager who had their back. If anything, Francona probably carried a little more weight in the room because he was a college superstar and had spent nearly a decade playing in the Majors. Little never played beyond the Minors. As the weeks went by, it was a revelation for the players to see how utterly comfortable Terry Francona was in his own skin. "He put the other coaches on his level without losing an ounce of authority," said Kapler. "He made everybody just as important as himself without ever losing his position as the leader in the room. It's not easy."

Millar tried to help Francona keep up the spirits of a struggling team, even though his bat completely betrayed him early in the season. In 2003, when Millar and his Harley-Davidson motorcycle showed up, life immediately changed in the Red Sox clubhouse, which was staid, to say the least. (Damon had been stunned to see the lack of interaction in the clubhouse when he had arrived in 2002, and he'd worked hard to bring life to the place, with the help of Carlos Baerga.) Once Millar arrived, nobody was safe, and Millar could pull it off because he was often the target of his own jokes. A Southern California native, Millar wound up making his home in Beaumont, Texas, where he developed—or created—a Texas twang. When things got stressful during the 2003 season and fans were angry that Derek Lowe came out of a game with a blister, Millar scolded the media and told them—and Boston in general—to "cowboy up" behind Derek Lowe. The phrase Cowboy Up would catch on like wildfire in '03, and Millar loved it.

By 2004, his teammates got tired of that slogan, so it went away. But Millar's personality did not. Although not particularly athletic, Millar had enough hitting ability for the Marlins to pluck him out of the Independent League, where he was playing for the St. Paul Saints. He became a solid hitter who could hit between fifteen and twenty homers and keep a clubhouse loose with the best of them. In the winter before the 2003 season, Boston fans couldn't understand why Epstein was spending so much time and energy trying to free Millar from an agreement he had made with the Chunichi Dragons of Japan. But Millar made up a story that he feared going to Japan because of a war that would soon start with Iraq. In truth, Millar just wanted to go to war with the Red Sox. Johnny Damon would come to love the presence of Kevin Millar. In Oakland, Damon enjoyed the fact that Jason Giambi could do all the heavy lifting when it came to bringing a clubhouse together. And it was the same dynamic in Boston once Millar arrived.

"Well, it definitely helps when you have another guy [to lead the clubhouse]," said Damon. "He can do it every day. I can't. There's some days you're beat up and you're like, 'Let me rest.' But here's Kevin. It was great having him. It was nonstop entertainment. Our team would not have won without Kevin Millar. He kept us loose the entire year and beyond."

Francona might have thought Millar was a little, well, nuts at first, but he soon learned that the madness got some results. "Millar was more valuable than his numbers," Francona said. "He probably did some things that would get you arrested, or at least fired, on the street, but in our clubhouse, it was relished. It was appreciated."

Though Millar's official title for the Red Sox was first baseman and middle-of-the-order bat, his unofficial one was equally important in several instances between 2003 and 2005. Millar was Manny Ramirez's unofficial babysitter. And it was something he took a legitimate interest in. "I like people, I like my teammates, I like to have fun, I like to laugh. I'm in a good mood most of the time," Millar said. "The moral of the story is, I felt a responsibility to keep Manny happy. Manny was a good guy back then. He got a little cuckoo later. But the years we had him, Manny was happy and funny, and I was a part of that. There's a little circle that Manny has and not very many Americans are going to be let into that circle because of that culture difference. I put forth the effort for him to open those doors to his circle and he did.

"Manny and I were very close those three years. We ate a lot on the road and we worked out a lot on the road and we went to breakfast on the road. We looked at car magazines. There were things you had to do besides the baseball and giving him a high-five in the dugout when he hit a three-run home run. There were things that went on to keep him kind of going. Manny, at that point, we knew what kind of hitter he was. There is an aloofness to Manny and you had to make sure that he was going to show up at the stadium. One day, you can wake up, and he might just be heading to San Fernando Valley to go buy a Nova, forgetting that we have a game against the Angels. There was a responsibility on my part, just to kind of keep Manny there and keep him accepted."

Ramirez seemed on board with all things Red Sox on May 11. The day after he flew to Miami to become naturalized as a United States citizen, the quirky left fielder took his position in front of the Green Monster at Fenway Park toting a small American flag in his hand. His teammates, undoubtedly with Millar leading the charge, had him do it. The crowd cracked up. It was another Manny-being-Manny moment.

And that was the same point of the season that Johnny Damon got hot and basically stayed that way the rest of the season. When Damon arrived at Fenway for the start of a home stand on May 7, he was hitting .245. Given that it was the first home game back after that tough road trip through Texas and Cleveland, Francona offered Damon a day off.

"He was kind of going through struggles, same as the team, and then all of a sudden, I don't know what got into him, because he was beat up and banged up, and one day, we were going to give him a day off and he didn't want it," Francona said. "I was like, 'Okay, great.' And he got some hits. And it was like he never turned back. As a manager, you've got to appreciate a guy that wants to play every day because he knew that he was leading off and he would see a lot of pitches and he knew that the other guys fed off of him, even if he wasn't feeling good. He'd find a way to get on base, and I loved him for that. I loved him for a lot of reasons, but that was one of them."

About halfway through the three-month lull, Garciaparra returned to the lineup after weeks of painful speculation in which some thought he was milking the injury because of lingering resentment he felt toward the team for trying to trade him the previous winter. It seemed ridiculous both then and now. Garciaparra was, after all, a pending free agent, so it would stand to reason that he would want to get back in the lineup to increase his value.

"I didn't understand any of it," Garciaparra said. "I was going, 'Well, why would I do that? It does me no good. It only does me good to play.' It was a free agent year; I wanted to play. That's all I'm about. Then you hear stuff that I wanted to be traded. I wanted to be this or that. I was like, this never has ever come out of my mouth. I don't think those words were ever muttered out of my mouth. I tell people, if you look at my actions, I always thought my actions spoke louder than any of my words. I go, 'Let me think, I was building a three-million-dollar house out there [in Boston] that off–season, I just got married.' I'm going, 'Does any of that say I want to be traded?'"

Years later, when David Ortiz would suffer the same injury in July 2012 and not be right again until mid-April 2013, Garciaparra wondered if maybe then people finally understood what he was going through in the early months of that 2004 season. Because of the lack of blood flow to the area, the Achilles is always one of the trickiest injures to recover from.

"Then they're going, 'Wait a minute, how long did David Ortiz actually take to get back?' I even remember talking to David about it," said Garciaparra, who would bump into Ortiz frequently during stints as an

ESPN analyst. "And I'm like, 'David, you're experiencing this, this, this, and this,' and he goes, 'Yeah.' He was looking at me, like how did I know? I was like, 'David, don't you remember? What do you think I was going through in 2004?' "

When Garciaparra finally did come back on June 9, the mood wasn't particularly joyous because of all the controversy swirling around him. Nonetheless, Nomar got back in there for a home game against the Padres and went 1 for 2 in an 8–1 loss. Perhaps his last magic moment at Fenway took place the night of June 22, when he belted a grand slam to help Schilling beat the Twins. Aside from that, there was little for Garciaparra to smile about in those months. His defense wasn't sharp, and fans clamored to see more of Reese. Bumper stickers saying "Pokey Would've Had It" actually popped up around Boston.

The entire situation seemed to come to a head on July 1, when the Red Sox and Yankees engaged in an epic "Instant Classic" type of game, one in which New York won 5–4 in thirteen innings to complete a sweep. But there was no Nomar. The shortstop had made three errors through the first two games, and decided to keep a scheduled day off in that series finale. Nearly a decade later, Garciaparra remains upset about how he feels the facts were distorted in that case. Yes, Terry Francona did ask him if he wanted to give up the day off, but Garciaparra remembers that the trainers had urged him not to play; he had played eight straight games before taking the down day in New York. The general plan for his return to action was that he'd play five in a row before getting a rest.

"I wanted to play that day," Garciaparra said. "The trainers kept me out. The trainers came in the day before. I limped in after the game and I got on the training table and you could see the swelling. You could feel it and you could see it; in that area, you could feel [that it was] really squishy and really liquidy. The trainers go, 'This is bad, Nomar.' I said, 'I know, but I've got to play tomorrow.' They go, 'You can't.' I said, 'I've got to play.' I remember when Terry came and asked me and I was distraught. I wanted to cry. I want to play and they're telling me I shouldn't. Terry goes,

'What happened?' I said, 'Tito, it's bad, I just can't. I need a day. I haven't had one [in a while].' I said, 'I'm sorry.' "

And there was Derek Jeter diving into the stands and bloodying his face to catch a Trot Nixon popup down the line in the twelfth inning. And the television cameras kept showing the contrasting images of Garciaparra stationed on the bench while the rivals squared off in the type of game he once took center stage on. Garciaparra's explanation for sitting on the bench while his teammates were on the top step cheering one of the great regular-season games of the decade was that it was his "lucky spot" and that teammates actually urged him to stay there.

But here is the craziest part of all. For all the controversy about Nomar not playing that night, he nearly pinch-hit for Nixon during that same at-bat when Jeter went into the stands. "What ended up happening was they had a left-hander warming up in the bullpen," Garciaparra said. "Trot was coming up and Tanyon Sturtze was in the game. It was tough on Joe Torre—he keeps in the righty instead of bringing in the lefty because he knew I was coming up."

Manny Ramirez had put the Sox on top in the top of the thirteenth. But John Flaherty won it with a deep fly ball that went down as a walkoff RBI single in the bottom of the inning. Francona, so proud of his team's effort, albeit in a loss, stood by the entrance to the clubhouse in an effort to encourage his players. Many media members witnessed the scene, and some took shots at Francona, trying to pigeonhole him as a softy. In truth, he was just trying to keep his team afloat after perhaps the most gut-wrenching defeat of the season. He didn't regret the reasonable gesture back then, and he didn't years after the fact, either. "I remember that night, after the game, because we had to travel to Atlanta, and I stood at the clubhouse door and I kind of patted everyone on the back as they came in," Francona said. "In my opinion, we had played our ass off. We didn't win. It was a crushing loss. But that didn't change how I felt. I remember the media, they had let the media down, but they stopped them at that one point. And a lot of the guys were making fun of me because here I am, sticking my head out the door congratulating guys. I wasn't congratulating them. I was telling them that I appreciated their effort.

"That was how I felt. I remember that it kind of, I don't want to say hurt my feelings, but when the media made fun of me about that, it made me mad. This was how I felt about that group and this was how I thought we could win. And we didn't start winning for a while. But if we played like that, we were going to be just fine. For me to turn my back on guys when we had a crushing loss like that I think is wrong. You can't just pat them on the back because of the W. You've got to reward the effort and that's how I felt."

This could have been a breaking point for the Sox. Epstein, worried about his manager, and, to a lesser degree, his embattled shortstop, hopped a flight from Boston to Atlanta two days later to take the temperature of his team. Francona remained unfazed, and did his best to convince his boss there was nothing to worry about.

"I remember Theo coming down and I think they were worried," Francona said. "I was more mad that we weren't winning, but I wasn't upset. You know what I mean? I didn't feel like we were losing the clubhouse or anything like that. We were losing tough games. I thought the only way to win was to stay the course."

During the pre-game hours on that Saturday night in Atlanta, Epstein also backed up Garciaparra's story that the trainers took the lineup decision out of his hands on July 1. "He was hurting to the point where he couldn't play," Epstein told reporters at Turner Field. "The day off did him a world of good. You saw how well he swung the bat last night. He was a medical scratch Thursday. He was not healthy enough to play that day."

And in his first two games in Atlanta, after the controversial sabbatical in the Bronx, Garciaparra raked six hits in ten at-bats, including a homer.

"What cracks me up is that the next few days, we go to Atlanta, and then, first of all, I go off, too. I do so well," said Garciaparra. "Why do I need a day [off]? Because this is the difference. And then, two days later, Theo sits in front of NESN and finally says, 'Well, yeah, with Nomar, it wasn't his choice, we made him sit down.' He does an interview, does all that, tells the whole story, but by then, it didn't even matter. I don't even know that people knew the interview took place, even though there is a record of it."

Dan Shaughnessy, the *Boston Globe* columnist who irked several Red Sox players that season with his hard-hitting opinions—from Garciaparra to Millar to Schilling to Martinez—was also in Atlanta that weekend. And he went to Garciaparra's locker the first day of the series and told him of the column he was going to print for publication the next day. The headline was: "Damaged Goods: Deal Garciaparra." Garciaparra doesn't mention Shaughnessy by name when he recalls the interaction he had with a writer in Atlanta. "He said, 'I'm writing an article, I'm going to say you should be traded and all that stuff. Do you have anything to say?' 'What can I say? I thought you were wrong? I thought you were wrong my entire career.' " Garciaparra said.

Something else happened during that weekend in Atlanta. Derek Lowe finally hit rock bottom, or at least seemed to. Pitching a Sunday day game on July 4, Lowe was a human firework, blowing up on-site. The righty gave up eight hits and eight runs over four and a third innings, as his ERA ballooned to 6.02. In a poor frame of mind, the normally chatty Lowe left Boston's clubhouse and headed straight for the team bus rather than talking to the media. Nothing Lowe thought on that afternoon was anything he wanted to share with the scribes who covered the Red Sox on a daily basis.

Lowe has a pretty good idea what he was thinking, though. "I am just costing myself millions," said Lowe. "I was looking at a four-year deal, possibly a five-year deal. You can really get pretty negative on yourself. Now you're thinking, 'I'm going to get a one-year deal for nothing.' "

Four days later, when the Red Sox were back at Fenway, there was obviously some interest in talking to Lowe. And that was when veteran WBZ radio reporter Jonny Miller, who asked the bluntest questions in Boston, and with the thickest Boston accent among the media to boot, set off Lowe again. "How is your head?" asked Miller. That lit a match within Lowe.

Three days after blowing off the media, Lowe not only wanted to blow off steam to Miller, but he wanted the entire media to come to his locker. As it happened, the rest of the press had just been filing out of Terry Francona's office after his pre-game session when Lowe suddenly provided notebook leads for everybody. With most of the conversation being dictated by Lowe, he spoke to the media for fifteen minutes, wondering why his psyche was always in question when he pitched poorly. From across the room, Nomar Garciaparra jokingly hollered to Lowe, "Don't do it!"

"My teammates are sick and tired of talking about Derek's head," Lowe said that night. "'Is he going to figure it out?' 'Is he an emotional wreck?' First of all, it should never be asked of them. I'm pitching like shit, bottom line. When Pedro pitches a bad game, or Curt, or anybody, they pitch bad. I pitch bad and I'm a mental Gidget."

Right there, that was classic Lowe. Mental Gidget? Nobody had ever heard that one before. Of course, nine years later, Lowe had no problem admitting that his head was exactly what was standing in his way of pitching good baseball games during that stretch. "It goes to show you where my state of mind was," said Lowe. "Everything irritated me. I probably said bad things to the waiter when he came over to give me my food. It was just a bad state of mind. But it was all self-inflicted and self-created."

At that point, there were just four days left before the All-Star break and Francona was just trying to keep his team's head above water, thinking maybe the break would help everybody. One last storm started innocently enough when Francona told Pedro Martinez he could return to the Dominican Republic a couple of days before the All-Star break. Martinez went seven strong innings to improve to 9 and 3 on July 7, and his turn in the rotation wouldn't come up again until after the break. Francona did poll several of his veteran players to make sure nobody was offended, and they all encouraged the manger to cut Martinez loose. There was one drawback. Manny Ramirez often sought out the same special privileges as the ace pitcher, only it was hard to reciprocate, because he was an everyday player. So on the Sunday before the break, Ramirez suddenly came up with a sore hamstring. His refusal to play came at a time when the Red Sox had started to show some promise as a team. They would close the first half with five straight wins.

Curt Schilling was not buying what Manny was selling. Both in the clubhouse and very publicly, on the field during BP, Schilling got in Ramirez's face and tried to get him to put the team above himself. Keep in mind that two days after Ramirez was apparently too sore to play in a regular-season game, he homered off Roger Clemens in the All-Star Game. When a player disrespected the game, it pissed Schilling off to no end. And when it hurt his manager at the same time, that made Schilling even more upset.

"We actually got in three separate fights between those two years," said Schilling, speaking specifically of 2004 and 2005.

By the point Ramirez was jettisoned from Boston via trade in 2008, nobody was more critical of him than Schilling. But in 2004, they had a relationship that was fascinating in the sense of how similar they were in terms of game preparation and how dissimilar they were in terms of behavior patterns.

"The hard part for me with Manny is I probably spent as much time next to Manny as I did almost anybody on that team because Manny lived in the video room, where I also was," said Schilling. "We always had conversations. I always asked so many questions about pitching and I learned so much from him. I'm sure he came across as just not an intelligent guy. But when you talked to Manny about hitting, he was a savant and it was otherworldly to talk about guys with him."

When Schilling was breaking down his opponent, he would get morsels of information from the man he considered to be the smartest hitter in baseball. Schilling mentioned that he would take some of what Ramirez said with a grain of salt, only because he knew that whichever hitter he was trying to break down couldn't be nearly as smart or gifted as Manny.

"So many parts of different game plans I put together were because of things he told me. But, there was the bullshit to deal with," Schilling said. "That was part of why Tito did such an amazing job that year. It wasn't just Manny and Pedro."

To be sure, the Red Sox were going in many different directions for the first four months of that '04 season. And after the All-Star break, Ramirez was still playing games with regard to his hamstring. He told Francona he could DH, but wouldn't play the outfield. That was exasperating, because Francona had no interest in having Ortiz play first base. That was when Francona let it be known to Manny that he could return to the lineup once he was well enough to play left field. Finally, when the Red Sox got to Seattle, the second stop on their road trip, Millar somehow convinced Ramirez to get back in left field. And something else happened in Seattle: Millar finally found his stroke, the one that had been missing all season, by picking the most unlikely person to imitate.

As he watched the Mariners take batting practice, Millar took note at the way Miguel Olivo, who would go on to have a journeyman career, was opening up from the right side. Millar could have imitated Edgar Martinez, one of the best pure hitters of his era, who was also on Seattle's 2004 team. But for some reason, he picked Olivo. And for some reason, it worked like a charm. When the Red Sox returned to Fenway on July 21, Millar had a decidedly open stance. And two nights later, he homered three times, even though the Sox somehow lost anyway to the Yankees. With his closed stance in 2004, Millar hit .269 with five homers and 25 RBIs in 297 at-bats. After he opened up, he hit .336 with 13 homers and 49 RBIs in 211 at-bats. Yes, baseball can be a crazy and unpredictable game.

"I'm struggling to death and basically we roll into Seattle and Miguel Olivo is raking in batting practice with an open stance and I looked at Varitek and said, 'Boys, I'm hitting open. That's it.' They were like, 'What?' Those were the kinds of things where you're just joking around and having fun," Millar said. "And we got back home, and I got on fire and the next thing you know, we're playing the Yankees, and I hit four or five home runs. And next thing you know, we just started rolling as a group."

July 24
The Day That Changed Everything

The spark had not only been elusive, but nearly invisible. It was like trying to light a damp match. For three months, the Red Sox tried to find one little thing to ignite them for more than three or four days, but nothing worked. Then there was July 24, a gloomy, rainy day in which the team was challenged in three distinct ways and came out on top in all of them. Three wins in one day? Maybe that's what an underachieving team needed to finally shake out of the doldrums that threatened to spoil their season. The first battle they won that day was simply getting the chance to play. Team executives huddled, and Francona and Yankees manager Joe Torre inspected the field with Dave Mellor, the leader of the grounds crew. Everyone seemed to be in agreement that the game should be postponed. Torre and the Yankees certainly weren't going to argue about a relaxing and free Saturday night in Boston, where they could have the dinner reservations of their choice. At that point, the Yankees were in cruise control in the American League East, and not getting much resistance from their rivals. But before a pitch would be thrown, the 2004 Red Sox showed their biggest fight of the season to date. When Francona returned from the field to his office, he found out that ornery veterans Jason Varitek,

Kevin Millar, and others had been in the faces of Epstein, owner John Henry, and club president/CEO Larry Lucchino demanding that the game be played.

"Our pitching was real thin that day," Francona said. "You play if you're supposed to. That's basically, I think, the way you look at it. If you're not, you don't. But our pitching was kind of beat up and the field was in bad shape. So I had gone out with Joe Torre and [umpire] Bruce Froeming and we were going to call the game, so I told Joe. And I came back in, and that's when I found out. John Henry was in there, and they're like, 'We're playing this game.' I'm like, 'What do you mean?' They're like, 'The players are dying to play.' So I was happy about that. But I was also, like, 'Somebody better call Joe.' I expected him to be furious and I think he was and I can understand why."

It's easy to understand why, as an organization, the Red Sox would have been fine with a rainout that day. After all, the team hadn't given anyone a reason to have huge faith in them by that point of the season. Just the night before, the Yankees had given Schilling a beatdown (10 hits, seven runs over five and a third innings), but they also belted Foulke around in the ninth, offsetting the three-homer night by Millar. At 52 and 44, Boston was nine and a half games behind the Yankees, and had their No. 5 starter, Bronson Arroyo, on the docket for Saturday's game. The perception of Boston's players was clear: The suits didn't have the faith they could win that day, and that's why they wanted to call the game. So the Red Sox got pissed. At that point, Arroyo, at the age of twenty-seven, was one of the least established players on a veteran team. Sometimes he got picked on, albeit in a good-natured way. In this case, it was almost like the Red Sox were sticking up for their little brother.

"That was the day the front office didn't really like the matchup, and we were like, 'No, no, Bronson's pitching.' And they wanted to go a different direction and take a day off," said Millar. "We were like, 'No.' It was like we laid our jerseys down on the table. And once again, that's how much we believed in ourselves. On paper, Bronson Arroyo vs. the Yankees, they might want to match it up with Schilling and Pedro or Derek Lowe, but we were, like, 'Bullshit.' We went in there and forced the front office to say, 'We're playing.' And what happened?"

Well, everything. Early in the game, it seemed Boston's malaise might be realized and the fear that Arroyo wasn't a good matchup might have been wise. The Yankees, ho-hum, took a 2–0 lead in the second. But in the third inning, the entire season started to change. Setting up the moment perfectly, Fox panned on Red Sox general manager Theo Epstein in the crowd right before the season-turning pitch and caught him yawning. Who could blame him? There's nothing more boring than a mediocre baseball team. But that was about to change, as Arroyo plunked A-Rod on the left arm. If it was a fastball up and in, the reaction of New York's controversial star would have been understandable. But a breaking ball? An incredulous Rodriguez mouthed expletives at Arroyo. And then Jason Varitek, the backbone and soon-to-be-captain of the Red Sox, intervened, telling Rodriguez to get to first base, adding in an f-bomb or two of his own. And that was when Rodriguez gestured to Varitek as if to say, 'Come on, let's go.' Bad move. Varitek engaged in the fight, lifting A-Rod off the ground with his catcher's mitt. It was go time for the Red Sox.

"There's always a spark when a team becomes united at once," said Pedro Martinez, sitting in an infield box seat at Fenway in August 2013, not far from where the fight took place. "Especially in a situation like that where it seemed relatively unfair for A-Rod to do that to Bronson Arroyo. It was like, 'Hey, don't touch that area.' It woke up a sleeping giant."

The Red Sox immediately charged out of the dugout to support their leader, and Schilling was out there faster than anybody.

"I remember thinking how stupid [Rodriguez] was. It was all a show," said Schilling. "He was doing that to get his teammates to think he was a tough guy, because no one on the planet other than him could have even conceived of that being an intentional pitch. It wasn't. To this day, everyone knows it wasn't. But he was looking to light a fire under their ass, which they didn't need. That was the thing. Like everything else, it was poorly timed and ill conceived. The only thing is, it did the exact opposite of what he intended it to do."

Because it was just the third inning, closer Keith Foulke was still in the clubhouse, finishing up his daily routine. But when he saw what had happened, he knew it was time to get on the field.

"The funny thing is, I remember that as the day I thought I killed Johnny Pesky," Foulke said. Foulke was preparing to go out to the bullpen when he saw the fight start, and he and a couple of other Red Sox went tearing out of the locker room. "I remember getting out the door and turning left to go down the stairs right as Johnny was coming up, and I hit him and knocked him back and we had to catch each other and stand him back up and continue on out there. That's what I remember about that. The fight turned into whatever."

Pesky, who died in 2012, was still a living legend in 2004, so it's easy to see why Foulke would still be horrified by nearly incapacitating the poor man so many years later. Pesky was the Red Sox ambassador. He worked in every conceivable role for the team, dating back to the start, when he was a shortstop on the great Red Sox teams of the 1940s with Ted Williams, Bobby Doerr, and Dominic DiMaggio. By '04, the Sox were still trying to sneak Pesky into the dugout when MLB would permit it. But when the fight broke out, it's easy to imagine Francona or one of his coaches warning Pesky to get out of the fray; after all, just one season earlier, Yankees coach Don Zimmer charged at Martinez, only to be dusted to the ground by Pedro in an unfortunate incident that everyone regretted, nobody more than Zimmer. Hence, the legend was heading away from the fight as the reinforcements charged toward it.

"We were in a dead sprint out the tunnel," Foulke said. "Right as I turned that corner, man, he's popping up and I hit him and I don't know how I caught him and I don't know how we both didn't just go tumbling down the stairs. All of a sudden you run out of the dugout and everyone is over to the left, and I'll go over there and do what you do. I remember getting spiked a couple of times."

Varitek was clearly the wrong Boston player for A-Rod to tangle with. "I mean, that's El Capitan right there. That's why I remember, when that happened, it was like, get there as fast as possible," Foulke said. "It just showed we loved each other. We were buddies and we were brothers. We were going to battle. That's how we were the whole season. We got along."

Varitek would officially be named the captain of the Red Sox on December 24, 2004, the day he signed a four-year extension. Unofficially, he had grown into his leadership shoes years before that. And everyone on the Red Sox knew it.

"Jason was and still is our backbone," Damon would say more than nine years after the fight. "That's how much respect we had for him. Whatever he said, we did. You couldn't have picked a better captain than Jason." The picture of A-Rod and Varitek, with the catcher's mitt planted on the third baseman's throat, would become symbolic of that 2004 season.

"I was just being a teammate," Varitek said at his retirement press conference on March 1, 2012. "It wasn't something that you're proud of. We've been down this road talking with my kids. I was just being a teammate. Things were going on, being said to my teammate. It just happened to happen that way."

There is one Red Sox player who isn't so sure how spontaneous Varitek's eruption was. Is there any chance the leader of the team was looking for a fight to wake up the team? "I tell anyone that will listen that that was premeditated by Jason," said Gabe Kapler. "It wasn't like he just lost self-control for a moment or he lost his temper. For me, it was clearly Varitek saying, 'We need something. This is what we need. And I'm going to give it to us.' "

Derek Lowe, who came up through the Mariners' farm system with Varitek before the two of them were traded together in a brilliant deal by the Red Sox in 1997, sounds like he could easily be swayed into Kapler's line of thinking. "Have you ever seen him do it before or after?" Lowe said. "I played with Jason since he got drafted in Seattle, I saw every game up until '04. But I think that showed you his leadership capability. We needed some spark here. We need something and it was just something that he just instinctively did because he felt like we all needed to do it. They were pretty much pushing us around up to that point."

Whether any part of the fracas was calculated on Varitek's part remains a mystery. Entrenched in his first year as a member of the baseball operations department for the Red Sox in 2013, Varitek declined to be interviewed for this book.

While Varitek vs. A-Rod received top billing, it might have actually been the undercard fight that day. Just as Varitek and A-Rod were being separated, another melee spun off, this one to the first-base side of home plate, toward the on-deck circle. Again, a Yankee—this time their starting pitcher from that game, Tanyon Sturtze—made a poor choice of who to tussle with. Somehow, he got into it with Kapler. And in this fight, blood would be drawn.

"Well, Sturtze actually pulled me out of the pile," said Kapler. "I actually, ironically, was face to face with Joe Torre. I was like, 'What am I going to do with this?' I was almost hands behind my back, expecting nothing to happen. And then I feel this big arm around my neck and then he's pulling me out of the pile and he's whispering into my ear and he's saying, 'Calm down Kap,' and meanwhile, while he's telling me to calm down, I can feel his grip getting tighter and tighter so his words weren't matching his energy and that's when we got into it."

And that's when the Volcano—aka Nixon—erupted with vengeance. Nixon ripped Sturtze to shreds on behalf of Kapler, and got an assist from big David Ortiz, who stood there almost like a bodyguard, keeping everyone else on the outside so Nixon could go to town with Sturtze. First, Nixon hit Sturtze, and then he ripped at his ear. By the time Sturtze emerged from the pile, he had blood dripping down the side of his face, under his left ear. If you search for Tanyon Sturtze on the Internet, one of the first images that pops up is the picture of him bloodied by Nixon. The native of Worcester, Massachusetts, had a fairly unremarkable career, but he was in the center of the action on July 24, 2004.

"And then as I watched the video of that fight, I noticed Trot's presence, obviously. I noticed David Ortiz's presence. And Kenny Lofton was throwing a wild haymaker at David. David was just on the outskirts of that little brawl. From that point on, I felt like we were brothers," said

Kapler. "That day, Trot turned into—not that he wasn't already a remarkable teammate—but in my eyes, one of the best that existed. When you
go back and watch the video of that fight and you see how we were protecting each other."

A star football player in North Carolina during his high school years,
Nixon would never pass up a fight. He was the ultimate protector. And
fortunately for the Red Sox, July 24 was one of those precious days in 2004
when Nixon was healthy enough to be on the field. "I ended up getting
drilled in the ribs because I don't think Sturtze liked too much what I did,"
Nixon said. "To me, Kap was kind of an innocent bystander in that whole
thing and all of a sudden, Sturtze came and grabbed him from behind the
neck. Then, I went over and grabbed Sturtze and I don't know if David
was around. I was right by Kap. And you're kind of just, you're not pushing anybody, you're not throwing any punches, you're just kind of sitting
there, you might be jawing back and forth, this, that, and the other thing.
And then I see him get attacked, so instantly, I'm going to jump on him
because Kap is my teammate, number one, and a good friend of mine.
When you've got the wrong jersey on, it's on like Donkey Kong. Sturtze
isn't a small boy, so you had to kind of get your spurs in him a little bit and
ride that bull a little bit. It was crazy."

Much like Varitek, Nixon will never back down from what he did
that day. But as someone who coaches his two sons, he feels a little sheep-
ish when people identify him with that moment. "Obviously, when there's
kids I coach, they're like, 'Hey, I saw you in this brawl.' I was like, 'You
don't need to be watching that.' You try to explain it to them and those are
professional athletes. 'This certainly doesn't mean that you guys need to
be doing this out here,' " Nixon said.

"The A-Rod–Varitek thing, it was cute," Millar said. "It was like, 'Go to
first,' 'No, you go to first,' 'FU,' 'FU.' Boom, facemask to the mouth, then a
glove to the face, then you kind of come around head-bobbing and mess-
ing around, but there was a real fight over there when Sturtze grabbed
Kapler around the neck on the on-deck circle and Nixon put Sturtze in
a chokehold and that's when he tried to rip his ear off and Sturtze went

out there and pitched with blood dripping down. That was the real fight."

So there it was, only the top of the third inning and the Red Sox had already won twice on that Saturday: first, the dispute on whether the game should be played, and then the fight, which any boxing judge would have given to the Red Sox on points. The game, however, didn't seem so promising. The Yankees erupted for six runs in the top of the sixth, and had a 9–4 lead. This would have been a deflating direction for the day to go in for the Red Sox, considering all they had put into getting the game played, and then clobbering their rivals in the fight. But back came the Sox with four in the bottom of the sixth, and now it was 9–8. By the time the Red Sox dug in for the bottom of the ninth, they were down 10–8, and faced with the task of beating future Hall of Fame closer Mariano Rivera, who was already a legend in 2004 and would only add to his reputation until his retirement in 2013.

Garciaparra, in one of his last big games with the Red Sox, started the ninth with a double off the Green Monster. Nixon followed and nearly tied the game, but his drive to right landed at the warning track, in the glove of Gary Sheffield. But Millar, who was in the early stages of his hot streak, laced a single to right to bring in Nomar. It was 10–9. And the right man was coming to the plate.

When you think of the 2004 Red Sox, Bill Mueller might be the tenth name that comes to mind, after Ortiz and Ramirez and Damon and Millar and Pedro and Schilling and Foulke and Varitek and Lowe. But that was exactly how he wanted it. Mueller loved playing in the shadows of the giants, where he could sneak up on an opponent that least suspected it. Even after his monster 2003 season, when he won the batting title while batting eighth, Mueller stayed in the background. When Walker departed after the 2003 season, Francona had a tailor-made No. 2 hitter in Mueller. But Francona would soon learn that Mueller didn't like hitting in a place of prominence.

So there he was on July 24, batting eighth. Rivera fell behind 3 and 1, making it a clear hitter's count. Mueller got ready from the left side and pounced on a high, meaty cutter, drilling it into Boston's bullpen, right into the glove of bullpen catcher Dana Levangie, who was crouched down and warming up Foulke. As the ball cleared the bullpen and the game ended instantly, there was almost a gasp that could be heard from the press box. It takes a lot to stun a room full of sportswriters from Boston and New York, but this was one of those moments. A crazy day had ended in the most joyous way imaginable for the Red Sox, allowing them to sweep their triple header of sorts. Finally, they had something to latch onto. And someone, in the person of Mueller, who they piled on at home plate in the walkoff celebration.

To say Mueller was low key would be the understatement of the century. An understated St. Louis native, Mueller had modest physique and seemingly no ego. He was a textbook player, though, one who did everything right. The Red Sox had taken to calling him "Billy Ballgame" and it completely fit.

Even Muller will admit his heart pumped with emotion during this particular home-run trot, the most memorable of the eighty-five runs he hit in his career. By 2013, Mueller, as an advance scout for the Dodgers, spent the final weeks of the season following the Red Sox all over the country in the event of a World Series matchup with Los Angeles. One afternoon before a game at Camden Yards against the Orioles, he took some time to reflect on his homer that people will always talk about.

"It's emotional for me, just because, one, I normally don't hit many home runs," Mueller said. "And two, to end the game. I don't know how many times I've ever done that in my life. And then, on top of that, to do it against a Hall of Fame guy like Mariano, nobody would have predicted that. That's why it was so amazing. There might have been a one percent chance of that happening and it did. It's an amazing feeling to help your team win, and to help your team win in the last inning of a ballgame. It was an emotional day, a long day. It's a thrill. It's an amazing thing."

For some reason, Mueller had his share of success against Rivera, producing a .353 average (6 for 17), including postseason. That was particularly impressive because Mueller, a switch-hitter, batted lefty against Rivera. And Rivera's cutter was especially nasty on lefties. But Mueller was his kryptonite, or so it seemed. Not that Mueller would ever admit it or give much of an explanation for why he was able to come up with big moments against an all-time great.

"He still got his outs on me and did his job and I just feel like some of the mistakes he made, I capitalized on, the small mistakes he made," Mueller said. "That's all. Other than that, there were many times my bat broke and it was a [ground out to second]. As long as I could try to put the ball in play, you had a shot. Like I said, he made some mistakes and I capitalized on them."

For a Red Sox team that talked a lot of trash—and often backed it up—there was never anything like that from Bill Mueller. It wasn't in his DNA. Not even a little bit. So if Mueller was underrated throughout his three years in Boston, there was a good reason.

"It's because he was so quiet," Kapler said. "He was the epitome of a guy that loved his role. I light up when I think about him."

You can only wonder how much Rivera's mishap against Mueller on July 24 would lead to another one three months later. But there is no debate about this from any of the Red Sox: That game against the Yankees, considering everything that was involved, was a turning point. Several players, without even being prompted, cite it as such.

"There was no question in my mind that the brawl with the Yankees was a huge turning point for us from a chemistry perspective," Kapler said. "Once a team eats and drinks together and spends a lot of time together off the field, then they bleed together. Let's call the fight 'We bled together.' It was midsummer. At that point, we needed a shot in the arm."

And they got it, via the triple-header sweep.

"We played," said Millar. "Then we get in a fight, we win the fight. A lot of good things happened that day. That was probably the day that turned around our year. Not just the fight, but the game. When Billy walked off Mariano, it doesn't get any better than that."

Even though the Red Sox did pick up some momentum the next night at Fenway by beating the Yankees again, led by the red-hot Millar coming through with three more hits and another homer, there was a bit of bad news before the game. Though Nixon had given the Red Sox everything he had in the fight the day before, he had nothing left to give on the field and he knew it. Nixon never said much to the training staff about the quad he tweaked while rehabbing his back in Spring Training. He just kept playing, hoping maybe it would just go away. "I went into Tito's office, and I never imagined myself saying this, but I just told Tito that I was in so much pain I couldn't play anymore. I just couldn't do it," said Nixon. "So needless to say, the '04 season was a bummer for me for the regular season."

But just as Nixon had Kapler's back in the fight, the reverse was true when Nixon went out of the lineup. Kapler patrolled right field with strong defense and got hot with the bat for a while. Kapler would simply try to hold down the fort until his friend was able to rejoin the fight. It's just that nobody really knew when that would be.

Add it to the list of suspenseful story lines in a season that was developing more spice by the day.

July 31
The Second Day That Changed Everything

I n Orlando Cabrera's last moments with the Montreal Expos, Hall of Famer Frank Robinson wanted him to play a guessing game. At that time, Robinson was the manager of the Expos, a team in perpetual limbo, one that would move to Washington, D.C., for the start of the 2005 season. In the visitors' clubhouse in Miami, where they were getting ready to play the Marlins, Robinson received word from his boss, Expos' GM Omar Minaya, that Cabrera, the starting shortstop, had been traded. That, in and of itself, wasn't a surprise. For weeks, Cabrera had been rumored to be on the go, with the Chicago Cubs appearing to be the most likely landing spot. Mostly due to the limbo of the Expos franchise, Cabrera had asked out of Montreal after declining a four-year contract extension. When he got to the ballpark on Saturday, July 31, the trade deadline, he was still an Expo.

"Well, it was really a unique day because I knew I was going to be traded," Cabrera said. "Frank Robinson called me in the office, he said, 'You got your wish, you got traded.' I said, 'Okay, let me know where I'm going'. He said, 'You can guess. I'm going to give you five guesses. You will never guess what team you're being traded to.' I said, 'What do you mean? Why don't you tell me right now? I need time to get the hell out of here.' He says, 'Oh no, guess.' "

Admittedly, after a stressful few weeks, Cabrera wasn't in the mood to play Trivial Pursuit. Instead, he wanted to pack his bags, get the hell out of Miami, and move on to a team that was actually in the pennant race. Nonetheless, Cabrera played along with Robinson. After all, a Hall of Famer deserves a certain amount of respect. "I said the Cubs because the whole time it was Chicago, Chicago," Cabrera said. "He said, 'No, it's not Chicago.' I mentioned five, maybe 10 teams; I remember mentioning L.A. Then he said, 'You got traded to the Red Sox.'"

At the moment he found out, Cabrera felt like he had been given a gut punch. Thinking he had a handle on what the situation was in Boston, Cabrera had as little interest in going there as he had in staying in Montreal. He was a shortstop and a damn good one, having played the position from the playing fields of his youth in Columbia, and all the way up to the Major Leagues, winning a Gold Glove in 2001. To go to Boston, Cabrera would have to change positions. After all, the Red Sox had Nomar Garciaparra. However, word hadn't gotten up to Montreal about the rise in tension between the star shortstop and his employer.

"I remember immediately the feeling that I had was I was really bummed and pissed off at the same time," Cabrera said. "I was really angry because one of the things that I told Omar was don't trade me to a team to play another position. I want to play shortstop. I was really, really bummed out. 'Why did you trade me there? I don't want to play second or third. I always play shortstop.' "

That was when Minaya gave him the news, telling Cabrera, "You're going to play shortstop." Maybe Cabrera was a bit slow to process the whole thing. He still hadn't figured it out. "I was like, 'How can I play shortstop? They have Nomar there.' He said, 'You got traded for Nomar.' I was like, 'WHATTTT????' I sat down and I was like, trying to think it through and I was like, what the hell is going on right now? Why did they trade this guy? He's like the face of the franchise. I was like, what the hell is going on? I had so many feelings, so many thoughts through my head," said Cabrera.

To be a shortstop in the Majors early in the twenty-first century meant that you looked up to Garciaparra, as well as to Derek Jeter and

A-Rod. At one time, they were considered to be the holy trinity at a position that hadn't been known much for offense before they arrived.

"Nomar was and still is one of my favorite players," Cabrera said. "He was incredible putting up those numbers and doing special things."

For a long time, New England had held Nomar, a Californian, as one of their own. He barreled the ball up at will, ran out every groundball like it was Game 7 of the World Series, and had the type of athleticism that had teammate Mo Vaughn calling him "Spiderman" early in his career. Children throughout Massachusetts mimicked their favorite shortstop, tapping their toes and obsessively touching their batting gloves when they got to the plate. When the Red Sox were eliminated by the Indians in the 1998 playoffs, Garciaparra came out of the dugout and saluted the fans for their support all season. It was a classy moment, one that showed how much he appreciated the Boston experience in his early years. And Garciaparra made it a point to tell new teammates what the fans expected.

"Nomar told me something the very day I joined the team at Spring Training in 2002," remembers Damon. "He said, 'These people pay a lot of money here to watch us play. If you bust your butt all the time, what can they say?' I said, 'Fair enough.'"

Blue-collar Bostonians appreciate players who go all out to aid the cause. They don't suffer pretty boys. The fact Garciaparra played like his hair was on fire and also hit with enormous grace, winning batting titles with glittering marks of .357 in 1999 and .372 in 2000, added to Nomar's enormous popularity. But a bad right wrist injury kept Garciaparra out for much of the '01 season. Garciaparra was back in 2002 and once again an All-Star, but he wasn't quite the same hitter. In fact, he would never recapture the greatness of his first four seasons ('97–'00), the glory years, when he seemed Cooperstown-bound and Bostonians really did think he could be the next Ted Williams.

Garciaparra was never healthy for the Red Sox in 2004. Sadly, he struggled to stay on the field for the rest of his career, save for one throwback season for the Dodgers in 2006 when he played for a manager named Grady Little. Always quiet by nature and consumed by his work,

Garciaparra was even more subdued in 2004. One week before he was traded—that same day that a clubhouse mutiny forced the game to be played against the Yankees—Garciaparra and agent Arn Tellem had a meeting with Red Sox ownership.

"They were saying, 'You don't seem to be happy.' I said, 'Well, of course I'm not all that happy. We had a deal. I want to be here for the rest of my career and I still don't have that contract.' I said, 'Look, is my unhappiness affecting the way I'm playing?' On the field, 'Am I who I am?' At the time, I think I'm hitting .324 or .3-something," said Garciaparra, who took a .314 average to the park on July 24, but would raise it 10 points that day with three hits.

"No. There may be other things I'm dealing with personally, but I go, 'It has nothing to do with me not wanting to be here.' I said, 'I want to finish my career here.' I go, 'I keep hearing that I want to be traded. I'm telling you guys right now, I don't want to be traded. I want to be here.' The only thing that I might be unhappy about, and I told them. I poured my soul [out] to them," Garciaparra said. "I said, 'All I ask is maybe you guys can help me with the media.' I asked for help with the media. I wasn't bitching about the media. I asked for help. 'For example, the day in New York, you guys came out two days later, Theo does an interview for NESN and sets the record straight that I wanted to play after everybody was painting me a certain way.' I said, 'Did it have to wait two days? Could it have not been the very next day?' I go, 'You know, there are ways, you could have called ESPN and told them the truth before they even aired all that. All I'm asking is for help.' "

If Garciaparra seemed distracted during his abbreviated stint with the Sox in 2004, it's because he was. And not just for baseball reasons. He had married soccer star Mia Hamm the previous winter, and she would spend much of the summer of 2004 abroad training for the Olympics. Garciaparra isn't too macho to admit he missed his wife. He would spend much of his clubhouse time that year sitting at his locker, waiting by his phone, because he remembers that was the only time his schedule coincided with Mia's where they could speak.

"There was one time somebody wrote, 'When you're in the locker room, all you see with Nomar is his head buried in his locker on the phone.' My wife is in another country and she's getting ready for the Olympics. The only window that we had to talk to each other every day was during the window I was talking in the locker room," said Garciaparra. "I was like, 'Did anybody bother to ask me why my head is buried there?' "

None of the players interviewed for this book said that Nomar hindered team chemistry. In fact, most players spoke fondly of him, even while acknowledging that 2004 was not the representative Garciaparra for a lot of reasons.

"He wasn't an outgoing personality, but I liked Nomar," said Kapler. "I thought Nomar was a great person, very supportive. Just not fiery. I saw him, at the very least, as a neutral presence in the clubhouse. He just wasn't performing like he performed in years prior."

In truth, Epstein had nothing personal against Garciaparra. But the way the Sox were underperforming as a team? That was something he took extremely personally. To Epstein, it was a direct indictment of the team he had built, and he knew a change was needed. He knew the Red Sox had to improve their defense.

Theo Epstein knew that championship teams not only caught the baseball with consistency, but also took hits away with regularity. So the GM worked the phones all day on July 31, exhausted every avenue, and finally struck gold on the trade that stunned Boston and the baseball world. Garciaparra was the one headed to the Cubs, not Cabrera. Cabrera would come to Boston. Doug Mientkiewicz, a slick-fielding first baseman who didn't lack confidence, would go from the Twins to Boston, which couldn't be any more convenient, given that the Red Sox were in Minneapolis the day of the trade. The Cubs would send prospects to the Expos to fulfill their part of the deal. In explaining the deal, Epstein felt that Boston's defense would become a fatal flaw if unrepaired. Despite the logic involved, the guts shown by Epstein to trade a franchise icon was rather remarkable.

"We had played .500 ball for three months and had been making costly defensive miscues at key points in the game on a regular basis,"

Epstein said. "We clearly needed some change to stop underperforming, but we weren't sure what shape it would take or whether we'd be able to pull off something big."

Oh, it was big all right. It was a monstrous trade, the general manager's version of a buzzer-beater.

"The Nomar trade was made with just seconds to spare, so we came close to remaining with the status quo, which concerned us," Epstein wrote as part of an e-mail in which he answered a series of questions for this book. "Probably not as much as trading our franchise player, but it concerned us! I do think the trade helped improve the defense and the clubhouse chemistry, but we probably would have played better to some degree had we stayed pat. The team was too good to keep playing .500 ball."

It was Epstein's job to always think about the big picture. At the moment the trade happened, the Red Sox were just trying to get their bearings.

"We don't really know what to say to Nomar," said Damon. "We're kind of saying, 'This is the biggest name for the Boston Red Sox and we just sent him packing.' And then Doug Mientkiewicz comes over all jolly and he's like, 'Hey guys, how's it going?' And it was kind of like, 'Holy crap.' We were still trying to figure out what's next. I think everyone figured, if Nomar's being traded, that means a few other guys could be moved at that point, too."

Without question, it was the most uncomfortable pre-game clubhouse dynamic of the season for the Red Sox. Garciaparra came to the ballpark that day planning on batting fifth and playing shortstop. As he sat at his locker during the pre-game hours, the clubhouse television blared with the news that he might be traded. Garciaparra stared at his phone, awaiting dialogue or information from his agent. And finally, manager Terry Francona had Peter Chase of the Red Sox public relations department usher the media out of the clubhouse. That was when Francona called Garciaparra into the office and delivered the news. As it turned out, Garciaparra had received a text from his agent moments before that the trade had been consummated. Despite the strained relationship Garciaparra had with ownership late in his time with the Red Sox, he definitely appeared shaken by the trade when he spoke to the media in a hall outside the clubhouse at the Metrodome.

"Still to this day, I kind of go, 'Wow.' I didn't know what to feel. I was just numb. I couldn't believe it. [I] packed [my] stuff and I addressed you guys [in the media], and I had to go," Garciaparra said. "That's the nature of it. All of a sudden, I think the business side of this game really hits you because you don't ever think of it that way. I never had to experience the business side of it. I get drafted, I come up with an organization, [I] give everything I have, this community embraces me, I embrace it. It's awesome. I love playing there. All the stuff you go through despite that, no matter what, I still loved it, I still represented it and then all of a sudden, [I was] traded. [I was] like, 'What?' [I] really [didn't] know what to say."

In the weeks, months, and years later, many Red Sox players—even the ones who were most fond of Nomar—think the trade was as big a catalyst as any to the success that followed.

"You want to talk about a move of the century," said Millar. "It's when Theo Epstein traded Nomar Garciaparra. That was like trading Ted Williams. He was an icon in that city. He had tremendous years. But you started seeing things wear a tad thin and Theo makes the move."

With a game coming up against the Twins within hours, the Red Sox really didn't know how to react, particularly players like Tim Wakefield, Martinez, Nixon, Varitek, and Lowe, who had teamed with two-time batting champion Garciaparra for several years, including a pair of playoff runs in the late 1990s. When that core had gotten together, the entire team was built around Pedro and Nomar. It was expected for years that when the team finally won it all, Pedro and Nomar—usually referred to by first name only—would be in the middle of it all. And here was Martinez, just months from free agency himself, watching Garciaparra exit, stage right.

"Given the fact that what we needed was a lot more pitching, I felt I probably wasn't going to get traded," Martinez said. "But I was sad for Nomar because I came over with Nomar. Everything was built around me and Nomar, and I saw Nomar leave and for a minute, I was like, 'I might be next.' But then I thought, 'No, I don't think they're going to break the nucleus.' And when I saw what they did, upgrade to defense, I said, 'OKAY, now I know what they're looking for.' It was sad for me too because Nomar was my colleague here for my whole time in Boston."

Once Garciaparra got to the team hotel in Minneapolis to pack his belongings, Larry Lucchino gave him a call. He reluctantly answered his phone.

"I got a call later on that night from Larry, and that's probably the last phone call I wanted to get," Garciaparra said. "He's like, 'How are you doing?' I'm like, 'I'm great.' He says, 'Great?' What was I supposed to tell him? 'This sucks? I'm miserable? It's awful?' You just traded me. You just changed my life in an instant. What am I supposed to tell you? Despite all this stuff, I never wanted to go. I cried in my room that night. Wow, I couldn't believe it. In the meantime, too, I have to make calls to my new team, 'What's the story, where am I going?' I have to go play the next day and try to win number three hundred for Greg Maddux." Garciaparra got to Wrigley Field in time for the day game on August 1 and had one hit in a Cubs' win. Maddux got a no decision, but he would win No. 300 a week later.

For the Red Sox, it wasn't just a matter of seeing their friend go. They were also trying to wrap their heads around the trade from a baseball sense.

"I don't know that anybody really fully comprehended the return on the trade at that point," Kapler said. "We weren't sure what it meant, what Doug Mientkiewicz was going to mean to our team. He was a new personality coming in, we weren't sure what to expect. Orlando Cabrera was going to be our shortstop and we had heard about Orlando Cabrera, and he turned out to be one of the great teammates."

While most of the clubhouse dealt with conflicting emotions, one man was relieved. Lowe was pitching that night against the Twins, and he was the other Boston player tied up in trade rumors for weeks. There was speculation, in fact, that he could go to the Cubs in exchange for Matt Clement. But Epstein hung on to Lowe, and that wound up being highly fortuitous, as Red Sox fans would learn that October and in the following season, when Clement did come on board and wound up being an injury-plagued washout for three disappointing seasons in Boston. Lowe might have been flaky and inconsistent but he was a big-game pitcher. That was something everyone agreed on. Considering the way Lowe had obsessed about his uncertain future the entire season, it wasn't hard to guess that he was consumed by trade rumors leading up to his start against the Twins on July 31.

The funniest thing of all is that Garciaparra is the one who told Lowe he wasn't traded.

"I remember coming out [of Francona's office]," said Garciaparra. "People were looking at me, and I said, 'D. Lowe, you can relax now.' Derek Lowe was just going on and on: 'Oh, I'm getting traded, I'm getting traded, guys. I'm gone, guys.' And I was like, 'Hey, you can stop saying that now because it ain't you.' I go, 'It's me.' He just looked at me, and everybody was like, 'What?'"

It was the weirdest pre-start day of Derek Lowe's life.

"Oh yeah, I thought it was fifty-fifty I'd get traded," Lowe said. "I think that my performance up to that point was probably a big reason why I didn't get traded. No one wanted you. Let's be honest. You're a free agent at the end of the year. You know you're going to leave. You've got a 6 ERA. There aren't a lot of teams going, 'Sign me up for that guy.' The day of the game, I didn't think about the game at all. It was just a matter of checking your phone every five minutes. Even when you go to the park, you're in there tiptoeing like, just looking around to see if the coaches are looking for you."

Lost in the shuffle of all that had gone on that day, there was another small move—or at least it seemed very small at the time—that Epstein made before the deadline. He got speedy outfielder Dave Roberts from the Dodgers for a marginal prospect hardly anyone had heard of named Henri Stanley. It was a true measure of the collaborative abilities of Epstein's staff that they could pull off this transaction even while working on the mother of all blockbusters. Zack Scott was the baseball operations employee who put together a list of pinch-running options for Epstein, and Roberts was near the top of his list. When Roberts was interviewed for this book on July 4, 2013, he couldn't remember the name of the player he was traded for. Stanley was 26 at the time of the trade and would never play in the Majors. The Dodgers were in a pennant race at the time and opted to acquire Steve Finley in another deal. If the Dodgers didn't trade for Finley, the Red Sox would have never been able to get Roberts. Just like Cabrera, Roberts was not thrilled about the trade when he first was told about it.

"I was very disappointed, to be honest with you," Roberts said. "I was surprised because I was on a team in Los Angeles that was in first place, had a great rapport, chemistry. I was pretty content being on the West Coast, to be honest with you. Obviously my wife [was a factor]; she was eight months pregnant. We had logistics on what we're going to do with that. After kind of being a little bit disappointed, we talked to the doctor; that was one of our first calls. He said if we get her on a flight soon enough we can get her out of here, so that kind of appeased me a little bit to get my wife and my newly coming daughter to Boston."

With the left-handed–hitting Roberts on board, the right-handed–hitting Kapler would have some help in right until Nixon returned. "With Dave, people were like, 'Trot, they're bringing in another outfielder.' I was like, 'I don't care right now. We just care about winning.' That was the beauty about Dave—he cared about winning. He was a fantastic team-mate," said Nixon. "Unbelievable teammate. It was a pleasure just having the opportunity to play with him, let alone become friends with him. He brought a dimension to our team that the Red Sox really didn't have. This guy was dynamic on the base paths. We were always worried about hitting a couple of singles and waiting for the three-run jimmy-jack. Dave not only brought a great defensive outfielder but also brought a dynamic, when he got on the bases, that all of a sudden, the pitchers start to worry a little bit more."

After the tradewinds blew for hours, leaving Garciaparra, Cabrera, and Roberts stunned in different ways, the Red Sox still had a game to play that night of July 31. With Lowe on the mound, Mientkiewicz patrolled first base and Millar moved to right field. Mientkiewicz was showered with a warm farewell ovation by the Metrodome faithful and went 2 for 4 as a visitor. The Red Sox lost 5–4, and still seemed distracted by the trades after the game.

But what the players felt that night paled in comparison to what was going on with Theo Epstein back in Boston. The whole thing might have been easier for the GM if the Red Sox were at home that day, or if he was with the club in Minneapolis. But there he was, in relative isolation, after making one of the most stunning trades in the history of the Boston Red Sox. And not even Epstein's twin brother Paul had any idea why Garciaparra was traded for what seemed a very underwhelming return. Theo and Paul Epstein grew up in the shadow of Fenway Park, living and dying with the team. While Paul would remain a fan, Theo would evolve into the team's biggest decision-maker, left to sometimes make cold-hearted moves that could result in a championship.

"After the press conference, I went back to the office expecting to see all the guys, but it was suddenly empty," said Epstein. "I forgot it was a Saturday. The only sound was a flat screen with ESPN News talking about the trade with a big picture of Nomar in a superimposed Cubs hat. My brother called and said not to turn on WEEI . . . he also asked why we had traded Nomar for a couple of .230 hitters. It was a pretty lonely time and I needed my first-ever Ambien to get to sleep that night."

The next day, however, the Red Sox got their energy drink—the one that would keep them going for the rest of the season. Sunday, August 1 was the morning that Orlando Cabrera joined his new teammates. Anyone who has ever met Cabrera can speak to his fast-talking, high-energy ways. The awkwardness that came with Garciaparra's abrupt departure and Mientkiewicz's land-speed record arrival from the home clubhouse to the visiting side seemed gone by the time Cabrera walked in the door.

"When I came to Minnesota, they welcomed me with open arms," Cabrera said. "Everybody was really excited. I was excited. From the first day, it was just extremely unbelievable chemistry with those guys."

Cabrera had an unforgettable introduction in his first game with the Red Sox. Facing Johan Santana, who would win the Cy Young Award that season, Cabrera slammed the first pitch he saw from the lefty and pounded it over the wall in left.

"First pitch, he hits a home run," said Millar. "It's storybook stuff. You can't make it up."

Well, except for the fact the Red Sox lost the game, 4–3. Here it was, eight days after the galvanizing fight, and Boston was 2 and 3 at the start of a four-city road trip. Though Cabrera's homer against Santana in his debut still sticks out, you might forget that the Twins scored the game-winning run that day when the shortstop had a cutoff throw bounce off his foot for an error.

Things don't always happen instantly. Though Cabrera's opening home run was certainly memorable, he had just two hits in his next 24 at-bats. Small sample size, sure. But when you're replacing Garciaparra, and the Red Sox still seem to be in a funk, it doesn't feel so small.

"It was crazy. One of the first questions I answered the first week was, 'Are you going to hit .350?' If that's what they traded me for, that's not going to happen," Cabrera said.

Francona tried to ease the early pressure his new shortstop might have been feeling by offering him a breather. Cabrera then demonstrated the type of fight the Red Sox would come to love in the coming weeks. "I said, 'Don't give me any days off. I want to be in there. I think I'm helping you at shortstop.' "

That was right around the time Damon gave Cabrera the type of pep talk he would never forget.

"I was sitting at my locker, with my head down. Johnny came to me, and said, 'Listen, we need you. We need you out there. What you're doing now out there on defense right now is priceless. We don't care about what you're hitting. You let us worry about the offense. You just worry about the defense.' When he said that to me, I was part of the team, I think," said Cabrera. "I was part of everybody. Everybody trusted me, and to me, it was just big words. He really gave me that confidence I needed at that time."

Cabrera responded to Damon's calming message by catching fire. In fact, his bat really didn't cool off the rest of the season. He came up with small hits, big hits, and everything in between, nearly all of them line drives. And he turned heads with his defense.

"I never saw Orlando Cabrera play before this," said Damon. "And then I'm playing behind him in center field and I'm saying, 'Oh my God, he gets to everything.' I'm like, 'This is incredible.' "

But Pedro Martinez had glimpsed it before, when Cabrera was a late-season call-up for the Expos in 1997. "Orlando was one guy who could play small ball and fundamentally perfect baseball and also help the pitching staff," said Martinez. "There were times I'd make pitches and he goes, 'You know what, don't throw that pitch again. Throw this one and I'm going to play in the hole.' He was limited with his arm and all that so he seemed to be everywhere the ball was hit, anticipation. The greatest anticipation I've ever seen in a shortstop was Orlando, and that's why he seemed to be in the right place all the time. Also, great energy. Great energy in the clubhouse. He was a loose guy. As soon as he got in, he filled in the space in there. He was really well liked by everybody."

By everybody, that meant Manny too. And this was no small thing. Cabrera instantly became a player that Ramirez liked, respected, and even listened to.

"I think what was important with him being a Latin guy, he was good for Manny," said Foulke. "He wouldn't take any of Manny's crap. He wouldn't let Manny get away with stuff. He was the first one to holler at him and keep him going, and that kind of fuels the fire."

The way Cabrera got Manny to buy in was fascinating. He didn't just give him the old rah-rah "Do it for your teammates" tongue-lashing. You see, Cabrera made Ramirez think he was dependent on him. Millar had performed such psychology on Ramirez for more than a season and a half, but in Cabrera, Ramirez now had a confidant with whom he could speak two languages.

"This was a guy but he was kid, a big kid," said Cabrera. "And he refused sometimes to act like an adult. Somebody else would have to act like an adult. I was like, 'Okay, I'll take that job. I'll tell you when you fuck it up and you're acting like a little kid. You have to bring your A game. You have to be here with us. I've never been in this situation. I want to be in this situation. If you want to be part of it, I'm going to make you do it, at least for me.' I became that person, like I was dependent on him. I made him believe that I was depending on his success."

Nixon will never forget witnessing one of these "pep talks" in person, though he coyly didn't mention Ramirez by name when retelling the story nine years later. It must have been one of those nights when Ramirez was opting to take one of his mental health days, perhaps citing his "hamstring" or "quad."

"There was a situation in the clubhouse one time, Millar and I were there, listening to it," said Nixon. "He said something to a certain player that wasn't playing. After that conversation, I looked at Millar, and Kevin looked at me, and I think there was one other person there, and my jaw started dropping and we were like, 'Let's go get something to eat.' I mean, it was impressive for him to call a certain person out like that, and instantly, we were like, 'That guy is a gamer.' That's the kind of guy that [when] you're going into battle, you want him on your side."

However, in retelling the same story in more descriptive fashion, Schilling left no doubt the identity of the man that Cabrera fumed at.

"It's a home game and it was the week or so after [Cabrera] got traded over here. Manny had taken himself out of the lineup late in the day," said Schilling. "And I was in the back, near where Manny dressed, which was back near the hot tub. And Orlando Cabrera comes around the corner and he looks at Manny sitting at his locker and he goes, 'What the fuck?' Manny says, 'What's up, Papi?' He says, 'Don't fuckin' Papi me. What the fuck?' Manny's like, 'What?' He thought he was kidding. Orlando goes, 'I'm not kidding. I'm not fucking around, dude. You're fucking with my paycheck. You put your fucking ass in the lineup right fucking now or you and I are going to fight.' I was like, 'Holy shit.' And he did. Manny was in the game. I remember thinking, 'Okay, now we go.' It was just perfect. That's when I knew. I knew. That was the day when I thought, 'Okay, this is going to work.'"

When the Red Sox departed Minneapolis and arrived in Tampa, the other new face arrived. And Dave Roberts, though not as fiery as Cabrera, was always smiling.

"I missed my flight going into Minnesota," Roberts said. "I left the next morning and met the team in Tampa. Right when I get there, Manny and David and Johnny give me a big hug and said, 'Hey, welcome to the team.' We had just acquired Mientkiewicz and Orlando Cabrera. There were some new pieces so I didn't feel on an island by myself. Tito, I knew a little before. I was like, this is a good group."

Still, it was impossible at that juncture to know just how perfectly it would all blend together. Years later, when Roberts spent some time in the Padres' front office before eventually becoming their first-base coach, he would come to realize how deftly Epstein had put the final pieces of a championship team together.

"I applaud Theo and his staff for having that vision for a winning team," said Roberts. "They covered all their bases in every aspect of trying to win to make a push. They got a shortstop to catch the baseball, a first baseman to fill in for Millar in the late innings who was a left-handed bat and a defensive specialist, and they brought me in to bring the extra outfielder for Trot when he was hurt. And if we need someone to do something on the bases, we've got a guy who can do that, too."

The Red Sox finally had it all. Now they just had to put all the pieces to good use.

August–September
The Arrival of a Juggernaut

t took one week. That's how long after the stunning trade the Red Sox began a season-ending stretch in which they played like a complete juggernaut. However, that one final week of mediocrity in 2004 was the most unsettling of the season for Theo Epstein.

"I got a little panicky when Cabrera made a big error right out of the chute and we continued to lose for a week or so," Epstein said. "Sometimes my mind would wander and I'd wonder what the hell I was going to do with the rest of my life. By mid-August, we got red hot and there was no looking back."

On the two-week anniversary of the Varitek–A-Rod brawl and the one-week anniversary of the trade, the pieces were finally in place for Francona's troops. There was little warning that August 7 in Detroit was the day that marked the start of one of the most scintillating fifty-five–game runs in Red Sox history. In fact, the day started with Millar not being a good clubhouse guy. Francona had opted to keep his hot right-handed hitter out of the lineup and Millar was upset.

"I wasn't told I was on the bench today," Millar told MLB.com, the *Providence Journal* and the *Boston Globe*. "I didn't know that was the situation. I didn't know they traded for [Mientkiewicz] to be the everyday first baseman. I wasn't told that. Once we got him, it was like maybe I'll play some right field against righties and first base against lefties, and here we are—El Bencho today."

And then, in a weird twist, Ramirez, perhaps trying to do Millar a favor, pulled himself from the lineup that night with flu symptoms. So instead of riding "El Bencho," Millar started in left that night, producing a hit and two walks and helping Martinez and the Red Sox to a 7–4 win. Millar apologized to Francona the next day for the "El Bencho rant." Perhaps the arrival of Mientkiewicz was the best thing that had happened to Millar. It kept him driven enough to keep the hot streak that had started on July 23 going until the end of the season. And he would settle back in as the regular first baseman, while Mientkiewicz would be used mainly for defense in the late innings.

Roles were starting to become clear and the team took off like a jet plane. Starting with that win in Detroit, the Sox played exquisite baseball for the rest of the season, going 40 and 15. From that point on, players seemed to be in a race to get to the park. The wins were piling up and the chemistry got better by the day. Cabrera created celebratory handshakes for every player, each seemingly more complex than the one before. Mientkiewicz would always come off the bench for the last inning or two, and would usually make a spectacular play or two. "We called him Mient-pick-awicz," said Nixon.

Mientkiewicz was so good with the glove that Francona started him at second base for an August 16 home game against the Blue Jays, which the Red Sox won, 8–4. Not only did he start a double play with a slick catch on a grounder, but he nearly got into it with Carlos Delgado, who forearmed him en route to second base. Mientkiewicz was a first-class battler, just like Cabrera and Roberts and nearly all of his new teammates.

"We were hurting. We were beat up. I think Ricky Gutierrez might have been our only backup that night and he was even beat up. His back was stiff," Francona said. "And one of the things I loved about Theo was he was never afraid to try something, like if it's outside the box or something. But when I told him that, I think he was like, 'Uh-oh.' And I'll be damned. First inning, groundball double play. They knocked Mientkie-wiecz on his ass, but he turned the double play. And I remember turning to [bench coach Brad Mills] and saying, 'He's the only guy on our team that makes that play.' "

Sinkerballer Lowe, with Cabrera playing behind him, settled into one of his few decent grooves of the season. And Epstein made one final move the night before the sizzling late-season stretch started, plucking lefty submariner Mike Myers off waivers from the Mariners, giving south-paw Alan Embree some support in the mid to late innings.

"You talk about Mike Myers; yeah, he's not going to ooohhh and aaahhh you coming out of the bullpen, but he makes it uncomfortable for left-handed hitters, I know that much," Nixon said. "Little things here and there. The organization just went out and said, 'These are our needs.' And they filled them."

For a team that had been unable to find a consistent winning mix in the previous months, it was striking how beautifully it all came together once it did. It was part chemistry, part ability, and a lot of probably just being overdue.

"And Manny was in good spirits, which was a huge thing," Kapler said. "David was in good spirits. Varitek had emerged at that point as the clear-cut, no-equal leader of our team, and in a way that was so unusual and so nontraditional in that you normally don't see leaders that quiet. It was just complete by example. Like, complete, 'Follow me, and I'm going to be selfless and put everybody else first,' and so yeah, a lot of those things were starting to happen all at once."

And the caveman who led off and played center field put together a glittering season offensively, although he was overshadowed by the over-powering Ortiz-Ramirez combo. "I just felt like every time somebody was on base, I was a home-run threat that year," said Damon. "I found my per-fect positioning and I opened up some. I crowded the plate. And pitchers kept making mistakes."

A Red Sox player might have felt he'd made a mistake if he hap-pened to walk into the clubhouse shortly before the game would start and Damon would be doing naked pull-ups. If it were anybody else, it would have been a stunning sight. But after all, this was the same guy who was chasing cars on foot back in January. "Well, it started because when I joined the team in 2002, we still had a very tiny clubhouse. We ate in the middle of the clubhouse and our training room was mixed in with our weight room," said Damon. "It was very tiny. If you wanted to get in the tub, you kind of had to wait. We're in a small little area. There's a pullup bar and no reason to jump in the whirlpool with my dry pants, so I would wait to get in, and do pull-ups while I waited. I started with the towel around me, but then it just became funny when that towel couldn't wrap around me, so I would do it, see how many guys I could gross out, and then jump in the tub."

The Red Sox had become the definition of a team, with everyone feeling they were completely vital to the overall success.

"See, the thing with Boston, I think everybody on the team knew how important everybody was. From Pedro to Schilling down to Dave Roberts and Kap, everybody had a job," Damon said. "Nobody had to be told what to do. Francona knew he was penciling me in every night, even if I'm in the tub ten minutes before the game. That was a team that understood each other."

So after spending four solid months searching for the right combination, Francona suddenly had the most enjoyable team in the world to manage. He even felt like a football coach in a way, because he had an offensive team he would start the game with and a defensive team he would finish with.

"All of a sudden, when we get to bigger ballparks or something, we could defense for guys. We could use our offense," Francona said. "We could use it and then we could substitute guys, we could pinch run, so we kind of had the best of both worlds and we used it. Everybody felt included because they all knew they were part of the team and it really worked. Once we got on a roll, we were using everybody. It's a fun way to play. We had that group of Kapler, Pokey, Mientkiewicz, Dave Roberts; we'd get a lead and then we'd flip-flop four or five guys and then we'd have the speed and defense in there and it became a weapon for us."

And the players didn't balk at any of the maneuvering because there was implicit trust in Francona.

"That guy was the perfect manager for that team," said Cabrera. "You could not find a better guy than that guy. Francona, he understood the team. He was out of the way. 'Just do what you know how to do.' He was amazing for us."

Francona knew better than to mess with the suddenly magic potion that had overtaken his team. "It was everything we had hoped for. Again, it doesn't always happen, but I'm a big believer that if you jump ship too quick or you panic, you don't give yourself a chance to let that happen," Francona said. "That doesn't guarantee it's gonna, but I think that's the only way it will happen. And once they got going, it was like, 'Hey, get out of the way and let them go.' "

The one thing everybody remembers is the confidence that spread like wildfire. The Red Sox had turned into a high-octane machine, and it didn't take the standings to realize it. They had an attitude, and it translated into near-perfect baseball. "We kind of felt that swagger that you wanted as a group. And you knew that we were a team now that nobody wanted to play," Millar said. "We had the same haircuts, we had the same facial hair. They just knew, when we rolled into town, it was like, 'We're the Sox.' When the Sox rolled, you knew now. We always knew we were good. But at that point, when we started rolling, and we have Pedro on the mound every fifth day and Schilling on the mound every fifth day and Bronson and Wakefield and D. Lowe, and Foulke was closing games like nothing with his changeup, it's just, we were almost, I don't want to say unbeatable, but we were balanced. There was not a hole with this group of guys. It was a group of guys that were healthy, cared about each other, and were pretty darn good."

Johnny Damon played parts of eighteen seasons in the Majors for seven different teams. But that stretch late in 2004 perhaps stands out from anything else he was ever a part of when you combine the amount of talent with the amount of brotherhood.

"It was the absolute best," Damon said. "We had fun on the field, had fun off the field, we cared about each other and just had a mentality —every time we went to a city—that other teams were scared of us. That's a pretty good feeling."

Even for Schilling, who had played for a National League pennant-winner in Philly in 1993 and a world champ for Arizona in 2001, this late-season stretch of 2004 was absolutely something to behold. He just wishes he could go back and relive it, so he could cherish it while it was happening. "Like a lot of my career, [I] just didn't get to enjoy it. It was fun, but it was hard because there was no letup," Schilling said. "Every day it was different. Every day you were back in the saddle. There was no sitting there, going, 'That was great.' It's one of the regrets of my career. I wasn't able to enjoy my career the way I would have liked because ... and I couldn't have. I don't think I could have done the things I did if I had been able to sit back and think how awesome it was."

Speaking of awesome, that's exactly what Schilling was down the stretch of that season. Though the ankle still barked at him at times, the righty couldn't be stopped. Over Schilling's final nine starts of the regular season, he was 8 and 0 with a 2.42 ERA. Opponents hit .188 against him over that span. And the streak didn't just happen. Somebody not only motivated Schilling, but also found a way to guide him through the home stretch.

"Chris Correnti came to me and he laid out a bunch of paper and he said, 'Listen, here's the data.' And he showed me basically the last five or six years of my career, from August on," said Schilling. "He said, maybe from a conditioning standpoint, we need to change some things. And if you look over the last six to eight weeks of that season, I didn't get beat. Every game after a loss, I won. I pitched probably my best baseball that last six weeks of the season because of him. I was very proud of that fact."

Correnti's role on that team should not be discounted. His main job was to keep the starting rotation healthy. Not one member of the rotation missed a start that year.

"Chris was amazing," Schilling said. "He had a ton to do with that. And when you think about the personalities of those five starters, you would not find five more different human beings. You had Wake, who was the knuckleballer, who was just on this otherworldly program. You had Derek Lowe, who was about a seven-year-old and it was like herding cats every day with him. You had Bronson, who was as dependable as anyone on the planet. He could throw five innings one day and five the next. But he wanted to play his guitar. And you had Petey and you had me, a Type A personality who never shuts up and puts his foot in his mouth.

"It was just an incredibly eclectic group of guys, but at the end of the day, one of the things you learn when you get older in baseball is all that other stuff is bullshit. What do you do at 7:05 when the ball is in your hand? Every one of those guys was a winner."

Though there were always whispers around baseball about how popular or unpopular Schilling was, he was a strong fit with the 2004 Red Sox. Players like Doug Mirabelli, Trot Nixon, and Kevin Millar loved to ride Schilling. And Gabe Kapler, who studied personalities more closely than probably any of the other players on that team, thought that Schilling was greatly misunderstood. "For me, I think you get to know guys less from their legacy and what they had accomplished on the field and more from who they are. I just found Curt to be misunderstood," Kapler said. "He is not abrasive. He is engaging. He is bright and he's articulate and he's smart. And he's a good teammate. You have to work to see it sometimes. You have to peel back the first layer and then what you've got is an extraordinary, special human being. There are some guys who just, on their surface, they walk into a room, and that's a great guy—somebody like Dave Roberts, for example. Curt, first of all, you have to give him what he dishes out. You have to be willing to go toe-to-toe with him. You earn his respect and then when you earn his respect, then you get to know him as a human being."

By September, behind their workhorse starting rotation, the Red Sox were in cruise control for a Wild Card berth. Hardly anyone noticed when they actually started tailing the Yankees. The day the 40 and 15 stretch started, the Sox were ten and a half games back in the East. Just one month later, on September 8 after a win in Oakland, Boston was only two games behind their rivals.

They rolled into Yankee Stadium on Friday, September 17, as a completely different team than the one that stumbled out after the epic thirteen-inning loss on July 1. Manny Ramirez made perhaps the best catch of his entire career, jumping over the wall to take a home run away from Miguel Cairo. They trailed Mariano Rivera in the ninth and came storming back. Roberts did that foreshadowing thing when he pinch-ran for Nixon and stole second.

"[Catcher] Jorge [Posada] went to the mound, had a meeting at the mound, and when he went back behind home plate, Mo came set, and held and held and held, and then delivered," said Roberts. "He did it again, and then I stole the base. So I knew that if I ever get that opportunity again, they're going to try to hold the ball on me to defense me stealing second base."

Rest assured, Roberts would get another opportunity to steal against Rivera. On this night, Roberts took the turn around third and came roaring home on an RBI single to right by Cabrera, who relished coming up with the game on the line. With two outs, Damon blooped one into center that Kenny Lofton literally watched drop at his shoe-tops as Rivera screamed in anger. In came Kapler and the Red Sox had the lead, en route to a 3–2 win.

It was an auspicious way for Boston to open the weekend series, but Derek Lowe got bombed the next day, his lowest of low points. Amid Internet reports that Lowe had been out carousing the night before because he expected a rainout, the righty recorded all of three outs in an abomination of a performance. Lowe gave up seven runs and made an embarrassing play on defense, when he looked to third and first, and didn't throw the ball anywhere. At a time everything else in the Red Sox' universe couldn't be better, Lowe was falling apart at the seams.

"That was terrible," said Lowe. "I remember that because I think that was when somebody said I was out all night long. Somebody said they saw me at some club at like three o'clock in the morning. I was like, 'This is just adding misery to my season' and then, you go out there and pitch one inning. In a made-up story, it actually in a stupid way gave it credibility because people were thinking 'Maybe he did.' There's no way that happened. That pissed me off."

The Yankees pounded Pedro the next day, and the division became an afterthought for the Red Sox at that point, which was fine. In 2004, the only difference between winning the division and the Wild Card was one extra home game in the first round. Eight years later, the rules would be altered, with the division champ getting more rest while two Wild Card teams would have to play a one-game playoff to see which one got into the postseason. There would be one final rivalry weekend with the Yankees before the postseason, and it came a week later at Fenway. It started with Martinez again facing his rivals, and the Yankees again getting the best of him. This time, Francona gave Red Sox fans nightmares of the Grady Little game the season before, keeping his ace in for 117 pitches and not pulling him until the lead had slipped away in the eighth. After the game, Martinez made news when he got so exasperated that he said, "I guess I just have to tip my cap and call the Yankees my daddy."

In his seven seasons with the Red Sox, Martinez would go just 10 and 12 against the Yankees, posting a 3.20 ERA. Boston's record in those games was an even more eye-opening 13 and 20.

"It was overexposure," said Martinez. "I was exposed to the Yankees too much. The same thing that's happened to Mariano [against Boston]. It doesn't matter how good you are if you are overexposed to someone, because a hitter can make an adjustment from one at-bat to the other. But a pitcher cannot switch mechanics from one month to another. You throw off whatever you know."

And what in the world ever inspired Martinez to call the Yankees his "daddy"? Allow the man to explain. "That terminology of daddy comes from winter ball," Martinez explained in 2013. "So I went on to use that. In the Dominican, let's say I owned Jay Buhner, they would say, 'Pedro is a papa to Jay Buhner.' That means daddy; he should have respect for me."

Despite the order of the standings, the Red Sox in no way felt inferior to the Yankees at that point in 2004. Instead, they were just hoping they could get a rematch in the playoffs. All that needed to be done before the regular season ended was for the Sox to get their house in order. One thing that was pivotal was getting Nixon back in the lineup. The gritty right fielder had been out of action from July 25 to September 6, and he served as an in-game replacement for four straight games before finally returning to the lineup on September 12. It was a long, hard road back for Nixon, but he was willing to do whatever it took to get back for the time of year everyone was waiting for. He worked with trainer Scott Waugh at Boston University daily. "Being on the disabled list, I think there were doctors saying I had zero chance, probably, of being ready for the post-season with the injury that I had," Nixon said. "My quad was close to rupturing. I told Scott that and I was like, 'Look, I want to get back on the field. If we go to the postseason, I need to be on the field.' I knew, and we both kind of knew, it was a situation where I needed to get back early enough where I could prove to the organization that I was healthy. We went hard, man."

Unbeknownst to Orlando Cabrera, the Red Sox clinched the Wild Card on September 27 with a win over the Rays. In fact, if you look at the video from the end of the game, the Red Sox aren't doing much more than their standard victory handshake line. But when they returned to the clubhouse, cases of champagne were waiting for them.

"I didn't even know we clinched. I remember [Dave] McCarty, the first baseman, he was like a crazy numbers dude, and before the game, he was like, 'I did some numbers and mathematically nobody can beat us or get to us.'" Cabrera took McCarty's word for it when he got to the clubhouse after the game, and saw the celebration unfold.

Besides playing the final six meaningless regular-season games, there was just one last order of business for Francona: It was time to plot the rotation. There was no doubt Schilling would get the nod over Pedro in Game 1. By that point in the season, he had clearly emerged as the team's best pitcher. And Martinez was coming off the two clunkers against the Yankees. The venerable Tim Wakefield was also sure to be part of the team's postseason rotation. Even though he stunk for most of 2004, posting a 5.42 ERA, Derek Lowe didn't seem to have any inkling that he was going to be the odd man out when it came time for Francona to shrink his rotation to four pitchers for October.

When Lowe got the news during the season-ending series in Baltimore that he was headed to the bullpen and Arroyo had won the final rotation spot, he blew up in the manager's office in front of not only Francona, but also Theo Epstein and pitching coach Dave Wallace. This was the cherry on top of what had been the most miserable baseball season of Derek Lowe's life. And now he wouldn't even have the playoffs to make it all right.

"And I threw a hissy fit and said a lot of bad words," Lowe said. "People can figure out which bad words I said. I told them I wasn't going to be on the team. I said, 'I'm going home.' Like, I'm not sitting in the bullpen for these playoffs."

If only Lowe could have seen it as clearly in Francona's office in Baltimore as he did on his living room couch nine years later.

"Looking back on it, it was all self-inflicted," said Lowe. "The reason why I wasn't in the playoff rotation was because of my own pitching. No organization is going to put guys in the rotation they don't believe are going to win. But again, this goes back to what we were saying earlier. That was just the bow for my season. I didn't really give myself a chance all season from a mental standpoint. Now, not only do you have a bad year, but the time you normally pitch well, when you can recover, now you're not even going to get that opportunity. I'm thinking I might have to sign a Minor League deal after this whole debacle."

Even when Lowe foolishly threatened to quit and abandon his team for the playoffs, Epstein and Francona tried to keep him on board. "They said something along the lines of, 'We're not going to basically hold those words against you right now. We'll give you a day to kind of think about it but we want you in the bullpen.' Again, I talked to Jason [Varitek], I talked to the guys," said Lowe. "They were like, 'Come on, man.' "

{92}   **IDIOTS REVISITED**

Of course, when it came to these types of chats, nobody could be more blunt than Curt Schilling, and he tried to give Lowe a wake-up call during batting practice in Baltimore.

"We were in the outfield and he and I were going at it," said Schilling. "I was like, 'Dude, you've got to stop. You've got to grow up. You will get the ball in your hand to help us win a World Series. You just have to keep your mind right.' You remember how Derek was. But that was the challenge."

When the Red Sox filed out of Camden Yards, they took their 98–64 record from the regular season and boarded a plane for the sunny skies of Anaheim, California, where the Angels were awaiting the start of the Division Series.

Division Series–Early ALCS
Sweep, and Then Almost Swept

hen the Red Sox got to Southern California to open their playoff run, Derek Lowe was in a foul mood. He got to the field early for the team's preseries workout and tried to run his anger off—from foul pole to foul pole.

"I got there super early. I ran, God, for like an hour and a half," said Lowe. "I did poles—angry poles. I was just, like, bitter at everybody in a way. But I took it as, 'I'm going to pitch to prove the Red Sox wrong.' That's the way I dealt with this. That's what I have to do to kind of get myself in the right frame of mind. When I do pitch, and I get a chance, I have to pitch to prove them wrong. As crazy as it sounds, that was my mentality. Then, of course, you're out there, I'm carrying the gum bag out [to the bullpen] before the game."

There was no anger within Curt Schilling. Instead, he was filled with pure determination. The championship he'd started talking about the previous November was finally within reach—a mere 11 wins away. And Schilling was going to get the party started.

"This is what I was brought here for. The regular season was awesome and that was great and I had fun but at the end of the day, I was brought here to win three or four games in October, period," said Schilling. "I didn't have a problem with that."

He even developed a catch phrase. Schilling went on to the Sons of Sam Horn website, where most of the most analytical and passionate Red Sox fans hung out in 2004, and started a thread in the fan forum section the night before the playoffs opened. Schilling surveyed the eight teams who were playing in the playoffs and wondered, "Why Not Us?"

"The whole 'Why Not Us' thing, I made the T-shirts because once you got past the goofy name, hey, why not us?" Schilling said. "What is stopping us? There has never been a curse. It's always been a curse of talent. You just had never been the better team, because I always believe the better team wins the biggest games. At the end of the day, we didn't have the better team. Now we did. Why not us? Give me a reason."

Indeed. Why not? The Red Sox were loaded going into those playoffs and had no detectable weaknesses. Playing in the postseason wasn't as old hat for everyone on that 2004 team as it was for Schilling. When Orlando Cabrera went out to shortstop for Game 1, he felt like his heart was going to explode.

"I remember, to be honest with you, I was really freaking nervous," Cabrera said. "I was like, so nervous. It was like I had been just called up to the big leagues. I was like, 'What the hell is going on? Why am I so nervous?' It was just the media attention and the whole atmosphere, I was like, 'Wow, this is what the playoffs is like. This is like what I watch on TV all the time.'"

Perhaps a sense of calm came over Cabrera once he looked around the field and saw the players he was surrounded by—the same ones he had dominated with for the previous six weeks.

"I was able to just pull myself down and level myself and just play the game the way we were playing it for the last two months and everybody was happy and we really felt like there was no stopping us," Cabrera said.

With lefty Jarrod Washburn on the mound for the Angels, Gabe Kapler got the start in right field, with Trot Nixon available off the bench. "Those games felt like the World Series," said Kapler. "They felt so important. We thought they had a really good club and we did."

But the Red Sox had a wagon at that point, one that seemed primed to steamroll over whoever crossed in their path. After a seven-run outburst in the fourth, the Sox were up, 8–0, reinforcing the question: Who could stop this team? The blowout in motion became kind of a snoozefest as everyone started to turn their attention toward Game 2, when Pedro Martinez would take the ball under the lights.

But there was a possible setback in the seventh inning when Garret Anderson hit a tapper toward the mound that Schilling charged. Then he planted, or tried to, and his right ankle gave out. The throw was wild, down the right-field line. But that was the least of Schilling's concerns. He clutched his ankle. As it would later be learned, his tendon sheath had ruptured on that play. Schilling stayed in for one more batter, giving up an RBI double to Troy Glaus. The severity of the injury wasn't revealed until a week or so later, so the Red Sox basked in the glow of their Game 1 romp, which ended with an 8–3 score.

Legitimate wonder about how he would perform caused a buzz in the air for Martinez's Game 2 start. The proud ace had been pounded in his final three regular-season starts, going 0 and 3 with a 9.35 ERA. For a prideful athlete, which Martinez certainly always was, this was the epitome of a statement game. And as you might expect, he came out throwing gas, his fastball in the mid-nineties, where it hadn't been for most of the season.

"It was crunch time," Martinez remembers. "I did what I was supposed to do. It's playoffs. Adrenaline will take you. You know that everything could be in jeopardy if you lose, so you let it all go. That's the reason you play the whole season—to get to that point and let it all out."

Martinez's night ended when he blew a fastball by Chone Figgins to end the seventh. Schilling erupted with approval in the dugout, elated by Martinez's having silenced his critics once again.

In the top of the seventh, the inning in which the Sox would take the lead for good, Dave Roberts pinch-ran for Bill Mueller and wound up not stealing. Instead, he was forced out on a grounder. To Roberts, it didn't matter that the Sox scored the go-ahead run anyway on a sacrifice fly by Jason Varitek; he felt that he hadn't done his job. "Francisco Rodriguez was pitching. It was a tie game and I didn't steal," Roberts said. "After that game, I was so frustrated in myself that I had an opportunity to run and I didn't run. So I said, 'If I ever get that chance going forward, I'm not going to miss it.' "

Meanwhile, Cabrera belted away any lingering nerves with a three-run double into the gap in left center in the top of the ninth, and the rout was on in the eventual 8–3 win. In the first two games, the Sox had hammered the Angels by an aggregate score of 17–6. And now they were coming home smelling blood. The Fenway faithful were in a festive mood on a warm Friday afternoon, salivating as the Red Sox tied to sweep Anaheim. Bronson Arroyo, deemed unflappable by this point in the season, got the nod and went to work, turning in a strong six-inning performance. Vladimir Guerrero silenced Fenway temporarily when he hit a stunning grand slam to right against Mike Timlin to tie the game in the seventh.

"Grand slam to right center and Fenway and I'm just like, 'Wow, what am I going to do?'" said Timlin. "The good part about it, it became totally irrelevant."

Not only that, but Derek Lowe was about to stop becoming irrelevant. The game was still tied in the top of the tenth, and Francona had already pored through his bullpen. All he had left was Lowe and Curtis Leskanic, a respected veteran whose arm was running on fumes in the final weeks of his career.

"I think they just drew straws," said Lowe. "The crowd was just unbelievable. They gave me a standing ovation when I came in there; they were yelling my name. I go out there and I was more nervous that game than any game I pitched in the regular season or playoffs. Just because, again, I'm trying to help the team win, but also kind of prove them wrong at the same time. And then I hadn't pitched in a long time."

It wasn't the prettiest scoreless inning of Lowe's career. He gave up a deep fly to center and then a walk. After a sacrifice bunt and an infield single, Lowe got Figgins to hit a ground ball up the middle. But Orlando Cabrera was there—of course he was. And Cabrera fired to first, getting the Red Sox back into the dugout. Damon singled up the middle to lead off Boston's tenth against Francisco Rodriguez and was erased on a bad bunt by Bellhorn. Ramirez struck out for the second out. Angels manaager Mike Scioscia then made an interesting decision, pulling out the reliever who had perhaps the nastiest stuff in baseball at that point in time and bringing on his Game 1 starter, lefty Jarrod Washburn. Scioscia also passed up his closer Troy Percival so he could go with the left-on-left matchup against David Ortiz.

After Washburn finished his warm-ups, the legend of Big Papi began on a national level, and it still hasn't ended. The lefty slugger walloped the first pitch he got from Washburn and put it into the Green Monster seats. Ortiz hadn't just walked off a game: He walked off an entire series.

"It was something that brings back a lot of memories," said Ortiz. "There's no better feeling than that."

The season before, Ortiz had started evolving into Boston's Mr. Clutch. He ripped a two-run double in Game 4 of the 2003 Division Series to overturn a deficit against his future teammate Keith Foulke, who was then with the Athletics. And in Game 7 that year against the Yankees, Ortiz put a David Wells fastball into the seats in the top of the eighth, putting the Sox up 5–2 before the roof caved in on Martinez and Grady Little.

In 2004, Ortiz turned into a megastar, hitting .301 with 41 homers and 139 RBIs. But the key stat was at-bats. Ortiz had 582 of them that year, the first time he had broken the 500 barrier in his career. Add in Ramirez's numbers (.308, 43 HRs, 130 RBIs), and the Red Sox had one of the great middle-of-the-order tandems of all-time. Ramirez would finish third in the MVP race that year, while Ortiz was fourth. When the Red Sox got right-handed hitting veteran Ellis Burks the previous winter, many wondered how much Ortiz would play against lefties, because that seemed a perfect role for Burks, who was too hobbled to play defense by that point of his career.

"I remember telling David in Spring Training, because I wanted to be honest with everybody," said Francona. "I said, 'There may be a lefty or two that I sit you against or I pinch hit you against,' but I said, 'Other than that, no need to worry.' I remember him looking at me with some skepticism, like, 'Oh boy, here we go.' We're into July and I told him, I said, 'I told you.' He was like, 'Yeah, I know, but I didn't know you.' I said, 'Hey, that's why I told you. I would never tell you something I didn't mean.'"

Ortiz's rise to stardom was impressive, considering Theo Epstein had signed him for all of $1 million the season before, after the Twins had foolishly released him. As Ortiz rounded the bases en route to clinching his team's trip to the ALCS, his teammates started looking at him like he was some kind of superhero. Ortiz tossed his helmet high in the air for emphasis just as he reached the plate, and allowed his teammates to pounce on him. "His status at that point, especially in the clubhouse and amongst the players, was almost otherworldly," said Kapler. "We almost expected greatness in those late-inning at-bats, perhaps unfairly so, like 'He's going to hit a thousand. He's going to get a hit every time. It was going to be an extra base hit and it was going to be a dramatic hit.' That was sort of what we came to expect from him. We bought into how Boston was feeling about David at that time."

Courtesy of Ortiz's missile into the Monster, the winning pitcher in the Division Series clincher was none other than Derek Lowe. Thanks to the three-game sweep, the Red Sox could await the result of the Yankees -Twins ALDS and know that they'd have three days off before taking the field again. After the post-game party in the clubhouse, some of the players went to another party right across the street.

"[Ortiz] turned into the greatest clutch hitter of all time," said Damon. "He was just on fire. He was hitting home runs. He was winning ballgames." At that point, it seemed apparent something special was happening with the Red Sox. They were putting on daily baseball clinics, and it didn't appear the increased stakes would faze them.

"We felt great because everything was working," said Francona. "We had pitching, we had hitting—timely hitting—[and we had] defense. Anaheim was a tough team to play because they ran, and they ran so aggressively and we played them so well that you had to be excited going into the New York series."

Yes, the New York series. After losing Game 1 to the Twins, the Yankees woke up and won the next three, setting up the rematch with the Red Sox that had seemed destined to happen for weeks. For the 15 players who remained from the 2003 heartbreak, this was a chance at redemption to salivate over.

"I think [that] going in, we knew that to secure our legacy, we were going to have to beat the Yankees," Kapler said. "That almost sounds obnoxious. But there's a lot of truth to that. To not be the whipping boy anymore, you have to kick the guy's ass. You can't go kick somebody else's ass. You have to beat up the big bully. And it's funny, it's ironic, that those first three games, we just got our asses kicked."

This wasn't what Curt Schilling had in mind when he held a press conference the day before the ALCS started and announced, "I can't think of any scenario more enjoyable than making 55,000 people from New York shut up."

For all the talk he had done all year—and Schilling never apologized for any of it—it seemed like he was going to finally have to eat some words. It was as if the dream that had been evolving for the last few weeks turned into an utter nightmare once the Red Sox got to Yankee Stadium for Game 1. Actually, the first horrible thing happened when Schilling walked out of the dugout, en route to the bullpen, and messed up his ankle even further. "Well, I knew when I walked out of the dugout, and I hit the top step of the dugout, I knew the tendon dislocated. I knew there was a problem," Schilling said. "I didn't know how or what we were going to do to fix it but I knew there was a problem."

When he started warming up in the bullpen, there was no comfort to be had. "I couldn't [get comfortable]," Schilling said. "I couldn't. I was just trying to survive." The Yankees pounced on the wounded pitcher, hitting one rope after another en route to a two-run first. By the third, after a three-run double by Hideki Matsui, it was 6–0. Gary Sheffield slid home with the third run and pumped his fist with such elation you would have thought the Yankees had already won the series.

There was another problem. Mike Mussina had the nastiest stuff possible that night. Dredging up memories of when he'd retired twenty-six straight batters at Fenway Park in 2001, the Moose mowed down the first eighteen in this one. Bellhorn ended his thoughts of a perfect game with a double in the seventh, and the Red Sox actually rallied for five in the inning, the last two coming when Varitek ripped a two-run homer against Kapler and Nixon's old pal, Tanyon Sturtze. A game that the Yankees once led 8–0 actually became 8–7 when Ortiz—who else?—belted a two-run triple in the eighth. The Yankees wound up preserving a 10–7 win, meaning that 99.99999 percent of the media attention after the game would be on Schilling and his gimpy right ankle. "If I can't do better than that, I'm not going to take the ball again," said Schilling, as downtrodden at that moment as at any point in his career.

The Red Sox couldn't obsess about Schilling's uncertain status. They had to try to climb back into the series. Initially, that was a failed mission. Martinez came out for Game 2, his first start at Yankee Stadium since his infamous daddy statement. With every pitch he threw, 55,000 or so people yelled in unison, "Who's your daddy?" Martinez actually stood up pretty well to the challenge and turned in one of his best games against the Yankees in a while, but lost 3–1, the difference a two-run homer by John Olerud.

Coming back to Fenway, the Red Sox felt reasonably confident they could get back in the series, and even got an extra day to lick their wounds when rain poured down in Boston on Friday, pushing Game 3 to Saturday. Yet not even that helped. Arroyo got shelled and the Yankees teed off in what looked like extra batting practice. People forget that after the Yankees scored three runs in the first inning, the Red Sox actually came back with four in the second to take the lead. But the New York bats piled on, leaving the Red Sox bloodied. It was only the fourth inning and Francona's pitchers had already given up nine runs when Tim Wakefield came trotting out to the mound.

Nobody could have known it at the time, but this was actually the first turning point of the series. Wakefield was supposed to start the next night. But in the most selfless act imaginable, he volunteered his services early in Game 3 so Francona could preserve his bullpen for the rest of the series. And Wakefield's brainstorm also created life for Derek Lowe, who would return to the rotation for Game 4, when his team's season depended on it.

"I just remember sitting on the end of the bench, I don't remember who all was down there, maybe Mirabelli and Derek Lowe," said Wakefield. "And we were just talking about how we couldn't use Timlin or Embree or even Foulke at that point. We can't waste these guys today because they had already done so much in games 1 and 2. I went down to Tito and asked him what he thought. I kind of said, 'Do you need me to go down there?' He said, 'Go ask Derek if he can pitch tomorrow.' I went down and Derek said, 'Yeah, I'll start tomorrow.'"

Certain images become blurry through time, but when Francona talks about Wakefield volunteering his services, it's as if he's right back in that moment. "I can still picture Wake standing behind me, he's like the little kid in Little League who doesn't get in the game," said Francona. "We're getting our asses kicked and there's Wake. He's got his spikes on and his glove in his hand, and he's like, 'Where do you want me?' It just gave me such a good feeling. That, to me, epitomized our team and that's what made me happy."

By the end of the 19–8 bloodbath, happiness wasn't a very familiar sentiment. The final score looked worse than it had to be, mainly because Francona was trying to keep his big guns ready for what was now going to need to be a miracle finish for Boston to get to the World Series. "To me, it didn't matter if we lost by ten or twelve," Francona said. "We got killed that game. Using Foulke for an inning that game is not going to help. I had trouble convincing people of that. I was like, 'Our goal is to win four games, not one.' "

In other words, it was a bit of a rope-a-dope strategy by Francona. And there was another boxing analogy that came to mind: Rocky Balboa. "It felt to me like the Yankees series . . . was like a Rocky fight," said Kapler. "You know how early in all the fights he just gets bloodied and beaten up and that's all you see for the first three minutes—blood and sweat flying all over the place? And then finally [he gets] some momentum the other way and he gets back in there."

Only this story wasn't part of an Oscar-winning movie. It was the setup to one of the most historic comebacks in sports history.

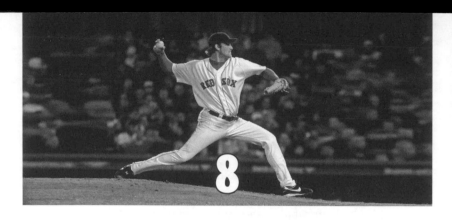

Game 4, ALCS
Man of Steal

eing the chief "Idiot" everyone knew and loved, Johnny Damon figured the best way to respond to being one defeat away from an embarrassing sweep in the ALCS was to pack his suitcase so he'd be ready to head home as soon as the Red Sox lost Game 4. In actuality, Damon was just goofing around and trying to lighten the mood by packing. He figured if he packed, the Red Sox would win—kind of like the guy who knows that if he doesn't bring an umbrella, he'll get poured on, and if he does, he would stay dry.

"Pack your bags," Damon said. "I always feel like if you do something like that, it won't happen, so I had my bags packed and ready, because I knew if we lost, I was in a car that day and I was gone. Then we all just kind of started saying, 'We're not ready to take our kids to school yet or get in the car line, so let's win.' "

While a lot of that talk seemed like reaching for a team that sure seemed headed to an early vacation, Kevin Millar put on the most convincing happy face, and it was even captured on camera.

"Don't let us win tonight," Millar told anyone who would listen during batting practice. "We win tonight, you've got Pedro in Game 5, Schilling in Game 6, and anything can happen in Game 7." Millar told this to bullpen catcher Dana LeVangie, a Massachusetts resident. He told it to fans sitting behind the dugout. And most passionately, he told it to *Boston Globe* columnist Dan Shaughnessy, who wrote that the Red Sox threatened to go down as a "pack of frauds" if they were swept by their forever enemies.

"When I read the article about Shaughnessy calling us frauds, it hit home. I said, 'Wait a minute, we're not frauds. They might be better than us, but we're not frauds.' One thing that team is not is frauds," Millar said. "The Yankees can be better, and they probably were better. But the fraud situation got me and that's what started the whole thing. . . . So when I got to the field that day, I wasn't going to change. I wasn't going to pout or start packing up boxes. We had to now fight."

One of Millar's closest friends on the team was Kapler. Yet Kapler still doesn't believe the rest of the team felt what Millar was feeling going into Game 4.

"Millar and I argue about this," said Kapler. "But the only time I can remember in the entire season where I felt like we as a unit didn't believe in ourselves was after Game 3 of the ALCS. And he says [on camera], 'Don't let this happen, don't let this happen, don't let this happen, let's get back in it.' I don't believe that was the sentiment. I think Kevin was incredible at presenting that. But I don't feel like that was the collective feeling in the clubhouse. So after Game 3, we go down three games to none, I think the feeling in the clubhouse was, 'Oh shit.'"

Only the biggest optimist of all time could have believed at that point. Through a 162-game regular season, the 101–61 Yankees had one four-game losing streak, from April 22 to 25. It seemed pretty simple when everyone got to Fenway Park on October 17, 2004. The Yankees would soon be headed to the World Series, and the Red Sox would soon be left to pick up the pieces of another season that would end in bitter disappointment. At about this time, nobody felt worse than Curt Schilling. He was the one who put the bulls-eye on his back and told the Red Sox and their fans they couldn't win a championship trophy without him. And his last act of the season was going to be that pitiful performance from Game 1 of the ALCS?

"I thought I was done," Schilling said. "We're down 3–0. I know everybody wants to tell you they thought we were going to win but I was devastated. I wanted to think we could win it, absolutely. I'm also not stupid. It wasn't about beating somebody four straight. It was about beating that team in four straight."

And that's why Kapler is absolutely unapologetic when he describes what he believes his team's true mindset was leading up to what turned into one of the most famous games in baseball history.

"This is the discrepancy between what has been reported and what actually was, because I think when we got to the park, it wasn't like, 'Don't let us get back into this.' I think it was more like a surrender," said Kapler. "'Okay, guys, we did everything we can. We've already done everything we could do. We can't practice anymore, there's no more cage work. There's no more meetings. Let's go and see what happens. Let's throw it out there one more time and see what happens.' I'm a realist in that way. I don't think anyone that was really honest with themselves was saying, 'We're going to come back and win this series.' "

But Millar kept talking the Sox into believing they could do it, even if he wasn't quite sure what the recipe would be for the win that got his team back into the series.

"I had no idea. Had no idea how we were going to win the game," Millar said. "Derek Lowe against the Yankees. They have left-handed hitters that drive the ball to left center. I knew we would be okay in [Games] 5, 6. Most of the time when you talk to me, I'm going to tell you the truth. You might not like it, but that was my true heartfelt feeling is that if we could find a way to win Game 4, 'Don't let us win, because Game 5 is Pedro, Game 6 is Schilling, and Game 7, anything can happen.' "

The first thing that had to happen was for Lowe to again take the mothballs off and try to find a way to cool off a Yankees' offense that had drilled nineteen hits the night before. The righty had another eight days of rest after his ten-pitch cameo in Game 3 of the Division Series and was going a little stir crazy. But when he came to the ballpark for Game 4 of the ALCS, he finally had a purpose again. Given the unlikelihood of the Red Sox coming back to win the final four games of the series, Lowe didn't have a hard time focusing on himself. This was one last chance to show potential suitors that he could still pitch. And if he pitched really well, it would also be good for his current team."You're down 3–0. This is my last chance. This is it. This is the end of the line here, kid," said Lowe. "I specifically remember standing in the outfield. They were getting ready to do the National Anthem. By the time I got stretched, I was in center field. I reminded myself, 'Take this all in because this is gonna be your last game ever at Fenway Park as a Red Sox.' I remember just sitting there, trying to take it all in. So it kind of put me in a cool place because it was like, 'This is my last game here. Let's just try to salvage something.'"

Looking back, the Red Sox are actually fortunate they got as much out of Lowe as they did in Game 4. Sinkerballers generally thrive on less rest, not more. But he was able to keep the ball down and keep the Red Sox in it early. Alex Rodriguez did hit an absolute rocket of a home run that went over the Green Monster to make it 2–0 Yankees in the third. The Red Sox, facing a big-game pitcher in Orlando "El Duque" Hernandez, finally rallied in the fifth, getting an RBI single by Orlando Cabrera and a two-run single by David Ortiz to take a 3–2 lead. After retiring Gary Sheffield to open the sixth, Lowe's night came to a sudden end when Hideki Matsui launched a triple out of the reach of a lunging Damon and into the gap in right center. Just like that, Francona came out to the mound and removed Lowe, who seemed almost bewildered as he left the game. Lowe had thrown eighty-eight pitches, but Francona quit while he was ahead. Mike Timlin came on and got nickel-and-dimed to death. Bernie Williams hit a game-tying infield hit that a charging Cabrera tried to backhand, but whiffed on. Ruben Sierra and Tony Clark also had infield hits that second baseman Mark Bellhorn couldn't make plays on, and the Yankees were back up, 4–3.

An interesting thing happened in the top of the seventh, when, with one on and one out, Francona called on closer Keith Foulke. Yes, there was the closer in the seventh inning, signaling that Francona was willing to do anything to try to save the season.

"That's why I didn't want to use those guys in Game 3," Francona said. "It was hard to explain to people, but it made sense to me. We knew if we were going to win, we were going to have to lean on some guys."

Foulke wanted to be leaned on at that point. In fact, more than any of his teammates, Foulke did not want the season to end, and he would do anything to keep it going. His reason was very personal: His wife Mandy had left him late in the 2004 season, and the couple was headed toward a divorce. Foulke didn't tell many people at the time what he was going through, but he was devastated. And the last thing he wanted was to end the baseball season and go home to an empty house.

"Motivation," Foulke said, when asked how the adversity in his personal life fueled his '04 playoff run. "It was one of those things where part of my life was not where I wanted it to be but when I went to the field, it was actually kind of a safe spot for me. I wasn't alone again. I'm back with my teammates and my brothers and stuff. It was good. It made me more focused. I was locked in. We had a goal and I wanted to do everything I could possibly do to help get us there."

Of all the big plays and key individual performances that occurred in that postseason, Foulke's performance in Game 4 was among the most underrated, even in hindsight. He threw fifty pitches over two and two-thirds innings to keep the deficit at 4–3, when his regular-season high had been forty-one pitches, and only five relief outings in his whole career had been longer. Pitch number fifty struck out Matsui, and that brought the Red Sox back into the dugout for what threatened to be the final three outs of their season. Joe Torre was going for the jugular on New York's side, and he had gone to the great Mariano Rivera to start the eighth. And when Rivera came back out for the ninth, there was a strong chance that the Red Sox were about to be executed. Entering that game, Rivera had a career postseason ERA of 0.69.

Asked what he had thought at the time, Lowe said, "We're probably going to lose. We're going to lose. And I hate to say it, but having seen him for all the years that we had been playing against him, this is when this guy shines. I mean, he's got a career ERA under 1. Why is he going to give up a run now?"

Millar, who had done all that chatting before the game, was the man who would get the first crack at Rivera in the ninth. The last time Millar had seen Rivera was Game 2, when, as the tying run at the plate, he struck out to end the game.

"I always say this, I enjoyed facing Mariano because there wasn't a devastating split or a changeup or that tremendous out pitch," said Millar. "What Mariano had was pinpoint control, but everything was hard. I enjoyed everything hard. My initial thought process was just try to get one mistake, middle in, and try to hit a homer. That's it. I was just going to try to pull a homer. You're not thinking walk."

The first pitch was high for ball one. Then came the pitch that brought Millar out of his shoes.

"He threw a 1-0 fastball—a hittable pitch—and I pulled it and yanked it foul," said Millar. Rivera was the one who yanked the next three pitches—all of them out of the strike zone. "The walk was something that . . . nobody saw coming," said Lowe. "This guy doesn't walk anybody this time of year."

The Red Sox had life. The leadoff man had reached base.

"He doesn't walk people," Millar said. "Most of them were up and in, which was surprising, because I thought, if anything, I thought they'd attack me down and away. The only place he could really get hurt was up and in. I think I had five home runs to right field in my life. At that point, it's all Francona and Dave Roberts and see what happens."

Millar had barely even touched first base before the speedy Roberts came over to take his place. Roberts was the only key participant in Game 4 who was even more rusty than Derek Lowe. He hadn't stepped on the field for a single play in eleven days—the regrettable experience in which he chose not to try to steal against Francisco Rodriguez in Game 2 of the Division Series. This time, he was running. And he didn't even need to look for the signs to know that. Francona had given him a wink of assurance as he left the dugout.

"It's a huge spot and I think that I've documented that Tito looked down at me in the dugout and gave me a wink and kind of a nod like, 'Okay, go for it. Do your thing.' So I go out there and it's just one of those things, there's a lot of nerves and excitement and fear," said Roberts, a gifted base stealer who was successful in thirty-eight out of forty-one attempts in 2004.

As Roberts got to first base, the voice of Maury Wills was literally ringing in his ears. Wills would steal 586 bases in his career, exactly twice as many as Roberts had when he retired after the 2008 season. When Roberts was with the Dodgers, there were numerous Spring Training mornings in Vero Beach, Florida, when Wills would be in the ear of Dave Roberts. As Roberts tells the story, this is what he remembers Wills telling him. 'D.R., one of these days you're going to have to steal an important base when everyone in the ballpark knows you're gonna steal but you've got to steal that base and you can't be afraid to steal that base.' Said Roberts, "Just kind of trotting out onto the field that night, I was thinking about him, so he was on one side telling me this was your opportunity and the other side saying, 'You're going to get thrown out, don't get thrown out.' Fortunately, Maury's voice won out in my head."

Roberts wasn't shy in the moment. He took a monster lead, prompting Rivera to throw over three times. Actually, Rivera was doing Roberts a big favor with the continued throw-overs, because he was allowing Roberts to rev his engine. And on the third throw, Roberts was almost picked off. He just got his hand back on the bag before Tony Clark swiped the tag.

"I think if Mo would have thrown to the plate first, I don't think I would have gone," said Roberts. "He threw over once, and the anxiety, everything started to dissipate a little bit. And then he threw over again and I was almost picked off. And then it was like, 'Okay, I've been in this game' and the game started to slow down."

On the near pickoff throw, Roberts made a classic reaction, as his mouth formed a tight circle, and it looked like he was saying, "Whooooooooo."

Then came the hard part—actually stealing the base everyone knew he was going to try to steal. As Rivera came set, Roberts made sure he was going to the plate before he took off. He still remembered the delay tactic Rivera used when Roberts stole off him exactly one month earlier in that comeback Friday-night game at Yankee Stadium.

"That's what I went into the ALCS with," said Roberts. "So after he threw over a second time and then a third time, I was pretty certain he was going to go to the plate and then I told myself, wait him out, wait him out, because he's going to go to the plate, so don't be too antsy, just wait him out. And that's exactly how it played out."

Rivera gave Posada a perfect pitch to throw Roberts out on—outside and a little high for a ball. Posada had a lightning-quick release— the fastest Sox bench coach Brad Mills had ever timed him at—and a near-perfect throw. Yet Roberts still dove in just safely ahead of the tag by Derek Jeter.

"I got a great jump," said Roberts. "I didn't even think was going to be a close play. And Jorge makes a great play. I just beat the throw."

"I always wondered why they didn't pitch out on the first pitch. Roberts is in there, he's in there to do one thing," said Lowe. "I would have just kept pitching out." Then again, Roberts might have beaten the throw anyway.

Francona often joked in the ensuing years that the play looks closer and closer every time he sees it. And Roberts, Francona, and the Red Sox will be forever grateful that second-base umpire Joe West got the call right. "It's funny, when I look at the video and the footage, it's like I didn't realize how close it was at the time," Roberts said. "Joe West jokes all the time, saying, 'I made you famous with the safe call.' So many umpires have come up to me so many times, saying, 'Man, do you realize how good of a call that was for Joe to be in position?' Honestly, initially I didn't, but after I looked back, I was like, that was a really close play. I definitely thank him for making me famous."

At the moment of the steal, Fenway Park roared with anticipation. Roberts had just executed what would end up being the most famous stolen base in the history of October baseball. Yet not enough people thank Bill Mueller for turning Roberts into the primary hero of that night. Mueller, the man who had tormented Rivera back on July 24, was back at the plate in the biggest spot imaginable. The most low-key player on his team was about to come up with the biggest hit of his life. After showing bunt on the 1-0 pitch, Mueller watched that pitch go by for a strike. "The season hanging on a bunt here," guest analyst Al Leiter, who was still an active pitcher in the Majors at time, told his audience on Fox.

Right as that sentence left Leiter's lips, the baseball left Rivera's hands and Mueller was not bunting. Instead, he hammered the ball straight up the middle. Out of desperation, Rivera wound up on the ground trying to field it, but the baseball was scalded. Fortunately, Bernie Williams had a weak arm and third base coach Dale Sveum knew it. He sent Roberts around from second and he slid in before going into a fist pump and a string of high fives from his teammates. "Bill Mueller has tied it!" Joe Buck exclaimed on television. The throw never even made it home. Rivera cut it off himself, knowing there was no play, and snatched the baseball with anger back into his glove. Amazingly, Rivera had once again missed his location badly with Mueller standing 60 feet, six inches in front of him. "Middle-middle cutter," is how Leiter described it.

As Fenway Park rocked with joy, Epstein got reflective. "When Roberts stole the bag, I flashed back to July 31. We were swamped with the Nomar trade and had put our pursuit of a pinch-runner on the back burner," said Epstein. "Earlier in the day I had asked Zack Scott to come up with a list of possible pinch-runners we could acquire—guys who could steal us a base when we absolutely had to have one. Roberts was one of the names at the top of Zack's list and he suddenly became available when the Dodgers traded for Steve Finley right before the deadline. Right in the middle of the mayhem of the four-way Nomar trade talks, we were able to acquire Roberts for Henri Stanley. As Roberts came around to score, I thought of Zack's list and all the great teamwork and camaraderie in our Baseball Operations department. It was a nice little moment during a really big moment."

If you think Roberts moving up ninety feet took some weight off Mueller, you'd be wrong. Aside from knowing he could no longer hit into a ground-ball double play, Mueller still felt like he had quite the job in front of him. "Nothing changes in your body when you're facing Mariano," Mueller said. "That is a tough at-bat. Without a doubt, it takes every bit of what you have to try and be successful off of him. Nothing changed. My senses were as high as ever with Roberts on first or second or third or wherever he would be. He's just a tough at-bat and you're hoping he makes a mistake and you're able to put the ball in play.

"It was out over the plate and I was able to make contact and that's what I was hoping, that he'd make a mistake. [It was] very fortunate that I was able to put that ball in play. I was thinking more of moving him over and doing my job and getting him to third base, almost to the degree that it would be a positive out because of how tough Mariano is. I was fortunate to find a hole."

There would be no fist pumps or signs of elation from Mueller. While the clutch hit fit perfectly with who he was, to celebrate with a game in progress would have been the anti-Bill Mueller. Much as Millar performed well in the spotlight by all but daring it to shine on him, Mueller's method was the opposite. He just wanted to play baseball the right way for nine innings every game, which usually entailed getting his uniform filthy along the way. "That was just my personality. That was the way I was able to handle the pressures and all that," Mueller said. "I was a little bit more quiet. Some of the other guys were more vocal, that was their personality, which was all good. I enjoyed a good time. I envied some of those guys that could have so much fun playing the game where sometimes, with my own insecurities, I worried about things too much and took things too seriously. To be on a club like that was enjoyable for me because it loosened me up."

If Mueller's place in Red Sox history has never been fully appreciated, he doesn't much care. Just as he seemed to enjoy the relative anonymity that came with being an advance scout during the 2013 season, he had absolutely no issue with being perhaps the most unheralded hero of the 2004 Red Sox.

"The credit is for the team," Mueller said. "We won the World Series. That's where the credit goes,. All the guys on that team contributed."

Mueller's teammates, on the other hand, loved to give him credit. "Obviously me getting on base is a big part of it, and obviously Dave Roberts stealing second base is the second big part of it, but Billy Mueller's base hit up the middle, you're exactly right, without that, we're not talking about any of this," said Millar. "If Billy Mueller pops up to short and the next guy grounds out, and the next guy strikes out, it's all irrelevant. Billy Mueller drove in Dave Roberts with a bullet up the middle that tied the game."

Unlike that thriller on July 24, Mueller didn't end the game this time. The Yankees were still in it. But it sure felt like the Red Sox were going to win, and Francona used his bullpen masterfully to put them in position to do so. Once Foulke was done, Alan Embree got five outs. When lefty specialist Mike Myers walked Hideki Matsui, the only batter he faced, to load the bases with two outs in the eleventh, Curtis Leskanic was the man entrusted to get Bernie Williams out and keep the game tied. This is the same Bernie Williams who would smack twenty-two career homers in postseason play while driving in eighty, producing an .850 OPS.

In Game 3, like all of Boston's pitchers, Leskanic didn't perform well, giving up two hits and three runs while retiring just one batter. But the next night, with the season merely hanging in the balance, he was supposed to save the season? At this point, Leskanic had put together a serviceable career, posting a 4.36 ERA in 603 games. But his arm didn't have a whole lot of life left in it by 2004. In fact, Game 4 of the ALCS would prove to be the final game Curtis Leskanic ever pitched.

After being released by the Kansas City Royals, Leskanic joined the Red Sox roster June 22, 2004. Leskanic fit right in from a personality standpoint. His long, stringy hair would always look like a grease factory after a few pitches.

"I knew he was from Orlando. I told Theo, I was like, 'This guy was put on waivers. This guy has a good arm. Please at least take a look. He did, and got him, and I was like, 'Sweet!' He was a great pickup, too," said Johnny Damon.

In the showdown with Williams, who could have prevented Boston's launch into history by coming through like he had so many other times in his career, Leskanic induced a shallow flyout to his pal Damon in center. The righty came back out for the twelfth and there was some concern when Jorge Posada led off with a single and Ruben Sierra bounced one off Leskanic's right leg. Leskanic was able to pick it up and throw to first for the out. Francona and a trainer actually came out to make sure Leskanic was fine to stay in the game. He nodded with approval and then mowed down the next two hitters, capped by a strikeout of Miguel Cairo.

As Epstein put it, Leskanic shut down the Yankees that night with "nothing but big balls."

Backed by the stellar relief of Leskanic, could the marathon Game 4 of the ALCS finally be building toward a conclusion? It sure seemed like it when Manny Ramirez led off the twelfth by belting a single to left. Big Papi was coming up, and he didn't let many opportunities go by in the postseason of 2004. Quantrill hung a nice meaty 2-1 offering at eighty-eight miles per hour and Ortiz deposited it into the Yankees' bullpen. The big man had come up big yet again. His previous walkoff had ended the Division Series against the Angels. This one made sure that the ALCS didn't end.

Ortiz again seemed almost mythical. While Ortiz has had a brilliant career, one that could land him in the Hall of Fame someday, he wouldn't reach the heights of 2004 again until 2013, when he fueled a third World Series title in under a decade by performing some similar magic. But '04 was the first time he had done things like this with the world watching.

"David at the point in his career turned into the greatest big RBI guy in the history of baseball," said Millar. "There wasn't a bigger RBI guy going than David Ortiz, period. You knew any situation, he was going to do something special. That's just the way he was. We knew at that point he was a superstar. David Ortiz at that point turned into a superstar. The '03 season put him on the map. In 2004, he is now a superstar. The stuff that he did doesn't make sense."

Ortiz has always been so matter-of-fact while explaining how he can continually come through, not just when baseball games are on the line, but when baseball seasons are on the line.

"I tell you what, man, postseason is something that can work both ways for you," Ortiz explained in October 2013. "It can go well, if you stay calm. Or it can go bad if you try to overdo things."

It was a mob scene Ortiz arrived to at home plate at the end of Game 4 of the 2004 ALCS. And if the Red Sox were still down 3–1 in the series, it no longer felt like that. That walkoff pile at the plate almost made it seem like Boston had just won the pennant. Millar no longer needed to provide a sales pitch to make people believe the Red Sox had legitimate hope. With one swing, Ortiz had threatened to swing a series.

"Yes," Kapler said. "Because now you can start to project just a little bit."

But the key to the eventual comeback would be to not do too much projecting, and Varitek and some other veterans stressed the importance of trying to win each pitch and each inning, rather than looking at the entire game or series.

"Each inning, we want to win the inning," Nixon said. "We want to win the top half. We want to get them up to the plate and out. We want to win more innings than they do. Simplify it like that and at the end of the game, we'll see where we're at. That may have calmed some things down. That may have put some guys in focus to say, 'Okay,' instead of going up there and saying, 'I need to get hits tonight,' now it's like, 'We're in battle mode. We're backed up against the wall.' Sometimes when someone is backed up against the wall, you don't know quite what they're capable of. They've got nowhere to go. So they're going to have to fight their way back out. And that's what we did."

Nomar Garciaparra, whose Cubs missed the playoffs by three games, was out with some friends from Boston watching Game 4, and he had a strikingly clear picture of where things stood once Ortiz had done his walkoff thing again. "I remember being out with friends, and they won the fourth game and I looked at them, and I said, 'Oh my God. They just won the World Series.' They looked at me like I was crazy," Garciaparra said.

"They were like, 'What?' I said, 'I know my guys, it's over.' I said. 'They just won the World Series. I'm just telling you, it's over. I know my guys. I know the mentality. I know the attitude. They didn't get swept. It's over.' "

In both 1999 against the Indians and 2003 versus the Oakland Athletics, Garciaparra had been part of Boston teams that were down 2–0 in a best-of-five Division Series and went on to win the next three games to advance to the ALCS. Nomar wasn't the only one feeling suddenly optimistic about the Red Sox.

And as a prophet named Millar promised, Pedro was lined up for Game 5, followed by Schilling in Game 6. And anything can happen in Game 7.

Game 5, ALCS
Trotting Toward History

Back in 2004, the news cycle wasn't nearly as frenzied as it would become just a few years later. In those days, Gary Sheffield could make derogatory comments about the Red Sox while his Yankees were playing the Twins in the Division Series and not have it come out until over a week later.

Speaking to Bob Nightengale for a *USA Today* publication called *SportsWeekly*, Sheffield described the Red Sox like this: "They're a walking disaster. . . . They act like they're tough, how they care so much about winning, but it's all a front. They're just a bunch of characters. They know what we're all about. We can still beat them, and they know it. Let's see what they do this time when it counts."

In today's world of instant journalism, USA Today would have tweeted an excerpt of Sheffield's eye-opening comments instantly, or Nightengale would have brought some attention to it to make sure somebody else didn't beat him with some similarly provocative comments. But in 2004, Nightengale was safe to file his story and wait for it to be published. And it just happened to reach the newsstands on Monday, October 18, the same day as Game 5 of the ALCS. Pedro Martinez was preparing what would end up being his final home start in a Boston uniform, and those comments caught his attention. None of the Red Sox knew that the comments were more than a week old, and that was probably a good thing. It gave them yet another rallying cry.

"I cut it out and I called a players' meeting," recalled Martinez. "And we wanted to really hurt someone that day when we realized all of that. I called a meeting, the first one and the only one I called myself. I said I wasn't happy about the fact we were losing to these guys and they were rubbing it in our faces. Everyone just got all together."

After pinning Sheffield's damning words on the bulletin board, Martinez got ready to pitch, this time on his turf, away from all the "Who's Your Daddy?" nonsense. It was a five p.m. game at Fenway, but it felt earlier, given that Game 4 had ended well after one a.m. on the same day. Martinez gave the crowd a quick burst of energy by striking out Derek Jeter and his buddy Sheffield in a scoreless first.

For Johnny Damon, it was very bad news that Mike Mussina was the man pitching for the Yankees in Game 5. Boston's leadoff man and catalyst all year, Damon was 1 for 18 through the first four games of the ALCS. And he blamed his slump squarely on one Mike Mussina. "He's was the one who actually put me in my slump I got in from Game 1," Damon said. "He was getting strike one, but he was on the corners or just off and getting that call and I was just looking everywhere and I had no confidence against him and then it went into the next couple of games. I started looking for the ball to be perfect and they don't pitch that way in the playoffs. The pitchers aren't giving in."

But even after Damon led off Boston's first by rolling over to second base, Orlando Cabrera and Manny Ramirez struck with back-to-back singles, and David Ortiz, who was just becoming otherworldly by this point, strode to the plate. In his first at-bat after his walkoff homer roughly 16 hours earlier, Ortiz clocked a two-run single against Mussina, and maybe the Red Sox did have momentum on their side.

They also had Trot Nixon on their side, and this turned out to be a very big development, considering the right fielder's minimal contribution throughout the season. As the ultra-competitive Nixon stood in right field, adrenaline flowing through his body, he finally felt that all the unglamorous work he had done in solitude with physical therapist Scott Waugh was worth it.

"We worked at an outside setting. We went to his offices, then we also trained at Boston University, did some strength and conditioning there, in the pool and on the field out there," said Nixon. "The beginning process was boring, it was the healing process I needed to just heal that stuff, and then just slowly strengthen the area."

After the monotony came the real work, which not only got Nixon back on the field, but allowed him to excel at times during the 2004 post-season. Waugh worked for the Boston Bruins as well as the Red Sox, and he trained Nixon like a hockey player. "Hockey guys, they get their RPMs and their heart rate up, they go real hard maybe for two minutes and then they'll come out for fifteen, thirty seconds, and then boom, they're back in the fight again," Nixon said. "So he kind of really did that with me and a lot of the stuff was difficult when we got more and more to the strengthening stage and got more active to the point where I started [to get better]. I remember that my body just did a great job of healing. That's the power of my prayer. I know my mom and my wife and everybody were praying for me. The power of prayer was unbelievable for me. It gave me the opportunity to play for that postseason."

It was one thing for the Red Sox to play without Nixon during the regular season. But it would have been strange for them to go to battle without their right fielder in October. Despite his thick southern accent, he embodied Boston with his work ethic.

"He was kind of like the heart and soul," noted Francona.

And ever since he had beaten Roger Clemens with a two-run homer in the top of the ninth at Yankee Stadium in May 2000, fueling a 2–0 win for Pedro Martinez, Nixon had become a fan favorite. Just like Garciaparra had told Damon, Boston loved the players who prioritized hustle. Nixon was the poster child for that. Unfortunately for Nixon, his body paid for the way he played, and it probably shortened his career. In 2004, though, none of that mattered. Nixon was caught up in the moment. Aside from

Red Sox–Yankees regular-season games, postseason baseball was probably the one time Nixon could feel that intensity that he so loved about football.

"There's nothing better than postseason baseball, for any ballplayer. If somebody goes ho-hum with postseason, then something is wrong with them," said Nixon. "You can be completely exhausted come the end of September, but if you have the opportunity to fight for a world championship and play in the postseason, the fans have a different decibel to them. They're a little bit more crazy, they'll heckle a lot more. There's a cool, crisp feel in the air. You know that fall is here, and winter is around the corner and it's postseason baseball. It was just great to be in that atmosphere and hopefully go out there and help my team."

Game 5 of the ALCS would be Nixon's signature game that fall. With one out in the third, A-Rod lined one into the corner in right and Nixon extended himself fully to make a sensational sliding catch on the warning track in front of the wall. At minimum, the hit would have been a triple if it had dropped. And the play loomed even larger when Sheffield followed with a walk and Matsui singled. Martinez got out of the inning unscathed when he struck out Williams, who had homered in the second to make it a 2–1 game. Nixon came back to the dugout with a filthy uniform, which matched his hat, which was always covered with all kinds of gunk. Befitting Nixon's image, his helmet was soaked so heavily with pine tar, you could hardly even see the "B" logo. It turns out that Nixon had a practical reason for all the pine tar on the helmet. Manny Ramirez told him to do it, explaining that if he continued to put pine tar on his bat, the bat would get increasingly heavy over the course of the season. Orlando Cabrera and Ramirez also had the pine tar–covered helmets, playing right in line with the grungy image of that Red Sox team, which was in such contrast to the clean-cut, clean-shaven Yankees.

Even buoyed by Nixon's fine catch, the Red Sox still couldn't solve Mussina, other than that brief breakthrough in the first. In the fifth, Martinez threw a purpose pitch to Matsui, a high-and-tight heater that finally told the lefty slugger he didn't have an invitation to just hang over the plate and blister Boston's pitching staff. Before the message pitch from Pedro, Matsui was 12 for 21 in the series. After that offering, he would go 2 for 12. Unlike Martinez's pitch to Karim Garcia the year before in the post-season that hit him in the batting helmet and caused one of the ugliest brawls in recent memory, this brushback pitch was executed like a pro.

"He had been lights out," Martinez said. "We had to do it. He was leaning and hitting everything out over the plate. He was feeling too comfortable. He needed to go back. And I made a statement, 'I'm going to pitch you inside and you need to move back, so that I can do what I need to do.' So I just busted him in and busted him again. Then the next day, everybody saw what I did and went on to do the same thing. So I cooled him off. We cooled him off that day."

But in the sixth, the Yankees finally became "Daddy" to Pedro again. With the bases loaded and two outs, Derek Jeter tormented and silenced Fenway Park all with one flick of the wrist—fisting a ball into the right-field corner that scored not one, not two, but three runs. And as he pulled into third on the throw to the plate, Jeter did his signature fist pump that, in Yankee-land, was the equivalent to the late, great Celtics legend Red Auerbach lighting up his cigar in the late stages of a win. The Yankees had a 4–2 lead, marking the first time they'd been in front since Mueller's hit brought home Roberts in the ninth inning of Game 4.

"Figures," said Martinez. "Typical Jeter. Just dumps one. But it was still early. We weren't going to give up, just like that."

However, the comeback that eventually occurred might have been unlikely if not for Nixon throwing his leather in the perfect place again. After the Jeter hit, Martinez hit A-Rod and walked Sheffield. Somewhat surprisingly, with Mike Myers warming up in the bullpen, Francona left the matchup with Matsui in Martinez's hands. And on 2-1, Martinez's curveball caught a little too much plate and Matsui hammered a sinking liner to right. But in came Nixon to make a sliding catch on the outfield grass, ending the inning. If the ball had dropped, the Yankees would have scored two on the play to take a 6–2 lead.

"They got to me, and they would have had the game [if not for the catch]," said Martinez.

By October of 2013, Nixon regretted that he hadn't gone back and watched the DVDs of all those 2004 postseason games with his sons Chase and Luke. He vowed to do it at some point, so perhaps he could appreciate what he'd accomplished.

"I didn't remember it until someone brought it up [recently]," said Nixon. "I think I have a picture of making that play, in my basement. I know Mr. Torre said something about it at one point. To me, I was just trying to do my job. At the time, I didn't realize the significance of it."

It became significant thanks in large part to an at-bat by Nixon later in the game. But before getting to that point, Keith Foulke was again called into action, this time with runners at the corners and two outs in the eighth. Here Foulke was, not even 24 hours removed from his 50-pitch stint in Game 4, ready to save his team from extinction again. He got Matsui on a flyout to left, perhaps giving the Red Sox the momentum they needed for what would be a game-turning, series-saving bottom of the eighth.

Tom Gordon, who still holds the single-season Red Sox record with 46 saves in 1998, was entrenched as the Yankees' primary setup man to Rivera by 2004. He had certainly done his job in the seventh inning of Game 5, coming on to get Ramirez on a double-play ball. But in the eighth, Gordon was at the centerpiece of the second Yankees meltdown in as many days. It started when he grooved a pitch to the wrong guy. Ortiz immediately put a charge into the crowd by leading off with a prodigious solo shot off the Volvo sign beyond the Green Monster. The Sox were down just a run, and it was now 4–3, the same score as the ninth inning in Game 4. And Millar, who had led the charge the night before with a walk, was essentially leading off again because Ortiz had cleared the table with his homer.

A walk didn't seem likely this time, as Gordon got ahead of Millar 0-2. Almost unfathomably, Gordon completely lost his control. His next three pitches were all in the dirt, and it was a full count. Millar took ball four, low and outside. He had done it again.

"A 3-2 breaking ball," said Millar. "Earlier in the year, that was the pitch I hit for a home run, and it was the third one I hit in that game. All these things, they play a factor. The reason I bring it up is Billy Mueller homers off of Mariano in the fight game. When you have success against a pitcher, it plays on their brain. At that point, Tom Gordon walks me on a 3-2 count, maybe thinking he'll get hurt on a fastball."

At times, Millar overshadowed who he was as a player with all his talk. The 2003–04 version of Kevin Millar is a man who helped the Red Sox win a lot of baseball games between the lines, and that's without even mentioning what he did before and after games in the clubhouse.

"I'm very comfortable saying that we don't win a World Series without Kevin Millar," said Gabe Kapler. "Very comfortable saying we're not that team without Kevin Millar. Even with just his performance on the field, even just his grind of at-bats, his never-quit act in the box. You need those types of plate appearances. He ground down pitchers. He was good."

Once again, Millar had set the stage for Roberts, who flew off the bench to replace him. Gordon was already frazzled. So the sight of the ever-enthusiastic, lightning-quick Roberts on first base was the last thing he needed to see at that time. And Nixon, who had already made an imprint on the game in the field, was coming to the plate. Dee Gordon, Tom's son, who is a Major Leaguer for the Los Angeles Dodgers, would tell Roberts later about the fear he saw in his father's eyes. Dee Gordon was sixteen years old during Game 5 of the 2004 ALCS.

"Dee has said that he's never seen his dad so nervous as when I was on first base," Roberts said. "You could see it. He was way quicker [to the plate] than he likes to be. He's a guy that likes to get loaded, deliver it. He was uncomfortable. For me, I was ready to run and steal but I wasn't going to try to run into an out. I was just hoping he would make a mistake to Trot."

The biggest mistake Gordon made to Nixon was to get behind him. Just like in the at-bat with Millar, Gordon threw a first-pitch strike. After the 0-1 pitch, Gordon threw over to first three times, giving Roberts the same chance to get his legs warmed up that Rivera had the day before. He also looked over twice without throwing, forcing more stops in the action. It seemed like an eternity between the first and second pitch to Nixon. Posada, who had already come out to talk to Gordon before the at-bat, was out to the mound again after the series of pickoff throws and pickoff looks. Following the conference, there was one more throw to first. And when Gordon finally delivered ball one, a whopping two minutes and 36 seconds had elapsed since his first-pitch strike to Nixon. Ball two and three were both in the dirt, just as they were to Millar. And now, Nixon, a dead-red fastball hitter, was in the driver's seat at 3-1.

The four-and-a-half-minute at-bat would conclude in dramatic fashion. Roberts was off on the pitch, getting every bit as good a jump as he did against Rivera. But this time, Nixon got a ninety-three-mph cookie way too good to pass up, and he hammered it into right center. Instead of a hit-and-run, this was a run-and-hit. And Roberts sprinted to third standing up, putting runners at the corners with nobody out. Yes, it was good to have Trot Nixon back.

"And Trot could hit a good fastball," Francona said. "There's something to be said for that in the postseason. Some guys can get their numbers during the year beating up on some middle-of-the-road pitchers, but Trot could still hit a good fastball and when you're sitting behind Ortiz and those guys, that's a valuable guy to have."

Considering that the trade for Roberts was such an afterthought the day it happened—a basic dot-dot-dot item in a beatwriter's notebook—his impact in two pinch-running stints was amazing.

"He got bigger with the leg kick and I took off and Trot swung the bat. I'm proud of the fact that Trot got the basehit when I tried to steal," said Roberts.

And this time, Rivera came on for a save situation that hardly seemed fair. Runners at the corners, nobody out, and Jason Varitek at the plate. After getting ahead 2–0, Varitek lofted one to center that was just deep enough to score Roberts for the tying run. This time, it was Jeter who cut off the soft throw by Bernie Williams in center.

"If I don't run, now it's first and second and he flies to center and it's just a flyout," Roberts said. "You just never know what could have happened."

After scoring the tying run of Game 5, Dave Roberts would never participate in another play for the Boston Red Sox. Yet his legacy is secure, and he'll probably never have to pay for anything in Boston for the rest of his life. But in that moment on October 18, the game was tied and still had several hours left. It was about to turn into an epic struggle with one team desperately trying to survive and the other trying to advance. Foulke came back out for the ninth and got the biggest break of his career. With two outs and Ruben Sierra on first, Tony Clark took his best swing of the series, and the best the Yankees had against Foulke, smashing a high drive to deep right that looked poised to score Sierra with the go-ahead run. But the ball bounced just in front of the wall, and then over it for a ground-rule double.

As Tony Clark stood on the field before Game 1 of the 2013 American League Championship Series at Fenway Park, he did so without a World Series ring on his finger. "I remember thinking after I hit it, 'Get out, get out.' Then after I saw it hit, 'Stay in, stay in.' It was just one of those situations where not being able to push another run or two across, it ended up being a little bit of a difference-maker," said Clark, who works for the Major League Baseball Players Association. "The irony is, even now as I travel around and I run into Boston fans or I run into New York fans, that still comes up. But you start looking at how things fell into place, and you realize perhaps it wasn't meant to be for us."

And from out of nowhere, everything was suddenly meant to be for the Red Sox.

"I've always maintained that you've got to be good. But you've got to be lucky, too, and then be good enough to take advantage of that luck," said Francona.

If anybody had earned some luck by that point, it was Foulke. The season wouldn't have even gotten to Game 5 without his herculean fifty-pitch effort the night before. And yes, that took a toll on him in Game 5.

"I remember I was having a hard time getting the ball down in the zone and had thrown a lot and I remember just being out there battling and just trying to get the ball down," Foulke said. "Clark hits it, it goes into the stands, and after that, it's second and third and two outs. I need to get one out. I've gotten thousands of them before. Just go back to work."

That one more out came on a popup by Miguel Cairo and Foulke's work was done for the day. Of that game, Foulke said, "It's like being in hockey, going into multiple overtimes. Who makes the first mistake and who can capitalize on it?"

The next moment to put a star next to for Game 5 occurred when Wakefield entered the game to start the twelfth. Remember, it was his self-less mop-up performance two nights earlier that had paved the way for many of the bullpen heroics that happened the rest of the way. And here he was, relying on his knuckleball to keep the Yankees in a funk.

"I don't really remember a whole lot of it," said Wakefield. "It was just basic survival mode at that point, just trying to get as many outs as I could and as quick as I could and not let them get any momentum."

When Wakefield started fluttering his knuckleball in the late stages of Game 5, a lot of people were probably thinking, "Poor Jason Varitek." He had barely caught Wakefield during that season. In fact, Doug Mirabelli had become Wakefield's personal catcher, a role he would hold from 2002–07. But in Game 5 of the ALCS, Francona had to ask himself what was more important: Mirabelli's knuckleball-catching glove or Varitek's bat? He chose the latter and nearly paid for it in the thirteenth inning, which started with Sheffield striking out, but still reaching base on the first of three passed balls Varitek would have in the inning. Wakefield's knuckleball was so good that day that Varitek, who was in the process of catching twenty-six innings in two days, was whiffing badly on it. The third passed ball was the one that pushed runners to second and third with two outs, meaning that another mishap would send in the go-ahead run. The 2-2 pitch to Sierra knuckled off of Varitek's mask, but he kept it in front of him. And Varitek squeezed the 3-2 pitch for strike three, and hopped out of the catchers' box and back to the dugout. Crisis averted.

It was a moment Francona loved every bit as much as the stolen base by Roberts or any of the walkoff hits by Big Papi.

"At that point, Tek was a force offensively. I didn't want to take him out of the game," Francona said. "I remember asking him, 'Tek, can you handle this?' He goes, 'I'll find a way.' You could see how proud he was, that he did it. Things like that, I got more of a kick out of than maybe some of the things that got all the publicity."

Wakefield and Varitek had a cruise-control fourteenth, sending the side down 1-2-3. And Big Papi was about to get even more publicity, meaning that the game—all five hours and forty-nine minutes of it—could finally end.

Damon, still heavily slumping, drew a walk. So did Ramirez. The table was set for Big Papi with two outs. As if the amount of outs even mattered any more, the way Ortiz was going. This time, he engaged with Loaiza for some ten pitches, including six foul balls. He ended the game by fighting off a pitch on the hands and muscling a bloop into center field for the single that brought joy to Fenway. "Damon running to the plate!" Joe Buck told his viewers on Fox. "And he can keep on running to New York. Game 6, tomorrow night!"

Gabe Kapler, who had entered the game as a pinch-runner for Nixon, had played the final six innings of that classic tilt. But his lasting memory is watching the struggle between Ortiz and Loaiza and knowing that, barring a walk, it was going to end with another walkoff pile at home plate.

"I'll tell you what I remember," said Kapler. "And with all due respect to Loaiza, it was, 'This guy has nothing to get David out with. He has no chance to get David out.' That was the sentiment. But that was very similar to most of the time. And that wasn't unique to that at-bat. It's just because that was what was going on for David at the time."

And as he was remembering what a special time that was for Ortiz, Kapler's mind shifted to another teammate he remembers fondly. "I think the case could be made that Wake was as valuable as anyone in that series," said Kapler.

Yes, it was Wakefield, the losing pitcher of Game 7 the season before, who earned the win in Game 5 with those three shutout innings out of the bullpen.

"We rooted so hard for each other and with Wake, he deserved that adulation," said Kapler. "He was the warrior who always had issues with wanting a certain level of respect for what he accomplished. And he deserved that respect. And even with that little chip, he still put everything aside for the team—always."

With the highly memorable Game 5 in the books, the Red Sox hustled out of Fenway Park and boarded their plane for New York. Mathematics claimed that Boston trailed the series, 3–2. But with everything in their bones, the Red Sox felt they were going to win.

"It's the equivalent of in Texas hold-'em, you pick up your two cards and you know you have better cards than the other team. And the other team knows you have better cards than them," Kapler said. "I think that's what was the feeling was. We knew that the pressure had shifted. We knew that they were panicky. And that we were no longer panicky and had nothing to lose. And so that was the feeling going into New York. And I'm very confident in my recall about how we felt about that."

Game 6, ALCS
Bloody Sock and a Foulke Hero

hile everyone in New England rejoiced over the Ortiz bullet into the bullpen that ended Game 5 and averted the sweep, Curt Schilling had a momentary sense of panic. With his Red Sox back in the series, Schilling was going to have to figure out a way to be able to pitch if his turn in the rotation came up again in Game 6.

"After the home run, when David hit the home run, I was like, 'Okay, this could be a problem," Schilling said. "It was just a couple of days of just trying to find a way and then it ended up working out."

Things were going on in the training room before Game 5 that most people didn't know about until a day or two later. For all the hype about the special high-top sneaker that Reebok had designed for Schilling following his disastrous Game 1, it did nothing to comfort his ailing right ankle.

"Nothing helped," Schilling said. "That was the thing. Nothing ended up helping. There was just no way to replicate the strength of the skin in that situation, in that place. Especially with what happens in my delivery at that point."

If not for the wonders of medical science—and a brainstorm by then–Red Sox physician Bill Morgan—it's doubtful Schilling could have made it to the mound for Game 6. But Morgan told Schilling about a highly unorthodox procedure in which he would literally suture Schilling's loose ankle tendon back into the skin. It seemed, well, barbaric. But the Red Sox did try it out on a cadaver first to make sure the idea had merit. There might have been countless athletes who would have vetoed what Morgan had in mind. Schilling, however, was desperate to be there for his team, and to complete the mission he came to Boston for in the first place.

Did he have any hesitation at all? "Nope," Schilling said. "As soon as he said, it, I was okay with it. I was okay because I knew I was going to get a chance. And that's all I wanted. I just wanted a chance. And he was going to give that. Then, it was nothing more than pretty strong faith in God, and getting out there and getting after it."

Looking back on it, Francona knows he should have been more worried about how his ace would respond. But Schilling had trained Francona long ago to trust him implicitly. And the righty just about never let his manager down. This time, Schilling reached even bigger heights in his manager's eyes.

"It's not fair to Schill, but I had known him for so long that I just figured he'd figure out a way to pitch and win," Francona said. "And looking back on it, that's not fair because he probably had no business pitching in those games, let alone winning. To be honest with you, I never really thought he wouldn't. I can remember him coming into my office because one of his staples was pinching, and he said, 'Hey, I'm going to undo one of these staples, so there will be some blood.' I was like, 'Okay.' I probably should have been a little more panicky, but I just figured he'd find a way to pitch. That was the Schilling that I knew. When it's all said and done, he probably shouldn't have been pitching. I guess I just always figured he would. I just figured he would. He had lived for that. He wasn't going to let something get in his way."

For years to come, anti-Schilling folks would joke about how it was ketchup on his sock, cackling that the righty just wanted more spotlight. For anybody who inhabited Boston's clubhouse in 2004, that line of thinking was an absolute joke.

"And it wasn't overblown," said Kapler. "When there was all that talk about, 'Was that really blood?' it's like, not only was it really blood, but what he endured and mentally overcame to perform the way he did may never be done again. I don't know that there's ever going to be a procedure like that to get a guy ready to pitch again. It was a little bit, like, science fictiony."

If Schilling's ankle procedure was of the science fiction genre, Millar continued to run Comedy Central in his corner of the clubhouse. Game 6 was a cold, raw, dreary, miserable day in the Bronx, and the first baseman barged into Francona's office and told his manager the players would hit in the indoor batting cages. Unlike the year before, the Red Sox had no interest in having their season end at Yankee Stadium. They were going to do whatever they could to turn the place into their house for the final two games of the ALCS. So why did Millar take it upon himself to cancel batting practice?

"Yankeeography possessed me to do that," Millar said. "When you take batting practice on the visiting field in Yankee Stadium, they play music for their batting practice and we get Yankeeography and have to listen to Yogi Berra stories and Derek Jeter and Bernie Williams stories. At that point, Yankeeography, I said, we're not falling for that. And it was a misty night anyway and cold. I told Terry Francona we're going to hit in the cages. He was like, 'What?' As I was walking down there, there was the Jack Daniels in one of the rooms. I just grabbed it and it started out as a joke."

There was a symbolic toast of Jack Daniels passed around by Millar, and delivered to various Red Sox players before Game 6 of the ALCS, perhaps just enough to warm them up a little amid the chilly conditions. You can be sure that Schilling didn't touch the Jack Daniels before Game 6. The righty would get so worked up on his game days that he'd barely even make eye contact with anyone, let alone engage in frat-house frivolity. He was glad to have the chance to pitch, but how could anyone know if his tendon would actually stay in place enough for him to get the push he needed off the mound?

"I was nervous," said Schilling. "I was nervous up until I started throwing and when I started throwing, I knew, in my mind, it was going to hold. At that point, I was good. It was just a matter of getting out there and getting after it."

In what would become a performance for the ages by Schilling, he would throw ninety-nine of the gutsiest pitches in baseball history, sixty-seven of them for strikes. But it was actually a ball well out of the strike zone that Schilling remembers most from Game 6.

"Probably the ball I threw to Alex, trying to knock him on his ass, and getting it up and in," Schilling said.

In a sign that Schilling was feeling damn good about himself, he buzzed Alex Rodriguez, the second batter in New York's lineup, in the bottom of the first. It was thrown with every bit of the precision as the pitch Pedro Martinez pushed Hideki Matsui off the plate with in Game 5. The Red Sox were not only beating the Yankees at this point in the ALCS, but they were marking their territory. A-Rod jumped back to avoid the pitch. And Schilling reveled in the fact he could finally get involved in the action.

"I felt like that's a hard pitch to command and I threw it exactly where I wanted it," Schilling said. "And I felt like, 'Okay, if I can do that, there's not a whole lot I can't do tonight.' "

By no means had Schilling and Pedro become dinner buddies by October 2004. But Schilling continued to capitalize on the education he had gained from watching Martinez at work. The pitch that he threw to A-Rod doesn't happen if he's not pitching in the same rotation as Pedro all year. "Yep, a lot of that I learned from Petey," said Schilling. "I don't normally do that. I didn't think I had to because I felt like I was good enough to win without that. But Petey showed me that it's not about being a tough guy. It's about making a statement in a certain way to win."

The Yankees seemed absolutely dead and out of statements. Even when they seemed to get some life, on a big swing by Jorge Posada in the bottom of the second, a gusty wind stopped the fly ball to right in its tracks, and Nixon grabbed it at the wall. Jon Lieber, who had outdueled Martinez in Game 2, had another strong performance going through the early stages of this one. But the tide turned in the top of the fourth when Millar jumpstarted a two-out rally with a double into the corner in left. And Varitek, somehow still functioning with his bat despite the most exhaustive workload of his career behind the plate, worked an eleven-pitch at-bat that ended with a line single up the middle to score Millar. Orlando Cabrera kept it going with a single.

And that brought Mark Bellhorn to the plate. To that point, Bellhorn was 4 for 32 (.125 average) in the 2004 postseason with no RBIs and 14 strikeouts. Though Francona did have him hitting ninth for Game 6, many Red Sox followers were stunned that he was still in the lineup, because the Sox had a serviceable backup in Pokey Reese, who played sensational defense. That was the beauty of Francona. He didn't lose faith in his players. And so often, they'd reward him for that.

"I remember me and Theo talking about it and I remember saying to Theo, 'I don't know if we can win but I know how we won't win.' And I said, 'If we start making changes, we're going to lose.' It wasn't that I had a crystal ball and I knew these guys were going to get hits," said Francona. "But I just knew that we needed to stay where we were. These were our guys and they were either going to do it or not do it."

Francona having confidence in Bellhorn allowed Bellhorn to have confidence in himself. "I appreciated it. I knew I was struggling. At the same time, it was just, what, six games. Just like during the year, all nine guys aren't going to be hot [at the same time]," Bellhorn said. "I thought he did a great job all the way around."

Just when everybody least expected it, Bellhorn made his mark in this ALCS. He went with the 1-2 pitch from Lieber and lofted it down the left-field line. Bellhorn sprinted out of the box with what he believed was a two-run double. "I just wanted to kind of come through for one time in the playoffs because I know I had been struggling," Bellhorn said. "He was pounding me in with everything and then he decided to go away with a pitch and I hit it fair. I definitely didn't think I hit a home run with the pitch."

But a home run is exactly what it was. A fan wearing a black pullover in the front row of the left-field seats caught the ball. Hideki Matsui saw it clear the fence, and at first, he made no effort to field it. The umpires huddled and eventually got the call right, and third base coach Dale Sveum, much-maligned by Fenway fans in 2004 for his propensity to get slow-footed runners thrown out at the plate, deserves most of the credit.

"I saw Dale at third running around and arguing with the umpires and yelling," Bellhorn said. "It's not easy to hit opposite–field home runs. I had a little bit of power but not a lot. Most times I hit them and I was just making sure I got to second base."

Francona also admits he didn't get a great look at it. But he knew that Sveum wasn't the type to argue just for the sake of it.

"I had a horrible view but Dale Sveum had a great view," Francona said. "By the time I got out there, he's like, 'Tito, you have to stay out here.' And the umpires did a great job."

And "great job" probably didn't do enough to describe what Schilling did on that chilly October night in New York. He tore through the Yankees with a fastball that had four to five miles per hour more on it than in Game 1, and a splitter that headed for the dirt as soon as a New York hitter took a feeble swing at it.

"I'm a man of faith and this was probably one of the most amazing times of my life, how I was tested and pushed," said Schilling. "It was just incredible. It's something I'll never forget."

Not that New Englanders will ever let him forget it. Schilling still lives in the Boston suburb of Medfield and not a day goes by that someone doesn't thank him for what he did in '04.

His teammates are equally grateful they had a front-line player who was willing to get stitched up in order to pitch.

"I mean, there's no doubt in my mind he was going to be out there, even if he had one leg," Millar said. "At that point, you become possessed as a player, as a professional, as a warrior—whatever you want to call it. But it's truly remarkable. The surgery he had, people don't really know what he had. The tendon going over the ankle bone and sutured up? The whole thing, you're like, 'What? What are you talking about here?' It's pretty damn cool."

Aside from a homer by Bernie Williams, a solo shot in the seventh, Schilling was virtually untouchable. The Red Sox hadn't seen a pitcher put together a performance like this through major injury since Pedro Martinez in deciding Game 5 of the 1999 ALDS. With inflammation in his throwing shoulder, Martinez came out of the bullpen that night to throw six no-hit innings, vaulting the Red Sox into the ALCS. He did it with a diminished fastball that barely cracked ninety.

"Desperation," Martinez said of his performance in 1999. "I was desperate to do whatever I could do for us to win. I had to do it at the right time or else it wasn't going to do it. And I put my career in jeopardy and all the shoulder problems that I developed later were related to that."

But Martinez wasn't complaining about what happened later. "No, I don't regret it at all. That's one of the highlights that people will take from the time I was here, was the All-Star game [at Fenway], the playoffs when I went out [hurt]. Those are the things that the people actually appreciate from me."

Ditto for Schilling, who is remembered a lot more in New England for his bloody sock adventure than the twenty-one wins he had in 2004, or the two hundred sixteen he notched in his career. His seven-inning, four-hit, one-run performance included no walks and four strikeouts. And it ended with Schilling whiffing Ruben Sierra on a splitter. When Schilling got back to the dugout, Francona and Kapler hugged him. Tim McCarver had an immediate grasp of the historic magnitude of Schilling's night, proclaiming on Fox, "Schilling's performance tonight will long live in New England baseball lore."

But things sure did get adventurous the inning after his departure, with Bronson Arroyo now pitching for Boston. Cairo lashed a one-out double to right and Jeter, who wasn't about to quit, ripped an RBI single to left and now it was a two-run game with A-Rod up.

In a completely different way, an Arroyo–A-Rod matchup was about to produce another memory that would never be forgotten. And yet again, Rodriguez was the villain. This time, he hit a little tapper to the mound, down the first-base line. Arroyo, one of Boston's better fielding pitchers, charged off the mound to get it. And then he chased Rodriguez toward first, where he probably would have been able to apply the tag-out. But Rodriguez did something completely unimaginable, using his left hand to slap the ball right out of Arroyo's hand. The ball squirted down the right-field line and Jeter, having no idea what his ill-intentioned teammate had just done, thought he had scored all the way from first. Epstein tore from Francona's office to the clubhouse, where he spotted Dave Roberts, and told him to make sure Francona knew how blatantly obvious the replay was that Rodriguez had flat-out cheated. Francona was already aware, and well on his way to another productive protest with the umpires.

For the second time in the game, the umpires got together and reversed the call. A-Rod was out for interference. Jeter was sent all the way back to first base. To put it nicely, Rodriguez had made a fool out of himself and the Red Sox again thanked their lucky stars that they got to play against him instead of with him in 2004.

"That was just, like, 'Wow, what next?' My question is, has anyone in history had so little self awareness?" wonders Schilling. "That's what it is. At the end of the day for me, just no self-awareness whatsoever."

And the image that remains forever in Schilling's mind is the incredulous look and dismissive hand wave Rodriguez gave when the umpires told him to get off second base and that he was in fact out. "That was embarrassing," said Schilling.

Once again, Francona was just relieved that the umpires got it right. "I actually had a real good view and I got out there as quick as I could, which isn't real quick," Francona said. "Joe West was the home-plate umpire and whatever he said to me, I know put me at ease. As I was going by him, he said something like, 'I've got this.' And I remember thinking, 'We're okay.' "

And by this time, Francona had to know he was okay going with Keith Foulke for the ninth, even though the closer had thrown seventy-two pitches over the previous two days. Foulke was in full hockey-player mode by this point. He would keep going out there whenever the team needed him, no questions asked. All Foulke needed to keep himself driven was to have that image of his offseason home empty, his wife nowhere to be found. If he could just keep throwing up zeroes, he could delay that trip home.

"That's why I wanted to pitch as much as possible," said Foulke. "I did whatever I had to do to get out there."

The ninth inning of Game 6 would be his most challenging frame of the entire postseason. It's usually not a good sign when a closer opens an inning with a walk, which Foulke did with Matsui at the plate. He bounced back to strike out Bernie Williams and then he popped-up Posada. But Sierra then worked him with a walk. Not only were the tying runs on base, but the winning run was at the plate in the person of towering Tony Clark, the same man who nearly took Foulke deep for the lucky ground-rule double just the day before. Clark would go on to hit 251 homers in his career, but none in the postseason. If he had struck with a blast there, he would have become every bit as legendary as Aaron Boone, and every bit as infamous in Boston, where fans still remembered the awful season Clark had as the Red Sox' primary first baseman in 2002.

It was 12:05 a.m. on Wednesday by the time of the Clark-Foulke matchup, and the Red Sox would need a good result to play in Game 7 later that night. Agonizingly, Foulke started Clark off with two balls.

"Again, I was tired, but that's when you rely on your experience," Foulke said. "You rely on your mechanics and stuff. To me, I know I'm tired but I'm still out there with the same mentality of pitching. Again, I know I was having a hard time putting the ball in my location but like I tell everybody, I tell kids when I work with them today, 'You've got to pitch.' I'm not in there trying to blow an eighty-eight-mph fastball by him. I'm going to pitch. I'm going to keep them off balance up and in and down and away and change speeds."

Foulke bounced back from 2-0 by throwing a called strike and then getting Clark to foul one off, bringing the tense at-bat even. But he came back with a ball in the dirt to force a full count. Suddenly, the possibilities were endless. There could have been a walk to load the bases or a home run to win the series, or many things that could have been exasperating to the Red Sox. Epstein, still in Francona's office, felt like a 30-year-old about to have a fatal heart attack.

There was one man who remained completely unflappable. And that was Foulke, who mustered back and threw a perfectly elevated eighty-eight-mph fastball that Clark swung right through to end the ballgame.

"I don't really remember how we got there [to 3-2]," said Foulke. "But I just remember, you know, obviously, what happened the day before. I don't really remember the pitch sequence, but I do remember when it came to the last pitch, I was like, I think he might be looking changeup right here, so that was one of those pitches like, here we go, rear back and I just want to let a fastball just fly. It was a little bit higher than I wanted probably, but it was also higher than he could handle."

An elated Foulke pumped his fist and embraced with Varitek. He could be heard on camera hollering to teammate Arroyo, "Had to make it interesting!" Foulke wasn't normally one to display a lot of emotion on the baseball field; in terms of body language, he was one of the more low-key closers around.

"After that out, I was pumped," said Foulke. The Red Sox had already made history the second Clark swung at and missed Foulke's fastball, becoming the first team to force Game 7 in a postseason series after falling behind 3–0. Foulke had just thrown a hundred pitches over a stirring, three-game span, giving the Yankees zero runs, one hit, and one walk while striking out five. It was a run that never quite got the credit it deserved, perhaps overshadowed by Dave Roberts and David Ortiz and Schilling's bloody sock.

"I remember after it was over, trying to explain to people that to win like we did, you have to have some players do some pretty amazing things," said Francona. "Foulkie was one of them. He pitched and he pitched and he pitched. Not only did he pitch, but he pitched effectively. It was, like, you need to have that happen to win. Guys like that have to do something like that and he was right in the middle of it."

In the middle of a personal crisis, Keith Foulke was pitching in the biggest games of his life, and just loving the intensity of the competition.

Foulke had inadvertently misled some people the day he signed with the Red Sox when he mentioned on a conference call that he wasn't a big baseball fan. That just meant he wasn't one to sit around and watch others compete. With his spikes on his feet and his glove in his left hand, Foulke loved the action.

"When I came in to pitch, it didn't matter what it was. I came in to pitch. That's why I played the game," Foulke said. "Everybody talks about how I don't like baseball. It's like, it's a tough game to sit around and watch. But I loved to pitch, that's why I played the game."

As Foulke set the stage for Game 7, it was fair to wonder what in the world had happened to the mighty Yankees offense, which had tormented the Red Sox so thoroughly in the first three games.

"It was weird because they had all the momentum but they started playing differently," said Lowe. "They started swinging outside the strike zone. They started making some plays that they normally don't make. Just by watching it, and every inning that went by, we got more confident. Not to say they weren't confident, but there was a different feel, like they should be stepping on our throats right now, they should have all the momentum. But they started chasing more pitches in the dirt. They started doing stuff that they weren't doing before."

Derek Lowe wasn't at Yankee Stadium when Foulke ended Game 6. He had been sent back to the hotel to rest up for the biggest baseball game of his life at that time: Game 7 at Yankee Stadium.

"Again, this is another opportunity to salvage this miserable year that I had," Lowe said. The man who was once out of the postseason rotation entirely was now getting ready to help determine if the Red Sox could at last erase the myth that trailing a best-of-seven series three games to none was a death sentence.

Game 7, ALCS
Miracle Accomplished

When the Red Sox showed up to the ballpark for Game 7, nobody felt more fortunate than Johnny Damon. The man who prided himself for most of his career on setting the tone for whatever lineup he was at the top of had done nothing with his bat in this ALCS. Whenever the Red Sox would lose a low-scoring game in those years, Damon would typically stand in front of his locker and take the blame, proclaiming that Boston's firepower "all starts with me." But even after falling behind 3–0 in the series, they had managed to strike their way back to a Game 7 without their spark, who was 3 for 29 through the first six games (.103 average) with three runs scored and two walks. All three of his hits to that point had been singles.

The beauty of Damon, however, was that he never panicked. So when he got to Yankee Stadium, he had the same easygoing demeanor as always, figuring that his time was going to come, now that his team had bought him some.

"I felt very blessed that we were able to get to a Game 7," said Damon. "I felt like it starts over. I knew my at-bats started to get better in Game 6 and then I felt good. There really wasn't anything wrong with my swing. I was being picky and not swinging the bat."

Damon could have overreacted by taking hours of extra batting practice. But instead, he just tried to keep it simple with hitting coach Ron "Papa Jack" Jackson.

"We were just doing our regular stuff, nothing crazy—not hitting a hundred balls or so," said Damon. "We're just trying to hit twenty perfect balls and just make sure the swing is there and the timing is there. That's always been my approach playing baseball. Why have a hundred swings? Try to focus on the ten to twenty perfect swings and then get out there."

The only person who seemed to keep calmer in the heat of the moment than Damon was his manager, Terry Francona, who kept his center fielder at the top of the order for the entire ALCS.

"I'm sure he got some pressure about sitting a few of us," said Damon. "He didn't waiver. He goes, 'Johnny helped us get here, he's fine.'"

Johnny certainly looked fine when he started Game 7 by slapping a single into left against Kevin Brown. Not only that, but he stole second. And just when it looked like the Red Sox were going to get off to a strong start in the winner-take-all game, Ramirez slapped a line single to left, and third-base coach Sveum waved Damon around. Derek Jeter cut off Matsui's throw and threw a bullet to the plate. Damon was out.

"I got thrown out at the plate because I had to freeze on Manny's line drive right past Jeter," remembers Damon. "He almost caught it. Then I get thrown out for the second out and I'm saying. . . ."

Whatever Damon was going to say, David Ortiz made him say something else. On the very first pitch after the Red Sox got a runner thrown out at the plate, the magnificent Ortiz hit a bullet into the right-field seats, and his team was off and running with a 2–0 lead. Brown was pitching Game 7 on three days of rest and didn't look ready for it. By late in 2004, he was a shell of his former self, showing his frustration when he broke his left (non-throwing hand) punching something in the clubhouse after a frustrating inning on September 3. As for the Red Sox, they were suddenly downright thrilled to have Derek Lowe pitching, even on two days of rest.

This wasn't the first time the Sox had gone to a starter on two days' rest in October. They had tried it with Jim Lonborg in Game 7 of the 1967 World

Series, but he didn't have it that day. And Lonborg was pitching against Bob Gibson, not a past-his-prime Kevin Brown. Lowe had thrown eighty-eight pitches in Game 4, but just ninety-eight in the previous twelve days.

"As far as arm-wise, none of that stuff has ever bothered me," said Lowe. "I had only pitched, up to that point, six innings in ten or twelve days. Fresh as a daisy."

The anger he felt at the start of the playoffs over being bypassed had now turned to giddiness. He was getting the opportunity he needed to all but make his regular season go away in the eyes of potential suitors on the free agent market. Lowe had also grown up as a Red Sox, and even if this was going to be his last hurrah, the team was playing a monumental game that he was pitching.

"Even going through your whole career as a Red Sox, at that time of year, you just kind of pitch when needed," said Lowe. "That's how we got to Game 7. Guys like Wakefield were stepping in. Guys were just raising their hand."

The theory about a sinkerballer is that he actually pitches better the more tired he is. But Jason Varitek, who mastered the art of game-calling throughout his career, decided to switch his attack a bit and keep the Yankees off balance. Quite a few veteran pitchers pretty much called their own games, Curt Schilling among them, but Varitek had always nurtured Lowe, dating back to their time as Minor Leaguers together with Seattle. And Lowe had the most trust you could possibly have in a catcher with Varitek. So when they decided to go with a breaking ball–heavy arsenal for Game 7, Lowe played right along and ran right through New York's suddenly slumping batting order.

"It's the beauty of Jason," said Lowe. "I bet we threw eighty-some-thing percent breaking balls. Because at that point, like I said, in Game 4, they started getting a little more aggressive. And as every game went on, they started getting ultra, ultra aggressive. We threw almost exclusively breaking balls to try to take advantage of their over-aggressiveness." It worked like a charm. Lowe breezed through the first 1-2-3, completing with a strikeout on a breaking ball of Sheffield.

By the time Johnny Damon dug in for this second at-bat of the game in the second inning, Kevin Brown had already exited the contest. He was imploding and Joe Torre couldn't bear to watch it. Brown had loaded the bases by giving up a single to Millar and walks to Mueller and Cabrera when Torre came out to get him. This turned into one of the most fortunate developments of Damon's career. Damon's single against Brown would be only one of two he had in his career against the nasty sinkerballer. Brown's replacement, Vazquez, was the type of pitcher who floated offerings in Damon's wheelhouse, and he would finish his career as a .345 hitter against the righty with four homers, eleven RBIs and an .897 OPS.

It took one pitch for that golden matchup to manifest itself. Damon cranked Vazquez's first pitch of the night into the right-field corner and just into the bleachers. Grand slam. The Red Sox had suddenly busted open the tension of this ALCS by taking a 6–0 lead. As he walked to the plate, Damon had some burning motivation. He was still haunted by Game 7 the year before. With his team up 4–0 in that one, Damon grounded into an inning-ending double play against his old foe Mussina, which turned out to be huge in the scope of New York's epic comeback that night. Damon wasn't going to let it happen again.

"I was glad we were at Yankee Stadium [with a short right field]," Damon said. "I think the biggest thing I wanted to at least do was get another run. I was going to hit a fly ball, hopefully to the outfield, and I got enough of it. I remember Game 7 the year before: We're threatening and Varitek strikes out. Mussina gets me to hit a hotshot double play, and it was like that one, 'Who knows, we could have continued to the World Series if not for that. Let's get a run this time.' But when you get four, rounding the bases . . . for the most part, it goes silent."

It was not silent in Boston's dugout. That little space of Yankee Stadium turned into an absolute uproar. Pedro Martinez was beside himself with joy.

"They had a fake Bambino in the stands and I dared that Bambino to just stay there but he knew better," Martinez said. "He took off, right after Johnny hit the grand slam. When he showed up, we hit a grand slam.

So that Bambino showed up and just took off. I was laughing. I was enjoying it so much—just a lot of joy."

Lowe was in the midst of a masterpiece. And in the fourth, Damon basically turned the lights out on Yankee Stadium for the season, this time ripping a majestic two-run blast off Vazquez that soared into the upper deck in right field. Amazingly, it again happened on the first pitch. So with two pitches and two swings, Damon had gone from goat to hero in the most emphatic way imaginable.

"It's crazy," said Damon. "The pitch I hit for the grand slam that barely got out was right off the plate, [inside], and the pitch that I launched was right off the plate [outside] so it's like I got the arms extended." Damon's second longball had given Lowe and the Sox an 8–1 lead.

"Johnny Damon goes ape crazy," said Nixon. "We didn't need Manny that night. We had Johnny Damon hitting jacks left and right."

The images that will always be remembered most from that history-making night were those of Damon, his long hair flopping, as he rounded the bases.

"Pretty incredible," Damon said. "That's definitely going to be the defining moment of my career. Yes, there are other great things but the fact that you helped get the franchise a chance to win a World Series, that didn't come around too often in Boston."

Yet Damon wasn't smiling. At least not yet.

"A little bit, but not really, because I knew what had happened the year before, how they battled back and I was like, 'We've got to keep pushing.' There's no smile, there's no nothing," said Damon. "It's just like, 'Okay, this is what I'm supposed to do. We're up six now, let's try to make it more.'"

Damon's teammates were just tickled by his timely breakout.

"It was huge. And I think Johnny was as dependable as anybody," said Kapler. "Even when he was struggling, we always thought he was going to do something big for us. He also was a warrior."

Lowe's night ended when he made Sheffield look foolish by whiffing badly at a seventy-seven-mph offering. Over six innings, Lowe threw sixty-nine pitches, giving up one hit, one walk, and one run. He probably could have given his team another inning, but on two days' rest, the Red Sox decided to play it safe.

For all the great things Terry Francona did in Boston—not just in 2004 but in his eight years on the job—the only move that his players ever seemed openly puzzled by happened during that Game 7 romp. Why in the world did Pedro Martinez come out of the bullpen in the seventh inning of that game, with the Red Sox holding an 8–1 lead? This is what we do know: Pedro Martinez did volunteer to pitch Game 7 with one day of rest. In fact, instead of traveling with the team after Game 5, he stayed home an extra day and used the facilities at Fenway Park to maximize his preparation. He got to New York in time to watch Game 6 with his teammates. Martinez certainly had every intention of pitching with the season on the line. But with his team holding an 8–1 lead? That's not what he had in mind.

The crowd got so loud with "Who's Your Daddy" roars when Martinez came into the game that even bench coach Brad Mills, Francona's best friend in baseball, wondered what he was doing. Said Francona in the book he co-authored with Dan Shaughnessy: "When Millsie asked me what I was doing, I said I just wanted to get the crowd involved."

That much he accomplished. The crowd was in an absolute frenzy. It got even louder when Matsui and Bernie Williams led off with rocket doubles. Kenny Lofton's single to center brought home the second run of the inning, and it was 8–3. The ill-fated experiment ended safely at least, as Martinez got a strikeout from Olerud and a flyout by Miguel Cairo.

"That's one thing that I've yet to have answered," Martinez said. "Why they chose me to go pitch and didn't even let me warm up. It was 8–1, and I had pitched [two days] before. Why would they use me? It woke up the crowd. I threw eight pitches and I had my cleats off when they said 'Pedro is in the game.' 'What? Why?' 'No, they want you in.' I don't know whose call it was. I don't know who asked for it. I heard that Tito said it was because I said I wanted to be in the game."

The one piece of Martinez's memory nine years later that was obviously fuzzy was his recollection of not getting proper warm-up time.

Upon inspection of the video archives, Martinez is seen warming up in the bullpen as early as the top of the sixth. He is again loosening up in the bottom of the inning, and in the top of the seventh. Francona is puzzled, and maybe even a little aggravated, that Martinez remembers the situation so differently than he does.

"I heard him say he was surprised he pitched [but] he came in and volunteered and I actually explained to him the circumstances of how he would pitch," Francona said. "And the reason we brought him in was because our bullpen was pretty well gassed and I wasn't as worried with a lead about the first few hitters of the inning but I was worried about getting out of the inning. Bronson was the one guy who was rested a little bit and if Bronson came in and struggled, then we'd have to go to Pedro, and I wanted to just work it the other way around. We had some guys who were on fumes and if Pedro had really gotten into trouble, we could have gone to somebody a little fresher and that was really why we did it. I always worried more about finishing an inning than starting it."

Martinez was on just one day of rest, and by not using him in Game 7, he could have pitched one of the first two World Series games. That fact was clearly not lost on Pedro, who spent much of his career motivated by perceived slights.

"Schilling ended up pitching the [second] game at Fenway, and Wakey pitched the first World Series game," said Martinez, who thinks the opposite might have happened if not for his unnecessary twenty mop-up pitches in Game 7. "It would have been Schilling in St. Louis and then me here. I don't know. That would be the only thing that would tell me, that would probably make sense, was the fact he wanted Schilling to pitch in Boston and not St. Louis."

It's doubtful Francona would have used Martinez out of the bullpen just to avoid bruising his ego by pitching him on the road instead of at home in the World Series. After all, Francona had already pushed Schilling ahead of Martinez in his pitching rotation at the start of the playoffs.

"To be fair, Pedro's revisionist history is probably a little different than mine," Francona said.

After all the misery that wound up happening when Pedro was left in to give up the lead in Game 7 of 2003, it created an unsettled feeling for players to see him put into the game this time around with a blowout in progress.

"If you look at the game, it obviously turned out great," said Lowe. "When they brought in Pedro, we are all sitting there as players like, 'Why? Why are we doing this?' We're up 8–1, and then the place is as electric as the place was. It was quiet. We brought a frenzy back into them."

"I think that was the loudest I've ever heard any stadium when Pedro came in," said Mark Bellhorn. "That place was rattling. They got a couple of hits and they were chanting 'Who's your daddy?' and I had never heard anything like that. Before that, it was the old Kingdome when Randy [Johnson] was pitching. That was really loud."

Give Bellhorn credit for quieting the place again. His suddenly dangerous bat connected at the start of the eighth for a towering home run off the foul pole in right. That made it 9–3 and the lead would swell back to seven runs when Cabrera's sacrifice fly scored Nixon in the ninth. All's well that ends well, right? Mike Timlin got the first two outs in the ninth and Alan Embree finished the party by getting Sierra on a grounder to Pokey Reese that won the Red Sox their first pennant since 1986.

The architect of the team, the man who had acquired David Ortiz, Curt Schilling, Bill Mueller, Dave Roberts, Kevin Millar, Mark Bellhorn, and Keith Foulke, saw all the fruits of his labor come together in one glorious stretch of baseball. Theo Epstein shared the last out with his trusted top assistant, Josh Byrnes.

"Out of superstition, Josh Byrnes and I were watching on the tiny, grainy TV in Tito's office in the bowels of Yankee Stadium," Epstein said. "We had been behind home plate for the Aaron Boone game a year earlier, so we decided to mix it up. We just hugged and made our way out to the clubhouse door to greet the players as they came in off the field. It was pure elation, and this odd sense that we couldn't believe what we had just done but we also knew we were going to do it—if that makes any sense. One year earlier in that same clubhouse you could hear a pin drop. Now, you couldn't hear anything, the celebration was so loud."

Those moments after the triumphant Game 7 were as sweet as humanly possible for anyone with the Red Sox, particularly for the hold-overs from 2003.

"It's the greatest joy ever," said Martinez, when asked to flash back to that moment.

Millar had served his lucky toast of Jack Daniels again before Game 7, and given how superstitious baseball players are, he'd have to keep doing it until his team lost. By the end of Game 7, the beverage of choice had shifted to champagne.

"I just remember finally, Trot Nixon running to center field, flipping off the center field bleachers after 10 years of getting abused out there as a Red Sox player playing in Yankee Stadium, in the Bronx," said Millar. "You can't have a rivalry and not let us win one. Then it isn't a rivalry. We have to win at least one series. Put all that together and it was like, wow, we did it, period. At that point, we're the best team in the American League."

This time, there would be no orange cooler for Nixon to flip over in anger as he left the dugout. "It felt like we won the World Championship," said Nixon. "It was probably fair to say that not only did we want to go to the World Series, we wanted to beat the Yankees. If you're looking at it, it's like getting to the top of the Grand Teton Mountains out in Wyoming, you had two things on your professional pinnacle baseball-wise. You wanted to beat the Yankees and you also wanted to win the World Series."

And believe it or not, Keith Foulke, he of the hundred pitches in the three days that preceded Game 7, was annoyed that Terry Francona didn't give him the ball for the last three outs of the series.

"Yeah, I remember running in from the bullpen and celebrating," said Foulke. "And as soon as I found Tito, I grabbed him, hugged him, and was like, 'That should have been me in there.' I was a little, I wouldn't say pissed, but I wanted that game. I had never been in that situation, like to celebrate and [experience] the dogpile. I wanted that."

But doesn't Foulke understand his manager was just trying to pre-serve him for the World Series? "Yeah, I understand," said Foulke. "But at the time, I wanted that for me."

◆ ◆ ◆

When Epstein thinks about the miraculous comeback that happened on those four consecutive October nights in 2004, a collage of images and emotions come to his mind. "There were so many times during the series I felt like I was dying. Watching Tek battle his ass off to catch Wakefield. Hardly being able to believe Leskanic pitching a huge inning with a bum arm and nothing left but big balls," said Epstein. "Praying the ball in the right field corner would hop over for a ground-rule double. Trot's catch coming in on Matsui's ball. Holding my breath every time Schilling delivered a pitch with his makeshift ankle.

"Flipping out before it became clear Joe West was going to rule A-Rod out after he slapped the ball from Bronson. I ran from Tito's office to the clubhouse and yelled at Dave Roberts to tell Tito how clear it was on the replay. He was already on his way sprinting to the dugout. Feeling Yankee Stadium ignite when Pedro came into Game 7.

"Probably the worst was Tony Clark's at-bat against Foulke in the ninth inning of Game Six. Foulke was unreal, but he was on fumes and the strike zone was shrinking a bit. He just kept challenging Clark with FB after FB and finally punched him out. Had Clark managed to find the short porch in right and end the series, I may have actually expired on the spot."

Every type of emotion possible seemed to swirl around once the Red Sox got back to the clubhouse.

"After Game 7 of the ALCS, I think Grady popped into the minds of a lot of people," said Kapler. "It was sort of like your friend that passed away. It was like, 'I remember how much of a contributor he was.' And Grady contributed to that 2004 World Series championship. And his influence was still felt. His warmth was still felt."

Though newcomers like Schilling and Foulke never felt a real connection with Garciaparra, a lot of his long-time teammates thought about him during that postseason. As the Red Sox were in the midst of their joyride into history, there would be calls made to their former star shortstop from the team bus.

"I wasn't, like, glued to the TV watching it during the playoffs. I'd peek at it," Garciaparra said. "I'll tell you the greatest thing for me was when these guys would win, they'd win a game and I'd get a phone call from some of the guys on the team, and they're like, 'Hey, man, did you see what we did?' I'm like, 'Yeah, I did.' Even when they're on their bus back to the hotel, guys are like, 'Hey, it's Nomar on the phone.' Guys are like, 'Hey!' screaming. Guys are saying, 'We're thinking of you.' I still get chills as I'm talking to you about it, what that meant to me."

Garciaparra credited Nixon, Damon, and Varitek as three players in particular who tried to keep him connected as the team achieved greatness without him.

As for the man who replaced Garciaparra, Orlando Cabrera was just hoping to finally get a night of sleep after Game 7. Never had his boundless energy been tested as in those final five nights of the ALCS, which were played in five straight days.

"One of the things people don't realize is I had a friend with me, a reporter from Colombia," said Cabrera. "So this guy from Colombia, they don't cover baseball that much. He was the only one covering baseball so every single news outlet was calling him to get this interview and this and that. I hadn't slept. I didn't sleep like for four days. We were talking about every single thing through the whole night, from like four in the morning until like eight or nine. I was doing interviews to every single news outlet in Colombia. It was crazy. Nonstop. This guy is going to call, this guy is going to call. My phone was ringing from like four-thirty in the morning. There was so much excitement—I couldn't sleep. I was talking and talking and talking and thinking, 'Wow, this is incredible.' "

The odyssey of coming back from 3–0 now complete, Cabrera was connected enough to his new teammates to see how big an accomplishment this was, considering who it came against.

"For the guys who were there the year before, it was like coming back from death, a resurrection for them," Cabrera.

Several veterans, including Lowe, Varitek, and, most fittingly, Wakefield, stood on the mound after the game and took in their surroundings.

Wakefield could now look at that pitcher's mound and know that it was now the place of one of the great triumphs in Red Sox history, instead of that knuckleball that Boone had put over the wall. "To be able to stand on that same mound where a year prior to that, I had to walk off in shame after giving up the homer, it was pretty special for me to be able to share that with guys that were there that year, or the guys that were there the year before, like Mirabelli, Derek Lowe, Varitek, and I remember them taking pictures of everyone when they were covered in champagne," said Wakefield. "That was pretty special."

But the thing that still stands out to Wakefield was what happened in the clubhouse.

"I think the most important part of that night was getting a phone call from Joe Torre in the clubhouse. I didn't know it was him," Wakefield said. "I'm like, 'What the heck?' I thought it might have been a reporter or my parents or something, but I had picked up the phone and he said, 'Hey, Wake, this is Joe Torre. I just want to congratulate you. You're one of the guys that I respect the most after playing against you all these years. You're a true professional and I just want to wish you luck and remember to have fun. You guys deserve it and I'm really happy for you.' That meant a lot that the opposing manager called to wish me luck after we had just beaten them. That shows what kind of class guy he is."

And Wakefield also found out some news from his own manager that night. He would be starting Game 1 of the World Series, something he would have done the year before if not for the pitch to Boone.

"It was unbelievable," Wakefield said. "When Tito told me I was going to be Game 1 starter, I just couldn't believe it. It was the opportunity of a lifetime to be able to do that, especially at Fenway Park."

Derek Lowe also got some news.

"I remember we were in the shower, getting ready to leave and Dave Wallace said, 'By the way, you're going to pitch the fourth game [of the World Series]. That was like the first time I hadn't either been told the night before or the day before the game. So yeah, at that point, you feel we're one start away from salvaging something. We had so much momentum and confidence at that point," said Lowe.

The Cardinals would soon find out that the combination of peak momentum and confidence is a lot to try to beat in the World Series.

Game 1, World Series
Bellhorn Rings Pesky's Pole

Curt Schilling knew the World Series was over before it even started. Really, he did. And that wasn't meant to disrespect the very worthy opponent the Red Sox were going to face, the team that won 105 games during the regular season, four more than even the Yankees. But he knew. While Cardinals manager Tony La Russa was getting bent out of shape about his team's shoddy travel arrangements—a mixup had left the Cardinals at the Quincy Marriott instead of in downtown Boston—Schilling was ecstatic over scouting reports.

"We knew," Schilling said. "I went to the advance meetings with the coaches and the advance scouts and then with the players and the pitching staff. It was pretty clear in the advance meeting, we weren't wondering whether they could win. We were wondering whether they could win a game. We knew that they did not have a pitcher on that staff, except for Dan Haren, that had swing-and-miss stuff. If you couldn't make this lineup swing and miss, you couldn't beat this team. From a pitching perspective for me, it was just about keeping them under ten runs, because we were going to score a crapload."

Schilling wasn't alone with the utter confidence he was feeling, even though the Red Sox were facing a team with productive hitters like Albert Pujols, Larry Walker, Jim Edmonds, Scott Rolen, and Edgar Renteria.

"But we felt a lot of confidence. We felt relaxed," said Kapler. "It was a good team but it's amazing, we did not think they could beat us. And I remember Tito's body language was really important and his countenance was that of a man who believed that we could not be beat.

"And that leadership was important. And when you saw Theo in the clubhouse, it was the same sort of thing. I think Tito and Theo, they don't get the credit that they deserve for the work they put into that season. Nobody worked harder than those two guys. And from a leadership perspective, we draw our personalities from our leaders. Theo walks into the clubhouse, everybody automatically looks at Theo to see what he's doing and what he's feeling. Is he stressed? Is he confident? At that point, he was immeasurably confident, as was Tito. And therefore that confidence just sort of trickled down to the players."

For Orlando Cabrera, who had never even sniffed the playoffs before '04, the opportunity to play in the World Series was dreamlike.

"I've been watching the World Series since I was a kid in Colombia," Cabrera said. "The World Series was always so special. The whole world was always watching. I was like, 'Man, I'm going there.' And of course, I had the feeling I would be back in the World Series every year for the rest of my career. And I never went back."

Mike Timlin had played in the World Series twice before, with the Blue Jays in 1992 against the Braves and in 1993 against Schilling's Phillies. But a World Series game at Fenway Park, the first in eighteen years? That was a feeling Timlin will never forget. "I remember walking out on the field and you know the smells at Fenway," Timlin said. "But since you've been around the smells of Fenway, sometimes you don't notice them. We were there for a couple of years and you stop [noticing] the ambient noises and all that. You get back out there in the World Series and it all becomes clear again. You could smell the hot dogs, you could smell the popcorn. Even in pregame for batting practice, you could smell everything that's going on. You hear everything. Your senses are so heightened. It's a great place to play, obviously. When you get into the World Series, it's just totally special."

The weather for Game 1, however, was unspecial. It was dreary, it was cold, and it was windy. The conditions couldn't have been much worse for Tim Wakefield's knuckleball. But Wakefield did work around a Larry Walker double in a scoreless first, and it wasn't until he sat on the bench that he quite realized what he was pitching into. "I remember sitting on the bench after the first inning watching Woody Williams have problems with his control," Wakefield said. "The ball seemed to be slipping out of his hand as well. He was missing high on a lot of stuff."

And the rejuvenated Johnny Damon, still riding high after his Game 7 hitting barrage, practically raced to the bat rack to get the bottom of the first started against Williams. "How many pitches was that at-bat I started the game off with? I think it was maybe at least, like, ten," said Damon. "And I think I got a single or a double down the left-field line."

It was a ten-pitch at-bat that Damon ended by lashing a double, as he recalled, down the line in left.

If there were a worse possible way the Cardinals could have started the World Series than facing David Ortiz with two men on base in the first, it would be hard to identify it. Living up to the legend he had created for himself, Ortiz punished a three-run homer into the right-field seats. Bill Mueller laced an RBI single before the inning was through and it was a 4–0 game. However, this was the one game in which the Cardinals displayed their mighty offense. Even though Boston held a lead of 7–2, the team's shoddy defense, which would make four errors on the night, helped the Cardinals climb back into the game. Wakefield was gone by the fourth inning.

Manny Ramirez had a nightmarish eighth inning on defense, making errors on back-to-back hits. The first was a single by Renteria that Ramirez fielded and overran, allowing pinch-runner Jason Marquis to score from second. The second was a disaster. Larry Walker hit a fly ball to left that Ramirez came in for. He easily could have caught it standing up, but instead, Ramirez went into a pop-up slide and got his spike in the ground. He fell down and the ball dropped and the Cardinals had tied the game at 9–9.

In this moment of tension, the Red Sox displayed the beauty of their team. The play by Ramirez was so horrific that his own teammates were trying to contain their laughter. "All I remember is Manny diving for a ball on his knee and taking up, like, ten thousand pounds of grass," said Trot Nixon. "Here we are in the World Series. He got into a popup slide but his knee hit the ground first, dug this hideous trench, and I think he dropped the ball or something but we were dying laughing. I covered up my face. You're in the World Series; that's not funny. But we were laughing. I remember Johnny. Johnny was laughing. That didn't faze us. You could score two runs off of that, that didn't matter.

"We'd just come back from 3–0 against the New York Yankees—you think that worries us? I think Bellhorn, who never made any facial reaction, turned around to me and I'm just sitting there laughing. My glove is over my face. It was hilarious. Manny didn't know what he did. He just came in, and we were like, 'Dude, how're your feet? Seriously, man, you dug up old bodies from way back with that one.' It didn't stop us. The train kept going. It was kind of an ugly game a little bit but I don't think there were any jitters. I just think it was an ugly game, but we kept swinging the bat, we kept hitting it. We kept pounding the ball."

And in the bottom of the eighth, with Julian Tavarez on the mound, Bellhorn would strike again, this time with what will go down as the most memorable hit of his life. For the third straight game, Bellhorn went deep. And for the second straight game, he nailed the foul pole. This time, he was at Fenway Park, meaning he had struck Pesky's Pole, named in honor of the Red Sox legend that Foulke nearly knocked out on his way to the A-Rod–Varitek brawl. Johnny Pesky would hit all of 17 home runs in his career. But as legend would have it, several of them hit that foul pole that is at an odd angle at Fenway Park, just 302 feet down the line. A lot of baseballs that curl around Pesky's Pole are cheapies, but that, decidedly, was not the case with the rocket that Mark Bellhorn hit.

"To hit that foul pole, as high as he did, that was a bomb, by the way," said Nixon. "We were like, 'Dude, I wonder where that would have landed if it didn't hit the pole?'"

Of the nine starting players for the Red Sox in that 2004 World Series, Bellhorn had the least accomplished career. He would hit .230 over his 731-game career, with 69 home runs. It didn't matter. He hit a two-run home run that led to an 11–9 win in a World Series game, and for that, he will always be remembered. Bellhorn gave a classic response when asked what he was thinking entering that at-bat.

"I don't think I was thinking anything. I, honestly, was so caught up in the moment, just concentration. But he threw me the first pitch and he threw that one, a sinker that starts that looks it's going to be inside and then comes back. He threw me strike one like that and I was like, 'Okay.' I figured he was going to throw another one, so he threw another one. I guessed it right, and I hit it, and I remember the wind was blowing, it was crazy that night, it was blowing like twenty miles an hour straight out from center field to right field," Bellhorn said. "I honestly hit that one better than I hit the home run. And the wind just got it and took it way right. Then he threw a ball. And he threw a slider, and somehow I was just trying to put it in play and caught it right in the middle. I thought that was going to be foul too, and it ended up that the pole got in the way."

Even on a loud and boisterous team, Bellhorn fit right in. The players could good-naturedly get on him about his lack of words. And Bellhorn, good sport that he was, would always laugh right along with it.

"He was quiet," said Nixon. "We used to tell him all the time to shut up. We'd be on the bus jawing back and forth and somebody would go, 'Yeah, Bellsy, shut up.' He would kind of turn around and kind of smirk."

Bellhorn thinks back to those bus rides and chuckles as if it was the best time of his life.

"All those guys always entertained me," Bellhorn said. "That was the best part, listening to Millar get on the microphone, or just all of them. It was kind of crazy how you had guys from totally different backgrounds, and everybody meshed, everybody got together. Everybody got along together."

When you had a team like that, everybody in the dugout would light up at a player breaking out a slump.

"Because, you know, for us, we know how hard Bellhorn worked," said Nixon. "We know how much time he spends in the batting cage. We know how bad he wants to come out of a slump because we didn't look at it as a slump. Hey look, it's an adjustment period. He hadn't gotten many hits, but guess what? We're winning. We'll pick you up because there's going to come a time when he needs to pick *us* up. He did that."

Of all the players *Sports Illustrated* could have put on their cover for the edition that covered the first couple of games in the 2004 World Series, they chose Bellhorn leaping in the air to turn a double play. The man who thought he might be stuck in the Minors for the rest of his career before being rescued by the Red Sox was an SI cover boy. "I didn't see that coming," Bellhorn said. "That was a nice surprise. I had a buddy that I grew up with and he called one of my other buddies and he's like, 'You're not going to believe what magazine you're on the front of!' I thank them for doing that. That was, not a dream come true, but pretty special to be on the cover of that magazine. Of all the people that have been on there, it was great. I love it."

At his home in Arizona, Bellhorn has a display case that features that magazine cover, along with the official World Series program. For the rest of his career, which ended in 2007, Bellhorn never tasted much success again. But it doesn't seem to matter. By 2013, he was playing a lot of golf out in Phoenix, but also working for a company that produced artificial turf—lawns and putting greens. Inevitably, Bellhorn will bump into someone during the course of his day who will mention the home run, and his place as one of the beloved "Idiots."

"The Red Sox Nation is everywhere," said Bellhorn "Everybody, they all ask about the home run. They all ask about the team. Everybody wants to know about Big Papi and all those guys and how it was. It's fun being able to tell everybody my experiences on that team and it's cool for me that people recognize that year and what I did."

Game 2, World Series
Bloody Sock Sequel

The thrill of winning Game 1 of the World Series was something that the Red Sox players and most of their avid fans were probably sleeping off at around six a.m. on Sunday morning, about 14 hours before Game 2 would start. But Curt Schilling, the epitome of a late riser in those days, was suddenly awake.

"I woke up a six o'clock in the morning, which I knew, there was a problem," said Schilling. "We generally are guys that get up at ten, eleven, twelve o'clock after a night game. But I woke up and I was thinking to myself, 'Why am I awake?' And I was just kind of looking around the room and I went to roll over and I don't even know how to describe it.

"It's like somebody took a hammer and hit that little pointy bone in my ankle and I looked down, and if you looked at my leg, no lie, my calf below the knee was the same size as my ankle. It went all the way down to my foot. And from the bottom of my calf to the top of my heel, it was [Arizona] Sun Devil red. I'm looking at it, going, 'Oh, my God.' So I can't do anything."

This made no sense to Schilling because Dr. Morgan had done the same suture procedure the day before that had worked so well prior to Game 6 in

New York. Had Schilling's right ankle finally revolted and said, "Enough"?

"So I woke up [my wife] Shonda and I had her get me the phone and I called Chris [Correnti] at like six-thirty in the morning. He was like 'Schill, this can't be good.' I'm like, 'I don't know what to tell you.' I can't fucking move. He's like, 'What do you mean?' I'm like, 'I can't . . . my leg, I don't know what happened.' So I was like, 'You need to call D. Lowe and let him know [he might need to pitch].' He was like, 'Yeah, okay.' It was like an eight o'clock game that night," Schilling said. "I tried to go back to sleep. Slept a little bit in the morning and woke up at about eleven, and I ended up leaving for the park at, like, twelve."

That was the longest drive from Medfield to Fenway that Schilling can ever remember. "It took me like an hour and fifteen minutes to drive to the park because I had to drive to the park with my left foot," he said. "And I'm listening to the radio and I'm hearing, like, on 'EEI, people are calling and talking about how awesome it's going to be, blah, blah, blah, and I'm thinking to myself, 'They have no idea.' "

Then there were the signs wishing Schilling and his team well that he saw during his drive, and it wound up serving as a pretty strong guilt trip for a man who thought he was going to have to tell his manager he couldn't take the ball that night.

"There were literally, from my house in Medfield to the ballpark at Fenway, there were five hundred signs next to the side of the road. Like, everybody knew how I drove to the ballpark," Schilling said. "Fire station, police station, everything. I was getting emotional because I'm thinking, 'Oh my God, all of this and now this. We had beaten them 11–9; it was a tough Game 1."

When Schilling got to the players' parking lot in the early afternoon, there was his pal Doug Mirabelli with a camcorder, chronicling the arrival of each player for posterity.

"I was like, 'Dude, turn it off,' " remembers Schilling. "He was like, 'What?' 'No, you've got to turn it off.' He's like, 'What's the matter?' "

The answer to Mirabelli's question was rather obvious when Schilling stepped out of the car.

"My foot was bare," Schilling said. "And he was like, 'Oh my God.' And I was like, 'Yeah.' He's like, 'What happened?' I was like, 'I have no idea. I don't know.' So he helps me into the training room."

Before leaving his home, Schilling had told Shonda to take her time coming to Fenway because he wasn't going to be pitching. Dr. Morgan arrived a little later and Schilling's problems would go away shortly thereafter.

"You've got to remember I'm a stickler for routine. Game days go very, very specifically," said Schilling. "At about three-thirty, Doc comes in and he's looking at it and he's hemming and hawing and he goes, 'Hang on a second.' and he goes, 'This is going to hurt for a minute but hang on a minute.' And he said, 'Lie down.' He does something and I'm like, 'What did you do?' He's like, 'Sit up'. Thirty seconds later, the color is gone. You can literally see it leaking out of my leg."

As Morgan would explain to Schilling, he had put an extra stitch in the day before and wound up puncturing a nerve. Suddenly, it all made sense. "Then, fifteen minutes later, I'm walking around, like, 'This is perfect, I'm great, I can pitch.'"

But there would be one more wave of panic when the preparation-obsessed Schilling realized that his typical game-day routine had already been altered.

"I get an immediate wave of terror. I haven't been getting ready to pitch. It's four o'clock, and I'm, like, panicky," said Schilling. "I go through my whole routine. I missed chapel that day and I ended up going up and sitting with [team chaplain] Walt [Day] for about a half hour for one of the most incredible times in my life from a faith standpoint. Said a couple of prayers and, you know, I just wanted to be able to compete."

So caught up in all of the moments that occurred that day, Schilling remembered on his way to the bullpen that he never did call his wife and tell her he was pitching.

"I'm thinking to myself, 'Oh, my God, I never called my wife.' She's in tears, bawling, because she has no idea. And the first time she knows I'm pitching is when she sees me walk out of the dugout," said Schilling.

When he finally did get to the Fenway mound, Schilling's first pitch of the night was a ninety-three-mph fastball to Renteria for a strike. Other than a double to center by Albert Pujols, the opening inning was uneventful and scoreless. But the Red Sox mowed their way through another St. Louis starter, this time Matt Morris, in their half of the first, Jason Varitek's triple off the wall in straightaway center gave Schilling a 2–0 lead.

The craziness of Schilling's entire day—not to mention his month—was summed up in the second inning. There were runners on first and second and one out. Reggie Sanders actually should have been on third on a well-struck single by Tony Womack, but he missed second base, so he had to retreat.

"So I'm on the mound, Reggie Sanders is on second base, and Mike Matheny is up," said Schilling. "And I wind up to throw a pitch and I see Reggie take off. He's got third stolen easy. And Mike fouls the pitch off. And I'm thinking, 'Okay, I'm going to turn and throw to second now on this pitch because that will pick him off, he's going.' And he didn't see me see him. And nobody said anything. So I had him picked him off. So I come set, and I've done it a million times, just rotate, turn, and go to second. I pick my leg up and I can't throw to second. I don't know why. I can't turn."

When you look at the video, Schilling's leg kick does take an awkward turn, but he just continued on and delivered to the plate.

"So I throw the pitch and Reggie goes, Matheny hits a line drive, Billy Mueller catches it, tags Reggie Sanders and the inning ends. I'm walking off the field and if you see the video, look at the video of me walking off the field and I'm laughing," said Schilling. "I'm thinking to myself, 'Okay, that's not funny.' It was one of those things." It was one of those things, Schilling reasoned, that only increased his faith in a higher power.

The Cardinals finally did score in the top of the fourth when the normally sure-fielding Mueller would make one of his three errors in the game. Aside from that, Schilling was untouched. This time, Terry Francona limited him to six innings, during which the righty further cemented his legacy by giving up four hits and an unearned run, walking one and striking out four. With a steady stream of offense, the Red Sox had themselves a 6–2 victory in Game 2, and a 2–0 cushion as the venue switched to St. Louis.

Foulke, who would close every game of the World Series, was perfect in this one, mowing down all four batters he faced and striking out two of them. The Red Sox weren't merely threatening to beat the Cardinals in the World Series; they were threatening to suffocate them. And it was looking all so easy.

"It was strange because it was almost like they weren't ready for us and I'm not sure why because they were a great team," said Mike Timlin. "We just seemed to be a step ahead."

It wasn't until after Game 2 when Schilling, in a press conference, told the general public about the ordeal he went through that day to be able to pitch. If there are fans, or even players from around baseball, who think that the whole bloody-sock drama was overdone, the Red Sox players who own 2004 World Series championship rings think otherwise.

"It was just like a raw steak," Nixon said of Schilling's ankle. "I went in there and looked at it at Yankee Stadium, and I was like, 'What's that?' They stitched him up. I was like, 'What?' I looked at him and I was just like, 'Dude, that doesn't look good.' I think a lot of us were just, I don't know what to say about it really. It was kind of unbelievable. You don't know a lot of guys who are going to get stitched up here and there and then go out and pitch. Yeah, there was blood on his sock and all that stuff but if you just saw it before the game, you would have been, like, 'My goodness.' Schill was a competitor, man."

That bloody-sock sequel game closed the books on Schilling's 2004 season. In hindsight, it was also the end of his reign as an elite pitcher. There would be an ankle surgery that winter and Schilling was slow to recover in 2005. He bounced back with a fifteen-win season in 2006, but carried an ERA close to four. In Schilling's final season, 2007, he pitched through arm problems and once again was masterful in October. He doesn't dispute that his post–2004 body of work suffered thanks to what he pitched through in the postseason. He also offers no hint of regret.

"I couldn't be [the same]," said Schilling. "I was okay with that. I'd do it again. I don't know that it cut my career short, but I think it made me less of a pitcher over the last couple of years. It was worth it. The kinetic change starts at the toe and the initial force of the delivery comes up through the ankle. And when you can't transfer that power through the ankle up to the leg, into the hip joint, everything changes. But again, I've never looked at the injury and even thought about it for even a second like that."

The ankle, by the way, is still bothersome. "Yeah, it's really bad now," Schilling said on a damp New England day in November 2013. "Especially with the weather."

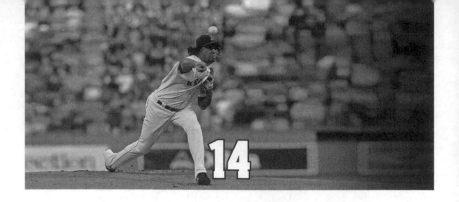

Game 3, World Series
Pedro's Last Stand

B y the time the Red Sox got to St. Louis, they were getting almost nostalgic about the end that they knew was coming in a matter of days. Would any of them ever have so much fun playing baseball again? Not only were they steamrolling the competition—something they had done since mid-August aside from the three-game hiccup against the Yankees—but also, they were crushing each other with trash talk. By this time, Millar no longer needed to bind the clubhouse together. He had just become the bartender, making sure those daily pre-game shots of Jack continued to flow until the streak ended. This team was one, and it was obvious to anyone who was around them.

"Here we are in Game 3 or Game 4 in St. Louis and you just can't wait to get to the clubhouse to horse around and talk some smack to Curt Schilling or Pedro and they'd dish it right back out to you," said Trot Nixon. "It was joking around but we cared a great deal about each other and it was a great portrait of a team that loved each other. From a military standpoint, that *Band of Brothers*, that movie, it's kind of like that, except we weren't fighting in a war. We were playing baseball but we cared about each other a great deal."

If you were one of the twenty-five players on that team, you could dish it or take it. "You'd check your ego at the door. We'll wear out Schilling, Timlin , Mirabelli, Millar, or Ortiz," said Nixon. "It didn't matter who you were. Even Tito and the coaching staff, they got it. Youk, we even tortured that poor kid."

It was Pedro Martinez's kind of team, and he was about to perform his final act for the Red Sox. Known for his icy demeanor on the mound, he was a clown in the clubhouse and on the bench during those days he wasn't pitching. Early in his time with the Red Sox, one of his teammates taped him to a pole in the dugout in the middle of a game. For a man considered by some to be a diva, Pedro knew how to yuk it up with his friends in the clubhouse. And his smile and laughter were infectious. As the hours ticked down to Game 3 of the World Series, Martinez was one hundred percent business. This was a big day—one in which he would finally pitch in the World Series.

In every Fall Classic, there was a player who had never been there before, and the media would build it up as the guy people wanted to win one for. Curt Schilling would search for a barf bag when he saw the story going down that road.

"And if you ever get a player alone, they'll tell you the same thing," said Schilling. "But I despise hearing we want to go and win it for so-and-so. That's such bullshit. Everybody wants to win. And in 1993, Pete Incaviglia [of the Phillies] was like, 'I've never been to a World Series, just, guys, help me get there.' It's like, 'Shut up, dude.' "

Schilling, however, knew the difference between Pedro Martinez and Pete Incaviglia. And Martinez never asked anyone to make the World Series about him. Like most players on the Red Sox, Martinez realized this quest was as much about the city of Boston, starved for a baseball champion, as any player on the team. Thanks to being up 2–0 already, Game 3 could essentially be about Pedro, and that was just fine with Schilling. He was looking forward to watching his co-ace go to work as much as anybody.

"That was fun to watch because he had a Hall of Fame career and this was his first World Series game," Schilling said. "This was my third. I knew what it was like to be on both ends of it. It was the first one that, to some degree, I got to really enjoy."

The spotlight had been squarely on Schilling and his bloody sock in Game 2, but it was all on Martinez in Game 3. Not only was it to be his first start in the World Series, but there was a sense this could be his final start in a Red Sox uniform. By the 2004 World Series, Martinez was already in decline from his years of Koufaxian numbers. It was clear that wherever he went as a free agent, he would never top his historic achievements in Boston. That would always be the team he'd be identified with. Martinez didn't completely block out that subplot as he got ready to take the ball, one day after his thirty-third birthday.

"That was my last game, I knew it," Martinez said. "I figured if it didn't happen earlier, it was probably going to be hard after all that teams would offer and all that."

Martinez was lined up to pitch Game 7, but there wasn't a soul on the Boston Red Sox who thought the World Series would make it back to Boston.

By the time Game 3 was getting ready to start, a ton of Boston players had had signature moments in the 2004 playoffs, from Big Papi to Mueller to Roberts to Lowe to Damon to Schilling to Foulke to Nixon and on and on. However, Manny Ramirez had just kind of been blending in, dumping in a single here or a double there, but really not doing anything to distinguish himself. As Ramirez dug in for a 2-2 pitch in the top of the first, Tim McCarver had another one of his well-timed statements: "This is the guy that Terry Francona says is going to break out and explode one of these games." Right after that sentence left McCarver's mouth, the baseball left Cardinals starter Jeff Suppan's right hand. And it was a pure Manny moment. The swing was textbook and it was beautiful, and the hitting savant hit a blast that landed in the second deck in left field. Doug Mientkiewicz was laughing in the dugout as he waited for Ramirez to cross home. Schilling screamed "Wow!" and pumped his fist. It would be one of four World Series homers Ramirez hit in his career, but it's the one people remember most.

"It felt like a steamroll," Kapler said of the latter stages of the World Series. "And I remember Manny getting really hot in St. Louis. Just like, boom, boom. And everything was gold."

Considering that Ramirez had made his teammates laugh at his defensive ineptitude in Game 1, it was eye-opening that he made a play in left in Game 3 that rescued Martinez from an early jam. In the first inning of his first World Series start, Pedro didn't look all that impressive. He walked Larry Walker and gave up an infield hit down the third-base line to Albert Pujols. When Scott Rolen walked, the Cardinals had the bases loaded and one out. That's when Jim Edmonds hit a fly ball between shallow and medium-depth left field. The Cardinals took a chance, and Walker tagged from third. Ramirez camped under the ball and made a perfect one-hop throw to the plate, where Varitek tagged Walker out to end the inning. In a humorous end to the play, Martinez, who was backing up in case of a poor throw, dusted Walker on the backside on his way back to the dugout. Walker and Martinez had been teammates in Montreal.

But Ramirez and Martinez had been teammates since 2001. In fact, Martinez isn't so sure Manny would have ever signed the mammoth contract from former Sox general manager Dan Duquette (eight years, $160 million) if not for their relationship. Though Martinez was just seven months older than Ramirez, he was clearly the big brother in that relationship.

"I influenced Manny coming over here. I was the one that Manny told when he wanted to come over here," Martinez said. "And then I went on to tell Duquette that Manny wanted to come here at the end of the year and that's how everything started." Perhaps Martinez didn't take it upon himself to keep Ramirez in line as often as Millar, or Cabrera, in his short stint with the team. But he did do his part.

"We all did," Martinez said. "I used to kick Manny a lot. I used to go, 'Manny, don't do that.' Sometimes he would come out of the game and take off his clothes and let go and all that and kind of forget about the whole team," Martinez said. "I'd tell him, 'Manny, what if we get into a fight or something?' Then he would get dressed. I said, 'Manny, you don't do that. You stay in uniform until we're finished.'"

Martinez took enormous pride in the players who would flourish outside of the Dominican Republic. Watching Ortiz and Ramirez go to work in the middle of their primes was one of the highlights of his career.

"I was right there, at the right time," Martinez said. "I'll tell you what: I've never seen a one-two punch more well combined than those two. Wow, lefty and righty. And both equally dangerous in the clutch. And also, they both had such a big role while winning it in '04. Nobody had a bigger role than David and Manny." Ramirez had done Martinez a huge favor with that perfect throw to the plate, and Pedro would hardly be touched for the rest of the night.

The Cardinals would give Martinez one more gift on the bases, and he would own the night after that. It happened in the third inning. Suppan led off with an infield hit and Edgar Renteria crushed a double to right field. With runners on second and third and nobody out, it seemed the Cardinals wouldn't be able to screw this rally up. When Walker hit a hard grounder to deep second, the Red Sox conceded the run, as Bellhorn fired to first for the out. But for reasons nobody will ever quite understand, Suppan hesitated to go home, and then tried to scramble back to third. David Ortiz, who had to give up his DH spot and play first base in the National League City, fired a perfect strike across the diamond, completely short-circuiting the St. Louis rally.

"Manny made a great play," said Martinez. "Suppan slipped, everything clicked. David hadn't played first base almost the whole year, then he goes and reacts and, boom."

The Red Sox got just enough timely hits to give Martinez some breathing room, opening it up to 4–0 by the fifth inning on RBI singles by Ramirez and Bill Mueller. That was a special hit for Mueller, a St. Louis native playing in front of his mom and dad.

"I was in my hometown and nerves were—was crazy nervous," Mueller said. "It was an emotional time because we just came off the emotion of beating the Yankees and then to be in the World Series, that's emotional. My goodness, it's the World Series. That's what I've been living for and wanting to be a part of my whole life."

To say the Suppan brain fart at third base was a pivotal moment in Game 3 would be the understatement of the century. Pedro Martinez didn't even give up another baserunner for the rest of his sparkling outing. And just as Francona so aptly predicted Ramirez was about to break out, he also mentioned this during his in-game interview on Fox, which was taped during the second inning: "If he can get through the first inning or two and find his rhythm, look out!"

The Cardinals should have scored against Martinez when they had the chance. The swagger he developed through the course of that night was still evident in his voice when he talked about it nearly a decade later.

"I remember just overcoming the first couple of struggles," Martinez said. "After that, I said, 'You know what, there's no way anybody can beat me here from now on.' I just got loose and I just went on and on and on and on and on to dominate. I let it all hang out. I just got on top. I got on top of it."

The highlights of Martinez pitching his lone World Series start in a Boston uniform are easy to distinguish from other games. His hair had gotten the longest it had ever been in his career, as he almost looked more like the late Pascual Pérez than Pedro Martinez.

"You saw that Jheri curl or whatever he had going on," said Nixon. "Floppy hair, long hair and all this stuff. He had a mullet out there. We didn't think about the opportunity that he could go somewhere else. We didn't think about that at all, as players. I know probably other people were saying, 'Hey, this could be pretty significant, it could be his last time pitching there,' but we didn't think about that at all. What better competitor and pitcher to have going into a hostile territory than Pedro Martinez? We were fortunate to have him there. It was awesome, seeing what Pedro was able to do."

Nixon was one of those players who was there for the best of Pedro. He was there the night Martinez fired the six no-hit innings in the deciding Game 7 against the Indians in 1999. He was there when Pedro fired a one-hitter with 17 strikeouts at Yankee Stadium in September of 1999, when the Yankees had an offensive juggernaut. Nixon was stationed in right field throughout the 2000 season, when Martinez posted a 1.74 ERA, the finest of his career. "I had front row-seats for some of those magical moments, when he was striking out seventeen in a game," Nixon said.

For Orlando Cabrera, who was with Martinez ever so briefly in Montreal, it was a thrill to rejoin him when he had already reached the living–legend portion of his career.

"To me, the most difficult guy to hit was Pedro Martinez," Cabrera said. "Pedro was a special guy. One of the things that always struck me was his attitude when he was pitching. He was a different person. You could never think that anybody could switch from that to this when he pitched. He was just like another person. You never see a laugh or anything. It's like, 'I'm here to beat you. I don't care what you do. That's it.' There's no laughing. The next day, he's like a clown. You're like, what the hell is going on? He was just like that in Montreal, the same way. He was so smart."

Gabe Kapler remembers almost feeling as if he had made it in the Major Leagues just because Martinez smiled at him in the middle of a game.

"My first experience with Pedro was when I was taking a lead off of first base in Arlington when I was with the Rangers and he was early in his career with the Red Sox," Kapler said. "And he picked over to first base and I dove back in. He picked over to first base again and I dove back in. He gave me, like, some random smile from the pitcher's mound. It lit me up. I was like, 'Holy shit, that's Pedro Martinez.' He's toying with me at that point. And that was the personality he brought to the mound. It was very playful but intense and extraordinarily talented. He was so kind to me. Very, very kind to me. A great teammate. From time to time, he could get a little bit narcissistic. Every superstar I've ever met had that."

Watching Martinez look like his vintage self in his World Series debut was something to behold. He was overpowering in his final inning, the seventh, punching out Edmonds and Reggie Sanders. The final pitch Martinez threw in a Boston uniform was a ninety-two-mph fastball that Sanders didn't even come close to touching. It was his ninrty-eighth pitch of the night. While Joe Buck and Tim McCarver speculated that Martinez might have another inning in him, it was clear his night was over when he pointed skyward.

"He was phenomenal," remembers Schilling.

After Timlin sent down all three batters he faced in the eighth, Keith Foulke—who else?—was entrusted with the ninth. This time, Foulke had the gall to give up a meaningless home run to Larry Walker that made the final score, 4–1. It was the only earned run Foulke would allow in the entire postseason. One out from winning it all, the Red Sox were ready to go for the kill.

"We were just locked in from [the first] pitch to the last pitch," said Foulke. "We got a couple of breaks in there and just never let them breathe."

Game 4, World Series
Is This Heaven?

ealizing they were closing in on history, the Red Sox were scurrying around for mementos in the hours leading up to Game 4 of the World Series. It all made Johnny Damon a little uneasy. Remember, Damon is the guy who packed his suitcase before Game 4 of the ALCS because he figured if he did, he wouldn't end up needing it. So why would he start collecting souvenirs from a championship season before it actually was a championship season?

"It seemed like everybody in the clubhouse before the game, they were trying to get things signed and everything," Damon said. "I'm like, 'We have to win one more and then we can do whatever the heck we want.' I just couldn't believe everyone going around, getting things signed and I was, like, 'Oh no, let's not count on the series before we win another game.'"

One thing was for sure: There was no chance of wiping the smile off of Derek Lowe's face. He was a picture of excitement when he arrived at Busch Stadium. In the space of a month, he'd gone from feeling red-hot anger to pitching perhaps the most-anticipated game the Red Sox had ever played in. During batting practice, Lowe sat on the bench with a relaxed look on his face and twirled a bat back and forth. If you wanted to have a conversation with Lowe that afternoon, it wasn't hard. He loved his time with the Red Sox and he knew it was ending. And he also knew that there was absolutely no better way to end it than to be the first winning pitcher in a World Series clincher for the Boston Red Sox since Carl Mays stifled the Cubbies on September 11, 1918.

"This is my last start ever [with the Red Sox]," Lowe remembers thinking. "This is literally my last start. This is it. There's no Game 8 in the World Series. I just said, 'This is my last start ever and just try to enjoy the day.' This is literally it. There's going to be no more starts for you. And not only that, as it turned out, I was never in a World Series again. Just take it in instead of thinking about where we are, up three, with a chance to win a World Series and a chance to beat the curse, all that. Enjoy the moment. Enjoy where you are."

Lowe hadn't even thrown a pitch in Game 4 and Johnny Damon gave him something to enjoy. As Damon said, he was all business going into what proved to be the last game, and he sized up the third pitch of the game, a ninety-two-mph fastball by Jason Marquis, and drilled it into the Cardinals' bullpen. Of the pre-game frivolity that made him feel uncomfortable, Damon joked, "That's why I felt obligated to hit a home run to lead the game off," Damon said. "I felt good. I had the count in my favor and I was like, 'I'm going to hit it hard.' It was a rope. I busted out of the box trying to get a double because I guess I just had some backspin and it carried out. I knew I hit it hard, but it was low and I knew Edmonds could bare-hand and try to throw me out at second."

But on a night the stars were clearly aligned—with a blood-red moon and the first full lunar eclipse in the history of World Series play—Damon's ball wasn't going to land where Edmonds could do anything with it. "I remember the St. Louis crowd was alive and they were ready for a comeback. They knew we had come back [in the ALCS]. Why couldn't their team? After I hit that home run, the place got absolutely silent," Damon said. "I thought we were going to roll the whole game, but it was a close game."

Yes, there were plenty of opportunities for the Red Sox to blow this one open, but the Cardinals kept it tight. It was the type of game that needed a big hit from someone else, not just Damon. And Trot Nixon, who came into Game 4 with a disappointing World Series performance (2 for 10), was going to become that someone. The foundation for Nixon's Game 4 breakout took place behind the scenes with a player who casual fans probably have no recollection of.

Adam Hyzdu was the definition of a Minor League lifer. This dedicated outfielder would play 1,703 games in the minors chasing down his dream. He had multiple stints in Boston's organization, and would team with Trot Nixon at Double-A Trenton in 1996 and Triple-A Pawtucket a year later. By 2004, Hyzdu was back with the Red Sox, and got a cup of coffee late in the season, playing in 17 games with the big club as a late-season call-up. As a reward for all his perseverance, Hyzdu did play in 221 Major League games from 2000 to 2006. He wasn't on Boston's postseason roster, but there are usually a couple of extra players who travel with the team anyway and participate in batting practice, etc. It is usually a reward for those who are considered good teammates.

So with Nixon in a slump and very eager to contribute something during the first World Series of his career, he knew which teammate he could count on.

"I told the hitting coach, 'Hey look, I'm going to go down to the cage, I'm going to bunt.' I said, 'You don't need to go down there. It's fine. I'm not working on anything hitting-wise. I just want to bunt.' He said, 'What are you doing?' 'I'm just working on my hand-eye coordination,' " Nixon told Papa Jack.

Nixon was bringing the philosophy of former manager Jimy Williams to the 2004 World Series.

"And Jimy Williams used to always go through the batting practice with Brian Daubach and myself, all the time," said Nixon. "And he would always make me start off drag bunt and bunting balls. He felt like what he had heard over the years in coaching that guys who did this just saw the ball a lot better in batting practice and when they're hitting. In bunting, you're sitting there, tracking the ball, you're laying it down, you're watching it hit the bat. Kind of the same things you want to achieve when you're hitting.

"So I grabbed Hyzdu. He wasn't active on the roster. I said, 'Du-Du, can you help me out?' I nicknamed him Du-Du for no reason, other than his name was Adam Hyzdu. I said, 'Look, can you throw me some BP?' He said, 'Are you going to hit?' I said, 'No, I'm just going to bunt.' I said, 'I want to start by just bunting and then I'm going to drag bunt. I know it's kind of grunt work. I'm just looking for somebody who's not throwing BP out on the field.' He goes, 'Yeah, that's no problem.' So he went down there and he was just pumping them in there hard, you know? I just kept working on laying down bunts, trying to be perfect with the bunts, drag bunting.

"You never know if I'm going to be asked to bunt in a game. I was more worried about my hand-eye coordination. And I did that both days, both before Game 3 and Game 4. It was amazing, I told the guy, 'It's amazing how much better I felt in that batter's box.' It's just seeing the baseball, and I'm going to tell you, in Game 4, the ball looked like a balloon coming in there."

By the time Nixon had stepped in for his at-bat in the third inning, the bases were loaded with two outs. Nixon had doubled just one inning earlier, but it didn't lead to a run. This time, he worked the count to 3-0. Third–base coach Dale Sveum gave Nixon the take sign. Nixon didn't see it, and that turned out to be a good thing. Nixon absolutely smashed the balloon-looking pitch from Marquis and deposited it high off the wall in right-center. Ortiz and Varitek both scored, and the Red Sox had broken out to a 3–0 lead. Pedro Martinez was beside himself, gleefully bouncing all around the dugout. Jimy Williams would be happy to know that when Chase and Luke Nixon, Trot's sons, take batting practice with their father, they start every round with twelve bunts.

With at least a decent cushion to work with, Lowe went to work and pitched every bit as brilliantly as he had at Yankee Stadium one week earlier. At that point, short rest or long rest didn't matter to Lowe. He was pitching like he had throughout 2002, the year he threw a no-hitter, won twenty-one games and finished third in the Cy Young Award voting behind Barry Zito and Martinez.

"His changeup was nasty that night," said Damon. "I could see it from center field. These guys had absolutely no chance."

To Lowe, the night was almost like a grand party that was going too fast. The last batter he faced in a Red Sox uniform was John Mabry. As Lowe struck him out to end the seventh, he literally hopped off the mound and sprinted into the dugout. It was the exact opposite of what he wanted to do.

"I remember running off the field," Lowe said. "And I remember telling myself, as I was running off the field, 'Why am I running? This is my last pitch ever for the Red Sox and in the World Series. Why am I running off?' I remember vividly, saying, 'Slow down.' and I just ran all the way in. Just take it all in, enjoy it. I wish I would have just walked off and maybe taken it all in."

Lowe would go on to earn the win with his seven shutout innings, in which he allowed just three hits and a walk while striking out four. Under baseball's new expanded postseason format, which started in 1995, Lowe became the first pitcher in history to win the clinching game of all three playoff rounds in one October. Andy Pettitte would do the same thing for the Yankees in 2009, but in far less dramatic fashion than Lowe. With Lowe's night done, it closed the books on the starting-pitching clinic the Red Sox had put on in the final three games of the World Series. Schilling, Martinez, and Lowe combined for 20 innings and didn't give up an earned run.

"And that was an insane offense. That was an unbelievable offense," said Schilling. "You had Renteria, Edmonds, Rolen, Pujols, and Larry Walker. And after Wake's first game, Petey, Derek, and I threw well and our pen nailed it."

Once Lowe left the game, the final two innings became a countdown for those who wore Boston uniforms and the millions who cheered for them. After pinch-running for Nixon, Gabe Kapler stood in right field for the ninth inning that would crown the entire season and he took note of the way his body was reacting.

"That, I actually recall like it was two minutes ago," said Kapler. "That was a physical feeling I felt, where it was very difficult getting a drop of spit in my mouth. My mouth was so dry and I was so nervous because nobody wanted to make the mistake that led to something that led to something that led to something. I think you want the ball. You do want the opportunity. You want to execute the opportunity. You feel very alive. Your eyes are wide open. You can feel the sensation in your body. So that's how I felt. That's how I felt in that last inning."

Mike Timlin didn't pitch in Game 4, but he remembered from Game 6 in 1992 how it felt to be the man standing on the mound when a World Series ended. This time, that man was going to be Keith Foulke.

"I can still see Foulke leaving the bullpen, going to myself, 'This is going to be it. I know, this is going to be it.' When he left, I had a sense of calm in my heart," said Timlin. "It's over. I know it's over."

By this point in the 2004 postseason, Keith Foulke was a cold-blooded executioner. He would throw the final pitch in all four games of the World Series.

"I remember going out of the bullpen, I was like, 'Let's get this done.' It was kind of the same thing as always. I'm going to try to make this as quick as possible," said Foulke.

Just before Albert Pujols was getting ready for Foulke's first pitch of the inning, Fox panned to a Red Sox fan standing at his box seat with a sign that said, "Is This Heaven?" It was getting close to that time. Pujols temporarily irked Foulke by hitting a fastball right through his legs, and up the middle for a single. That hit heightened Foulke's senses and put him into the mode of a hockey goaltender. "What I do remember is, after Pujols hit that ball between my legs, I was like, 'That ball, in order for that to happen again, it's going to have to go through me,' " Foulke said.

After Pujols reached, Foulke quickly dispatched Scott Rolen, who hit a fly ball to Kapler for the first out. That closed the books on an 0 for the World Series by Rolen, yet another sign of how awesome Boston's pitching staff was in those four games. Foulke carved up Edmonds, striking him out on three pitches. The World Series was coming down to one final out, and third baseman Bill Mueller decided to take a look around.

"I remember standing at third base and looking up in the stands and saying, 'I can't believe it, we're going to be World Series champions.' Just seeing the Boston Red Sox fans standing up in Busch Stadium," said Mueller. "I'm like, 'Man, what an unbelievable thing. I never want to forget this feeling. I never want to forget how I'm feeling right now at this moment.' That was a dream come true."

Foulke didn't leave much time for his teammates to soak in what was going to happen. He was locked and loaded and ready to go for the kill. There was one ball to Edgar Renteria. And then came the play that will live on forever. Renteria chopped one back toward the mound, and Foulke wasn't going to let this one get past him. "As soon as he hits it, it's coming back to me, and it's like, that chopper," Foulke said. "So I jump and don't necessarily need to. It's that split-second reaction. I remember getting the ball and it wasn't until later that I kind of realized, I didn't even really catch the ball. The ball was like, on the outside of the glove. But as soon as he hit it back to me, that's when everything went from here to just like that, warp speed. It happened so fast. I just remember the double pump and the flip, I don't even know if I remember seeing him catch the ball."

Mientkiewicz, who was again in at first for the late innings, corralled it and 86 years of coming up short for Red Sox fans ended just like that.

"As soon I tossed it, I turned around and was looking for Jason," said Foulke.

Just before the sturdy Varitek jumped into Foulke's arms, the closer was saying something. You can see it every time the video of the last out is played. What was he saying?

"It's not really book appropriate. It was just kind of my thing," Foulke said. "It was a lot of joy. That's a lifetime of stuff being released into the culmination of joy."

The players stormed the field from their positions, and from the dugout and the bullpen. Pokey Reese showed his athleticism one more time by leaping to the top of the pile, where he propped himself stomach-first as if he was lying facedown on a bed.

"I actually remember that well, it was like an out-of-body experience running in from the outfield," said Kapler. "And almost like, a mantra playing in my head. 'Is this really happening?' Almost like a dream state where you want to pinch yourself, like 'Is this really taking place?' And then as the days and the weeks passed, I remember feeling, seeing it as a movie instead of something as, we were there. It started to unfold like somebody else's story."

This was the third of Mike Timlin's four World Series titles, and the second in which he'd bolt in from the bullpen to join his teammates. The other one was when Joe Carter ended the 1993 World Series in Toronto with one swing, a home run against the Phillies.

"I got there as fast as I possibly could," said Timlin. "I secured my glove because I didn't know if anyone was going to take my glove. And I just wanted over the fence. I didn't go through the gate. We all just jumped over the fence and ran out there."

When a player reaches the pinnacle of sport, thoughts race through the mind. And at the end of 2004, Johnny Damon was seeing things a lot more clearly than his concussed October 2003.

"Everything we went through, that's what you start thinking about. Everything you went through to get to that point to win it all, all the ups and down, all the bruises, all the hard work through the years, and I guess that's why always, when my team has been eliminated, it hurt because you know all that sacrifice you gave, being away from your family was for naught," said Damon. "The only reason I ever started playing was to win. And to be able to win that World Series for the Red Sox after all the pain and heartache through the years. You can't top it."

It's hard to believe there was anyone with more conflicted emotions at the moment Mientkiewicz squeezed the last out than the man he was traded for. Nomar Garciaparra had long-standing friendships with Jason Varitek, Trot Nixon, Tim Wakefield, Pedro Martinez, and some others. And the fact he even watched the World Series on television displayed his loyalty and fondness for them.

"I only watched two World Series while I played. It was the one in '04 because of the way the guys made me feel," said Garciaparra. "And the other time was when the New York Mets and the Yankees played [in 2000] because Jay Payton was a center fielder and my roommate in college, and I wanted to follow him and watch him. That was it. I never watched it, because that was where I wanted to be."

Garciaparra, who once seemed destined to be the ultimate and life-long Red Sox player, doesn't dispute that his emotions were mixed when the 2004 World Series ended.

"Yeah, for sure, I definitely wished I was there, there's no question about that," Garciaparra said. "You wanted to experience that. As a player, your goal is to win a World Series. And I realized when I played in Boston after a few years there and growing up in that organization, it's not about me winning the World Series. It's bigger here. These people deserve a World Series. And I realized right then, 'Good for them, because they deserve it.' But I definitely wished I was there celebrating with the guys, no question, and being a part of that."

Because he was stoic by nature during his playing days, particularly with the media, Garciaparra's passion for the game and for winning was sometimes underplayed. When Lowe punched out the Athletics to end the dramatic 2003 Division Series, the image of Garciaparra, his arms pumped high in the air at shortstop as he roared with joy, was a great example of it.

"That's all I played for," Garciaparra said. "I didn't play for stats, money, or anything like that. I never wanted to hear my stats. I just wanted to go play. My mindset was always, 'Did we win?'"

Instead, it was Orlando Cabrera who was right in the middle of a World Series–winning celebration. And he could relate perfectly to the "Is This Heaven?" sign that was in the stands during the ninth inning.

"I truly thought that I was on top of the world. And probably I was," Cabrera said. "This is the world of baseball and we were on top. The feeling was incredible. It was something that I had never seen before and I never saw again. It was just everything. All the feelings were there. Every accomplishment was there."

Cabrera's double-play partner, the quiet Mark Bellhorn, must have suspected he would never be part of anything like this again. "You have so many celebrations throughout the course of the year," said Bellhorn. "It's like the last one is kind of a downer because it's all over and the season is over. It was a great ending. It couldn't have happened to a better group."

And once they retreated to the clubhouse, the champagne poured all over the place. Manny Ramirez, aside from his monster home run in Game 3, hit .412 in the World Series and was named the Most Valuable Player. The consensus in the clubhouse is that the trophy should have gone to Foulke, who was simply magnificent not just in the Fall Classic, but for the entire month.

"When they named Manny the MVP, we were all trying to think what he actually did," Damon said. "Millar and I were joking that Manny won the MVP and he actually almost cost us Game 1."

The man who helped save the season by having his foot stitched together for his final two starts found Johnny Pesky and lifted him up in the air and embraced him in a bear hug. For Curt Schilling, the moment with Pesky is still one of the most memorable moments of his career. Not long after that, Schilling gathered most of his teammates together for a toast.

With champagne bottles bunched together by the players who surrounded him, Schilling proclaimed, "To the greatest Red Sox team ever assembled!" The word "ever" was then echoed by a few teammates before they gulped down the bubbly.

"It was a time when less was more," said Schilling. "And in my mind, this was the greatest Red Sox team they had ever put together. People will say, 'On paper, this,' or 'On paper, that,' but year in and year out, it's proven that you don't ever put a championship on paper. We beat a team, on paper, that should have killed us. They had us beaten three games to none. People argue this but the best team always wins the championship. The best teams find a way to win the most important games."

And nobody could have been more satisfied than Schilling to see the championship come to Boston. After all, he was the only person who promised it would happen.

"Was it nerve-racking?" Schilling said. "No. It was exciting. But I was literally a David Ortiz home run away from failing miserably."

Once the champagne had run dry, the Red Sox headed to their nearby hotel, packed their belongings, and got ready to fly home. Everyone wanted to get back to Boston and see what that would be like. And when they got off the bus on the morning of October 28 at Fenway Park, Pedro Martinez had the trophy in his hand.

"I know Ellis Burks wanted it and people like that, but I wanted to bring it out just in case," Martinez said. "I took the trophy off the bus, handed it out to Boston. "I went, 'Here, Boston, you have it.' "

The Red Sox were awed that there could be such atmosphere in the air at a time when people are typically still sleeping or getting ready to start the work day. But when they got off the bus, there were people lined up waiting for them.

"It's crisp, it's cold outside. We're all bundled up, wearing beanies, you can still smell the champagne on our hats and our clothes," Kapler said. "The brotherhood is really, really strong. You go through the World Series champions in history, you're going to have some teams that are like, 'We didn't really like each other. We couldn't wait to get home.' This group of guys could have spent eternity together."

They had one last chance to spend an entire day together, and it was October 30, 2004, the day of the first Rolling Rally. Due to the magnitude of this parade, Boston Mayor Thomas M. Menino decided that the Red Sox would go through the city on duck boats, which can travel by land and sea. It was a gloomy New England day, but the joyous atmosphere made it feel like it was sunny and 85. There might never be another parade like it. Estimates had over three million fans scattered throughout the city for one more look at the iconic "Idiots." Every player seems to remember something different. For Trot Nixon, it was the old man on the rock.

"It's freezing cold. There are people waiting down in the water," said Nixon. "I remember seeing an old man that had a blanket, he was standing on a rock. This guy, he had been around a long time. He had seen some Red Sox games in his life. He had seen some Red Sox misery, I'm sure. He may have been around here when doggone Babe Ruth was around. That's how old this guy was. He had his Red Sox stuff on, just waving at us. It was unbelievable, it really was."

Dave Roberts remembers everybody doing stolen-base imitations, which might have been hard to pull off in a run-of-the-mill parade, but not at this extravaganza.

"People were imitating me stealing the base and diving on the grass, as we were going in the duck boats into the Charles River," said Roberts. "That was kind of funny, and comical."

Pedro Martinez only stopped laughing momentarily, when someone hit him in the head with a thrown baseball. It was a free-for-all.

"The parade never goes away from my mind. I couldn't believe I would see so many people all at once," Martinez said. "It was a magical day seeing so many people lined up all over Boston. I saw this guy jumping off the bridge into the Charles River, into frozen water. Someone dropped a ball and hit me straight in the forehead, boom. I had such a headache. It was worth it, though."

"Cold day, shirts off, people jumping in the river," said Millar. "You can't describe it. It was fifty to one hundred deep, all the way down and around. It was just one big celebration and we were all part of a family— Red Sox Nation."

Bill Mueller missed the parade. He was welcoming a new member into his family, a son.

"I was home for Tucker's birth. So I had to fly back. My wife was actually having contractions when we were playing in the Yankees series," said Mueller. "That's why I was completely drained by St. Louis. So, really, I might have been the only guy that's ever won the World Series and then that night, spent the night with his mom and dad. I went home to my house in St. Louis because we won there and then I took like a six a.m. bird back home to Phoenix."

Idiot Exodus

iven the perfect fit he had with the team, and the fact he was the definition of a "glue guy" in the clubhouse, it was somewhat surprising that Gabe Kapler was the first member of the 2004 Red Sox to leave. Perhaps for the same reason, it's not surprising he was the first to return. Less than a month after the World Series ended, Kapler signed with the Yomiuri Giants of Japan.

"It was a financial decision and an itch that I had to scratch," said Kapler. "It was based on playing time. It was based on who I thought I still was. I was probably wrong. I probably thought I was still a guy that could take down 550 or 600 plate appearances. And I never had that opportunity. I did have that opportunity to play every day but I had never put together the season that I thought I could put together. I came closest in 2001. And I still was short about seventy-five plate appearances. I still thought there were 20-20 seasons in there. The financial numbers weren't close. What Japan was offering me was three times what Boston was offering me, even though Boston was, for me, at that point, my home. I realized right away, 'What did I do?' "

Kapler was back with the Red Sox by July 15, 2005. Less than two months later, he ruptured his left Achilles tendon running out a two-run homer by teammate Tony Graffanino.

"If you think about the way it unfolded for me, do I tear my Achilles tendon in '05 if I didn't have the wear and tear from the beginning of the season [in Japan]? Was my body just not prepared for that? Baseball and life are just a series of forks in the road. I always think that we make the right decision," said Kapler. "It's always the right decision. It's what we were supposed to do in that moment. I shared a quote, it was on my locker all through 2004: 'This moment is exactly as it should be.' And I remember it having a huge impact on Millar. Every once in a while, if he's down or something, I'll send him that text. Every now and then, he'll send me a text: 'This moment is exactly as it should be.'"

Kapler bounced back quickly from the Achilles injury and was back on the field for the Red Sox by June of 2006. It would be the last of his four seasons with Boston. Kapler retired prematurely to scratch another itch, managing the Greenville Drive, a Class-A affiliate in Boston's farm system during 2007. But he made a comeback for the Brewers the following season and would spend the final two years of his career with the Tampa Bay Rays before retiring after the 2010 season.

"I have zero regrets," said Kapler. "I'm so blessed."

By 2013, Kapler was a baseball analyst for Fox Sports 1, and had also done some consulting work for the Rays.

Dave Roberts wound up with eighty-six at-bats in a Boston uniform and six stolen bases, including the one that no baseball fan will ever forget. But by December 2004, after the glow of winning the World Series was replaced by the business of plotting his future, Roberts didn't think it made a lot of sense to stay with the Red Sox. The entire starting outfield was under contract for the 2005 season. While being a super sub for an eventual champion was something Roberts relished for the final couple of months of 2004, he knew that being a full-time sub was not for him.

"I was like, 'Theo, I love it here, I'm so happy but you've got to trade me. I really appreciate everything but I'm in the middle of my career and I don't want to be a fourth outfielder.' I understand, I'm a nice luxury to have. At that point in my career, I wanted to be a starter," said Roberts. "I wanted to leave. I just am so grateful because he knew that I wanted to go to San Diego and he made it happen. Because of his ties with Kevin Towers, they kind of facilitated that. I remember being at Robin Ventura's retirement party up in San Louis Obispo, in wine country, and my agent called and said you're going to go to San Diego. That was like the most amazing thing. That's why I'm so happy the Red Sox had a chance to win in 2007 because he did it right. You just don't see that in baseball. A lot of times you see guys so worried about their own club. For him to kind of step aside and give me an opportunity to do my thing and have a career for myself, I was forever grateful."

In a way, the trade the Red Sox made for Roberts was the one that led to the club reacquiring Kapler. When Epstein made the deal with the Padres, he got back Garciaparra's old college roommate, Jay Payton, who seemed like an offensive upgrade over Kapler as a right-handed hitting platoon to Nixon in right field. But Payton was absolutely miserable being a bench player and had a dugout tirade in early July that led to Francona not allowing him on the team plane from Texas to Baltimore. He was designated for assignment the next day and traded to the Oakland Athletics about a week later, leading to the re-signing of Kapler.

Roberts returned to Fenway Park in June 2007, as a member of the San Francisco Giants. Predictably, he got an applause that brought down the house. There would be some rumors in the ensuing years about Roberts resurfacing with the Red Sox, but he is happy it never came to fruition.

"It's a lore that I just love and I cherish, and I think the fans cherish that. I don't ever want to diminish that," Roberts said. "Whether I came back and played well or came back and didn't play well, it would have changed it. I want to leave it just the way it is."

In March 2010, Roberts, by then a member of the San Diego Padres' front office, was diagnosed with Hodgkin's lymphoma. He is still touched at the way the Red Sox reached out to him during the most difficult time of his life. "Going through my fight with cancer, the well-wishing from Red Sox Nation, that's stuff that I'll never forget," Roberts said. "It's just genuine, sincere, 'We care about you, we're thinking about you. Get well.'"

Larry Lucchino, a fellow cancer survivor, was also there for Roberts during that time, on behalf of the Red Sox. "Larry is one of the first guys I called when I got diagnosed. He had gone through it before," said Roberts. "He was like, 'You know what, I'm going to get you in touch with my doctor and put you up in the Trilogy [housing facility],' and he put me up for the month I was here, getting radiation treatment. He said, 'You're one of ours. Whatever you need.' He brought me into his suite during a game when I was here and the thing is, he didn't have to do that. This organization has just gone way, way above and beyond."

After three years of coaching first base for the Padres, Roberts was set to become their bench coach in 2014. No matter where he is, the stolen base always comes up.

"If I leave the house, someone is telling me about it," Roberts said. "I could be in my hometown in San Diego, I could be in Milwaukee, Wisconsin—someone is thanking me. And let alone, obviously, if I go to the ballpark. And I get fan mail and thank-you cards and holiday cards. It's endless. A lady named her dog Dave Roberts."

Pedro Martinez basked in the glow of the World Series for a little while, but then it was time to get down to business. After seven magical years with the Red Sox (117-37 record, 2.52 ERA), the man regarded by many as the best pitcher in team history was a free agent. Though Martinez really didn't have a whole lot of interest in pitching with the New York Yankees, he did at least play the game with Yankees owner George Steinbrenner, who would die in 2010. The offseason after the 2004 season was one of the last in which Steinbrenner was still healthy enough to be in control of his empire.

"Steinbrenner wanted to meet with me," Martinez said. "He said, 'Do you want to play for the Yankees?' I said, 'I don't have a job, sir.' He goes, 'Would you cut your hair to go play for the Yankees?' I said, 'Once I'm an employee, I'll do what my boss tells me to do.' He goes, 'Goddammit, you gave me a lot of headaches, I don't want to have to face you ever again.'"

In truth, Steinbrenner's Yankees had done their fair share against Martinez over the years. But it was equally true that the Boss simply got off on prying star players away from the Red Sox. He did it with Wade Boggs and, indirectly, with Roger Clemens, who was traded to the Yankees two years after he had left Boston.

"I want you to become a Yankee," Martinez remembers Steinbrenner telling him. "He goes, 'Money is not the issue. You can always come here and if you want a job with the Yankees, you have a job. Let me know.' And I said, I was really honest, I said, 'I appreciate the offer, I will consider it, but at the same time, I'm committed to Boston. My best interest is in Boston and I think the Red Sox are going to give me what I want and I will go back to Boston. But if I don't, first, I need to talk to Omar Minaya, because I promised him I would give him a chance. And if I don't get it sold with Omar Minaya, my countryman, I'll get back to you.'"

Omar Minaya, the same man who had traded Orlando Cabrera to the Red Sox just four months earlier, was the general manager of the Mets by the time Pedro Martinez was a free agent. Minaya needed a star to rejuvenate interest in the club and was putting a full-court press on Pedro Martinez, even if he was in decline.

"Minaya filled up all the expectations I had with the Red Sox," said Martinez. "Then I told the Red Sox after I spoke to Minaya, I said, 'You have fifteen days to match this contract.' I didn't get into specifically who it was with."

And around that time, in one of the chance encounters of all time, Martinez bumped into John Henry and Larry Lucchino at an airport in the Dominican Republic. Henry and Lucchino were making a trip to their academy in the Dominican to show off the World Series trophy. They hoped to bump into Martinez while they were in town, but nothing was set.

"I remember receiving Lucchino, and Mr. Henry coming in, getting in off the plane. I was getting on another plane in the Dominican. It's not that we were supposed to meet," Martinez said. "We happened to bump into each other. They were bringing the trophy, but I didn't know about that. Nobody told me about that. I saw Mr. Lucchino and Henry coming off the plane. And I had no choice but to wait. There was a small office there that they had for the planes, or whatever, so we sat down. Some of the people, once they saw the trophy, wanted me to hold it. And there was a reporter from the Dominican who came in as soon as he saw me and saw me with the trophy. He wanted to take a picture with me and Lucchino and the trophy. So I took the picture with the trophy but I had a scheduled flight.

"Lucchino asked me if I wanted to come back, and what it was going to take. I said, 'It's going to take you three years.' He goes, 'But you didn't have the best year.' I said, 'Larry, I have four years, guaranteed, all of them, somewhere else.' And he goes, 'No, that's bullshit.' Those were his specific words. And I took off my glasses, and I said, 'I have four years, and you have fifteen days to match it. Honest to God, I have four years.' And John Henry said, clearly, I still remember it now, 'Come on guys, just get it done. Just get it done'. Larry respects me a lot [now] because of that. I was straight honest to him."

Looking back on it, the most remarkable thing about Minaya's offer, which proved to be very real, was that it was kept out of the media until the deal with the Mets was all but complete. As baseball's Winter Meetings were wrapping up on the final day, rumors spread like wildfire that Pedro Martinez was headed to the Mets on a four-year, $52-million contract. The news stunned everyone. Just days earlier, David Ortiz had told the *Boston Herald*, "Pedro ain't going to no Mets." Yes, Pedro was very much going to the Mets. They had flooded him with the type of affection he loved, not to mention the dollars.

In Theo Epstein's last-gasp effort to keep Pedro Martinez in Boston, something that John Henry wanted more than the baseball operations department, he offered the ace two years with a club option for a third year that could bump the total up to about $40 million.

"My agent calls and he goes, 'I don't think the Red Sox are going to do it. They haven't said anything, they haven't done anything. I think we need to move forward because the Mets need an answer right now.' I had no choice but to commit. Once I committed, the Mets said they were going to send a plane early in the morning to pick me and go to the physical. Theo called at one-thirty, maybe two in the morning, at three years. They were shocked when I got four years, guaranteed, like I told Lucchino. At the very last instant, they came in with two years and an option," said Martinez.

As hindsight shows, Theo Epstein played the situation one hundred percent right. Martinez would go to the Mets and have a pretty good season in 2005, going 15-8 with a 2.82 ERA. But his 2006 season was riddled by injuries, as he went 9-8 with 4a .48 ERA. One of his lone highlights from that year was when the Mets came back to Fenway Park for an Interleague series. Martinez was a spectator in the first game, and the crowd went absolutely crazy when they saw him in the dugout. The next night, he was showered with an equal amount of love when he took the mound against his former team. But it was sad in a way because the Red Sox absolutely shelled him.

There wasn't a Red Sox fan out there who wanted to see Pedro Martinez humiliated. By the end of the 2006 regular season, with the Mets en route to the playoffs, Martinez had to undergo rotator cuff surgery. That was the unofficial end to his time as an ace. Martinez would make just five starts in 2007 and twenty in 2008, looking nothing close to the legendary performer he once was. Pedro's career did end with some nice moments. The Philadelphia Phillies picked him up halfway through the 2009 season and Martinez pitched some inspired baseball, going 5-1 in nine regular–season starts and putting together a vintage performance against the Dodgers in the National League Championship Series. Martinez got to pitch in the World Series again, and at Yankee Stadium. After proclaiming himself to be the most famous person to ever set foot in the new or old Yankee Stadium, Martinez lost Games 2 and 6 in New York, the latter performance coming on the night the Yankees won it all. Pedro Martinez would never pitch again in the Majors.

But he is back with the Red Sox, hired in January 2013 as a special assistant to Ben Cherington. Martinez works with Minor Leaguers and some Major Leaguers and spends a good chunk of Spring Training with the team. His bitter parting with the team is now a distant memory. Martinez has said he wants to be like Luis Tiant or Jim Rice and stay with the Red Sox forever.

And, in 2013, Martinez finally signed the Green Monster on a day he was at Fenway filming a commercial with Elliot Tatelman of Jordan's Furniture.

"I refused to sign it until I finally realized that I won it. I left [the Red Sox], and I knew I had a chance to come back and sign it but it never crossed my mind until I was recording a commercial down here in left field," Martinez. "I told Elliott, 'You know, I never signed the wall. And one of these days, I'm going to stop by and sign it.' He goes, 'Why don't you do it today?' I said, 'It looks like a good day for me to sign it.' So I went in and signed it."

As it turns out, Derek Lowe was right about one thing. When he turned down that contract extension in the spring of 2004 and wound up having the worst regular season of his career, he cost himself any chance at returning to the Red Sox once he became a free agent. All of the Red Sox, including Theo Epstein, were very grateful for the postseason he had, particularly after his late-season tantrum in Baltimore.

"He was going through a tough time in September and we had to give him bad news about the postseason rotation," remembers Epstein. "We tried to do it in a way in which we wouldn't lose him. He took the news hard—as you would expect. But he hung in there and ended up saving the day. I was proud of him."

However, as Epstein proved in the Martinez negotiations—not to mention the Garciaparra trade—he wasn't really the sentimental type. He couldn't make a positive evaluation of Lowe as a free agent because of a small sample size, like four starts in October. The Red Sox didn't even negotiate with Lowe after the 2004 season. Both sides knew they were moving on, and Lowe went to the Dodgers, where he would wind up playing for Grady Little again in 2006, and with Nomar Garciaparra and Bill Mueller. Manny Ramirez would also join the fun in Los Angeles via a trade from Boston in July 2008.

Lowe would pitch in the playoffs in three different seasons for the Dodgers. But he would never get back to the World Series. He would also come to miss East Coast baseball, where everything mattered so much. "It's funny, I haven't played there in ten years and it's still one hundred to one, fans come up to me and talk about the Red Sox instead of the Dodgers or Braves or anyone else I ever played for," Lowe said. "It's funny when I think about the season because it was my worst year. And people think I won twenty games and won the Cy Young. It was my worst year. There was so much that went into that season that people probably remembered at the time but don't remember now. Even when I was in L.A., in Manhattan Beach walking around, and people would say thank you for '04."

Shortstop Orlando Cabrera wound up having a short stop in Boston. Even though he fit in like a glove with that 2004 team, the Red Sox outthought themselves, bringing in a fellow Colombian, the same man who hit the ball back to Keith Foulke to end the World Series. On the strength of a four-year, $40-million contract, Edgar Renteria came to Boston. That left Orlando Cabrera to sign with the Angels for four years at $32 million. He wanted very badly to stay in Boston, but the Red Sox knew they could get two draft picks as compensation if they let Cabrera go. And they also felt Renteria was a better hitter.

"One fundamental priority of our off-season strategy was to accumulate as many high draft picks as possible in order to build up the farm system," Epstein said. "That steered us away from Orlando and toward other players."

Cabrera remembers posing for a picture with Epstein amid the euphoria after winning the pennant at Yankee Stadium. "He thinks we won the World Series already after we beat the Yankees," said Cabrera. "He said, 'I want a picture with the guys I traded for.' So we grabbed Mientkiewicz and he grabbed Dave and he grabbed me. He said, 'Thank you. You just saved my life.' He said that to me. I didn't even know. I was like, 'Wow.' He said people were going crazy wherever he was living. They were saying some shit to him and he was scared. So he said, 'Thank you for saving my life.' I was like, 'All right, dude, no problem, my pleasure.'"

That gave Cabrera some false optimism.

"So when it comes down to November, I remember, my agent was like so excited because he was like, 'I don't have anybody with Boston.' We thought we were in a great position," said Cabrera. "My agent sat down, he said, 'What's up, let's talk about Orlando.' "

The conversation didn't go much further. Epstein already had eyes for Edgar Renteria, not to mention the draft picks he would get for losing Cabrera.

"I was really okay with that because I really believe at that time, Renteria was a better player," Cabrera said. "He was absolutely a better player than me. I was like, 'That's a good move for them. They want more offense. They're going to get more offense from him.'"

Here is where the story gets a little fuzzy. Cabrera insists that Epstein disparaged him as a player to agent Dan Lozano. But Epstein flat-out denies that his conversation with Lozano was anything but cordial. He simply wanted to go in a different direction for a variety of reasons.

"There was just one phone call to the agent, Dan Lozano, in which I told him I appreciated everything Orlando had done for us but we were likely to pursue other alternatives," Epstein said. "There really wasn't much of a negotiation at all with Orlando because of the desire for the compensation picks, which we ended up using to draft [Jacoby] Ellsbury and [Jed] Lowrie."

At any rate, when Cabrera signed with the Angels, he was mad enough at Epstein for not retaining his services that he listed the Red Sox as the only team he couldn't be traded to.

By the time Cabrera returned to Boston with the Angels, on June 3, 2005, Renteria was already proving to be a bad fit for the Red Sox. His defense was shaky and his offense was inconsistent. And unlike Cabrera, the hypersensitive Renteria took offense every time he heard some criticism. The ovation that the Fenway faithful gave to Cabrera in his first game back, and in all three games of that weekend series, was deafening. "It was an amazing feeling because I wasn't expecting it, and to tell you the truth, it was probably my first–ever standing ovation," Cabrera said. "The way they stood up and clapped was just amazing. And the captain was behind the plate and I tried to tell him to get back in the catcher's box. But [Varitek] said, 'Um um, take it in, enjoy it.' I was like, 'All right, thank you.' It was special. It was really, really nice, an incredible feeling."

Renteria, who was a stud during World Series runs for the 1997 Marlins and the 2010 Giants, simply couldn't figure out how to cope with the pressure of playing in Boston. Cabrera, on the other hand, was a natural.

"You have to take it slowly," Cabrera said. "It's not a hard place to play. I don't think it's difficult. You just have to know how to take it. You can't take everything at once. You can't take everything personally. You need to understand that people [in the media] need to do their job. That's it."

While the Renteria experiment was in the process of failing badly, rumors started to leak that maybe some off-field problems had something to do with the Red Sox declining to keep Cabrera. If that innuendo was leaked by someone from Boston's front office, Cabrera didn't appreciate it one bit.

"Listen, you know what's so crazy about it, the whole bullshit they came up with about off-field stuff was after Renteria messed up," Cabrera said. "When they signed Renteria, nobody said anything. Nothing happened. I never did anything. I never did anything that Youk didn't do or Manny wasn't doing. It was the same thing as everybody else, you go to a bar, have a couple of beers, go back to the hotel. I was doing nothing. There's nothing I could do [about the perception]. People would never ask me. I can't control that stuff."

Part of life as a general manager is taking risks. So if Epstein hit a home run on his blockbuster trade of Garciaparra, he struck out with his belief that Renteria was the right fit to replace Cabrera. He also stands by the process he used to make the decision. After all, Ellsbury would help the Red Sox win the World Series in 2007 and 2013. "In hindsight, we probably should have signed Craig Counsell, as we considered, rather than Renteria, but that's life," Epstein said.

Not only did the Red Sox trade Renteria to the Braves in December 2005, but they paid $11 million of his remaining salary over the next three seasons. That's the only way the trade could be made, and that's how much they felt the need to get rid of a man who made thirty errors in his lone season with the Red Sox. Shortstop would become a revolving door in Boston for the rest of Epstein's time as general manager. Alex Gonzalez held the position in 2006. Julio Lugo was an even bigger failure than Renteria after signing a four-year deal with the Sox prior to the 2007 season. Halfway through the 2009 season, he was traded, and Boston was on the hook for some of his existing salary, just as with Renteria. Jed Lowrie and Marco Scutaro would come later, followed by Mike Aviles. When the Red Sox won it all again in 2013, it was with Stephen Drew, who came in on a one-year deal. Xander Bogaerts, who looked like a star in the making in the '13 playoffs, could wind up at shortstop in Boston for a long time if he doesn't switch positions. The last time the Red Sox had this much excitement surrounding a young shortstop was when a guy named Nomar came up in the mid-1990s.

Nomar Garciaparra suffered a gruesome injury on April 20, 2005, his first and only full season as a member of the Chicago Cubs. The injury, a torn groin, sidelined him for over three months and limited his season to sixty-two games. So much for that marquee rematch against the Red Sox, who visited Wrigley Field for the first time in Interleague play in June 2005. Though Garciaparra was still rehabbing his injury in Arizona at that time, he flew to Chicago for the weekend series, both to see his former teammates and to make sure others weren't forced to answer questions about him for three days. Everybody who played even one game for the 2004 Red Sox received a championship ring, and Garciaparra was approached about receiving his on the field in a ceremony at Wrigley Field. He hated the idea.

"That's not going to happen," Garciaparra remembers relaying to the Red Sox. "I said, 'I am not about to get a World Series ring in front of these great people in Chicago when all they want is a World Series. Are you kidding me? You think they really want to see that or deserve that?'" I said, 'No, that's not going to happen. I don't want that.' "

Instead, a group of Red Sox players met up with Garciaparra in Chicago after one of the games. Jason Varitek, Garciaparra's former teammate both with the Red Sox and at Georgia Tech, handed it to him. There were many fans and media members who wondered how Garciaparra could take any joy in collecting a ring after such an acrimonious departure, particularly when there was a perception that the trade was a pivotal reason why the Sox won the World Series. To understand why Garciaparra was proud to receive the ring, perhaps you need to know what he would tell his Boston teammates during the first meeting of Spring Training every year. He would look at a room full of players and tell them that a team needs everyone to win a World Series—not just the twenty-five players who are on the team at the beginning of the season or those who are fortunate enough to be part of the ride in October. It takes everyone, he told them. And by 2005, when he got his ring, he still believed it to be true. And eight years after getting the ring, he was still adamant in that belief. "I think a lot of people forget, it's a championship season," Garciaparra said. "It's not just a championship series. It's 162 games. It's over eight months just to prepare to get there. And it takes an entire team. I did that speech in Spring Training when I would see everybody. It's like, 'Listen, it's not the twenty-five guys, it's every single one of you guys in here who can make an impact.' Look at Bogaerts [for the 2013 Red Sox]. He wasn't there when the season started. Every year, there's somebody. K-Rod with the Angels [in 2002]. Every time, there's someone who comes in and plays the role at some point. It's not always what you start out with in Spring Training. There're guys along the way. That's why every single guy gets a ring. There's a reason for that."

Does Garciaparra ever wear the ring?

"Every once in a while, if I go out to an event, I'll wear it," Garciaparra said. "Sometimes I'll just put it up on the mantel and look at it. For me to not feel a part of it? That's crazy. And the other thing, too, that people forget is that 2004 wasn't won in one year. This wasn't just getting lucky one year and winning it. This was building up to that. We were one game away from the World Series the year before. One game away. This was a great team. We won ninety-five games the year before, we won ninety-three games but didn't make the postseason the year before that. Guys like Keith Foulke, guys like Curt Schilling, don't come to a team if there isn't already a winning attitude there. You don't get these other pieces without being winners already. At that stage of their careers, they would have gone somewhere else. The reason that's built up is from the attitude of the core guys who have been there for so long. There was a lot who kind of changed the mentality but the way the Boston Red Sox are perceived—there were guys who changed that."

By the time Garciaparra's Cubs met the Red Sox in June 2005, Cabrera wasn't even around anymore. But there was a humorous encounter between the two shortstops during a Cubs-Angels game in Spring Training of 2005.

"Either he got on second or I got on second and he was probably wondering what I was going to say," Garciaparra said. "I look at him, I'm like, 'Hey, man, thanks for getting me a ring. Great job. You did awesome, by the way. That was awesome.' He was like, 'Thanks, man.' "

As it turns out, Epstein and the Red Sox were fortunate they didn't sign Garciaparra to that four-year deal that appeared close at one point. Nomar would spend most of his post-Boston years battling nagging injuries. The one All-Star season he had left in him was in 2006, for Grady Little's Los Angeles Dodgers. By then, Garciaparra had become a first baseman.

The final season of Garciaparra's Major League career was in 2009, with the Oakland Athletics. Two significant things happened that year. The first was that Garciaparra and Orlando Cabrera became teammates. Cabrera told Garciaparra then how much he loved the "ring" comment back in Spring Training of 2005.

"I always remembered what you told me," Cabrera told Garciaparra. "My God, that was awesome."

"So we hung out, we were pals over there with Oakland," Garciaparra said. "We had had a blast. We chatted a lot."

Back in the American League after all those years, Garciaparra finally got to come back to Fenway Park and play against the Red Sox. And July 6, 2009, felt like it was July 6, 1999. The fans forgot whatever awkwardness surrounded Garciaparra's departure and stopped debating whether his exit was actually the reason they won the World Series.

Instead, they embraced Garciaparra and thanked him for his hitting artistry, particularly during those magical first four seasons of his career. Suddenly, everyone remembered things like the three-homer, ten-RBI night from 1999. Or those days in July 2000 when he flirted with .400.

When Garciaparra stepped to the plate to lead off the top of the second, he got the longest and loudest and most heartfelt standing ovation of his career. In five years, absence had indeed made the heart grow fonder. John Smoltz, pitching for Boston in the twilight of his career, stepped off the mound and gave Nomar plenty of time to take in the moment. Varitek, much as he did for Cabrera four years earlier, also took a self-imposed delay so Garciaparra could get all the love he deserved.

"I'll tell you, I can't tell you how special that was," Garciaparra said. "I can't even put it into words. I was emotional before talking to all of you guys in the press conference. And that ovation . . . you really don't know what kind of ovation you're going to get."

While walk-up music started to become common in the late 1990s, Garciaparra preferred crowd reaction.

"I didn't want a walk-up song. The only walk-up song I ever had was when I went to the Dodgers," he said. "But anyway, I didn't want one at Fenway because I always wanted my first at-bat, I wanted to hear what the fans felt about me that day. I wanted to hear them. It was a cheer every single time. So that time, you just don't know what it's going to be like. You don't know what was being said. You don't know what they believed. You get an ovation like that and it was just emotional. I can't describe it and put it into words how great it was. I remember looking at Tek after wiping the tears from my eyes and going, 'I'm supposed to hit after this?' And then I go, 'Hey, can you do me a favor and tell Smoltzy I said thanks.' That's respect from the pitcher to understand the moment."

Garciaparra even hit like it was 1999 that night, producing a two-hit game while leading the A's to a 6–0 victory.

"That was something that was definitely special and something I'll never forget. There's a reason why I retired a Red Sox—moments like that," Garciaparra

In Spring Training of 2010, Nomar came to Fort Myers and signed a one-day Minor-League contract so that he could retire as a member of the Red Sox. Theo Epstein took part in the press conference, as did Larry Lucchino. There was another interesting moment for Garciaparra in the context of 2004, and it happened late in the 2012 season. As part of a two-day extravaganza to commemorate the one-hundred-year anniversary of Fenway Park, the Red Sox held an eight-year reunion for the 2004 team the first night and then unveiled their all-time team the second night. Nobody was surprised when Garciaparra was named the shortstop on the all-time team.

However, there were some raised eyebrows when Garciaparra participated in the '04 reunion, which included riding around on duck boats at Fenway Park during the pre-game ceremonies. Garciaparra held the trophy in his hands and was flanked on his boat by Pedro Martinez, Kevin Millar, Tim Wakefield, and Mike Timlin. According to Garciaparra, his former teammates were the inspiration behind his participation in the ceremony.

"Guys were like, 'Oh man, it's good to see you.' We went out there to celebrate 2004 on the field," said Garciaparra. "I was like, 'I don't know if I should go.' They were like, 'You better come with us.' The guys were all like, 'You better come; you better sit with us.' Pedro made me grab the World Series trophy and take a picture with him. He made me. He goes, 'This is the only picture I want. This is all.' And he made me take it with him. He said to whoever took it, 'You better make sure I get this picture.' "

When you consider that the Red Sox won ninety-five games in 2005, it was a decent attempt at a title defense. This, even though they were bounced in a three-game sweep by the White Sox in the Division Series. But for certain players who were coming off the euphoria of '04, the season proved to be a big letdown, and a depressing time. Keith Foulke topped the list of players in that category. He would never again be an elite reliever after catching that final out in St. Louis. In fact, he didn't even come close. A lot of people suspect that throwing the hundred pitches in three days during the ALCS took a toll, much like Schilling and his ankle. But Foulke is adamant that that theory is dead wrong. The real story, said Foulke, is that he was blatantly stubborn regarding the state of his knees. There was a red flag right away, when Foulke went through his Spring Training physical in 2005.

"The doctor was asking me what was bothering me, and I was like, 'My knees.' He does the exam and next thing you know, I get called into the GM's office and I walk in and it's like the brains of the Sox are there, and the doctor," said Foulke. "I'm like, 'This isn't good.' The doc tells me, 'I don't like how your knees are. I don't see how you're doing it and I don't see how you're going to make it through the season at this point.'"

If the end of Foulke's marriage helped inspire him to greatness in the postseason of 2004, the reality of it all was tearing him apart by 2005. It impacted his rationality when it came to ignoring Dr. Thomas Gill's recommendation about his knees.

"I needed baseball. The last thing I wanted to do was be sitting around rehabbing and kind of being by myself again," Foulke said. "I'm like, 'No, I'm going to battle through it.' I regret that decision.

"I don't really remember what they said. All I remember was hearing those words of the doctor and I remember just thinking, 'You know, I can't do it.'"

If 2004 was the pinnacle of Foulke's baseball life, the following year was the complete opposite. The decision to pitch through pain at the start of the 2005 season was the lowlight of Keith Foulke's career, the moment that basically set up the downward spiral that ensued in the following years.

"Tough," said Foulke. "It still haunts me to this day and it will haunt me until the day that I die. It's upsetting for me to think about it now because that's basically the decision that killed the rest of my career. It went on for however long it went on before I [had to stop]. I was hurting."

When you play on the West Coast like Derek Lowe did in 2005, you get to watch a lot of East Coast games while you're in the clubhouse getting ready for a game. Lowe couldn't believe what he was watching when he saw Keith Foulke on the mound. The image was so startling that Lowe called his close friend Chris Correnti, the trainer who was in his final season supervising Boston's pitchers in 2005.

"I remember Derek calling Chris Correnti," said Foulke. "And he saw me pitching on TV one time and he was like, 'What is Foulkie doing? He looks like an erect penis out there. What is he doing?' "

Lowe's point was that there was little to no bend in Foulke's legs during his delivery. As Foulke took a beating, his mood worsened. Meanwhile, the Fenway faithful gave him a hard time, booing his collection of blown saves. And things hit their low point on June 29, when after a blown save against the Indians, Foulke vented against the fans.

"Of course I heard it," he said in front of his locker that night. "And I'm not inviting them to my World Series celebration, either. They have all the right. They can boo, cuss me, and tell me I suck. Go ahead. If they don't want me to do the job, tell them to tell management. I've done a lot of good for this team but, you know, let them boo. They pay their money. They can boo; they're fans. They pay me to do my job and I didnt do it. Like I've told you guys plenty of times, I'm more embarrassed to walk into this locker room and look at the faces of my teammates than I am to walk out and see Johnny from Burger King booing me."

The Johnny from Burger King portion of the statement made Foulke sound like a guy who was disparaging the common man. That's not how he meant it to come out. Nevertheless, Foulke didn't regret the statement some eight years after he said it.

"No, what it was meant to mean was I still believed in our team," Foulke said. "I still thought we had the team to win it again. It was not about belittling the average working people. It was like, 'I'm still going to have a World Series party and you're not invited. If you don't believe in us, then I don't want you there.' "

The truth of the matter is Foulke wasn't the only '04 hero to struggle mightily. Schilling's ankle made him a shell of his former self that year. Alan Embree and Mark Bellhorn performed so poorly that they were released. Kevin Millar never got his bat going. But Foulke was a scapegoat, and he didn't help reverse the situation with "Johnny from Burger King"–type comments.

After yet another blown save on July 4, 2005, at Texas, Foulke finally had to shut it down and have his left knee operated on. Without a closer, the Red Sox turned to Schilling for a couple of months. When Schilling returned to the rotation in mid-August, Mike Timlin closed for the rest of the season.

As for Foulke, the damage was done, and a quick-fix surgery wasn't going to save his season or his career. By pitching on the bad knees for another few months before the surgery, Foulke is convinced he did himself irreparable damage. He pitched just six times in September after his return, only to be shelved again with knee woes, this time for the rest of the year.

"I should have probably taken '05 off, because even after I had it done, they had to go in there and scrape that bone out," said Foulke. "Because my joint, there was a defect, so it was, like, huge craters. The cartilage was gone, so it was bone on bone. But it wasn't smooth. It was jerky. My knee would lock up and it's like you had to kind of pop it. Scraping the bone like that, it takes a while to heal. I was trying to battle back from it and I was in more pain. I had to get my knee drained every week."

Foulke was given a chance to have the closer's job back in 2006, but Jonathan Papelbon unseated him just three games into the season. When the Red Sox won their next World Series in 2007, Papelbon was the man standing on the mound. In fact, '06 would be another disaster for Foulke, plagued by injuries and ineffectiveness. The Red Sox did not pick up his option after the season and Foulke actually signed a one-year, $5 million deal with the Indians for 2007. But his body was still barking. And in one of the more stand-up moves you'll see, Foulke told the Indians just before Spring Training that he was retiring. He could have gotten to camp and gone on the disabled list and taken the $5 million. But Foulke knew that was the wrong thing to do.

"I remember trying to train," said Foulke. "I couldn't train more than two days in a row. My elbow would start swelling up on me. I remember telling my second wife at the time—we had just gotten married, the cars were already in Florida, I'm in my closet packing for Spring Training—I felt like I was going to prison. I was like, 'I can't do it.' I kind of made that commitment to myself and immediately felt better and told the wife and called my agent and he was like, 'You're crazy.' I ended up calling [Indians general manager] Mark Shapiro and told him, I was like, 'I'm not healthy and I'm not going to take your money.' I was like, 'I appreciate the offer, but I can't do it.' "

By 2008, Foulke felt better, and pitched his final Major League season for the Oakland Athletics. He was pissed when the A's didn't bring him back for '09 and wound up spending part of that summer with the Newark Bears, an Independent League team. The man who threw perhaps the most famous pitch in Red Sox history pitching in Newark, New Jersey? It didn't seem right. If Foulke had stuck with it, he thinks he might have wound up back in the Majors. Instead, he left the Bears and tried to save his second marriage—to no avail.

"Things happened at home again and I didn't want to make the same mistake twice, so I kind of chose family life over baseball," Foulke said. "She splits. I've got no baseball, no family, I'm like, 'Wow, I should have still been playing.' It was tough because I kept getting flak from home. I would pitch and catch a flight home for a few days and go back. That was a joke. I should have chosen baseball."

After falling off the map for a few years following his retirement, Foulke resurfaced for the grand hundred-year anniversary celebration at Fenway at the beginning of the 2012 season. He now comes to Boston a few times a year, taking in some action at Fenway and making community appearances on behalf of the club.

For one of the only times in his career, Mark Bellhorn came to Spring Training in 2005 knowing that the starting second baseman's job was his.

Instead of seizing the moment, Bellhorn had a terrible season, hitting .216 and striking out 109 times in just 335 at-bats.

"It was tough," said Bellhorn. "For some reason, I guess I couldn't put two good years together in my career. It was disappointing. I obviously wanted to repeat what I did the year before and I just never could get it together."

The Red Sox released him on August 19, 2005, and the Yankees, of all teams, picked him up eleven days later. Just one month earlier, Alan Embree had been released by Boston, only to wind up in New York, too. Neither player would make any type of impact in pinstripes, which had them feeling a little odd when the Yankees clinched the American League East title in Fenway Park on the second-to-last game of the regular season. Don't bother trying to find footage of Embree and Bellhorn spraying champagne all over the place in the Yankees' clubhouse that day because you won't find any. It was an odd afternoon for both of them, not to mention a brief existence in New York.

"It was different but I'm sure both of us were probably glad the other one was there," Bellhorn said. "I think both of us knew it was so far from the same feeling we'd had the year before."

What was the difference between playing for the Red Sox and Yankees? "It's kind of what it appears on TV," Bellhorn said. "The Red Sox are more of the blue collar and the beards and getting dirty and the Yankees are more professional and all business."

By 2006, a much more prominent "Idiot" would switch to pinstripes.

If you ask Red Sox fans when Johnny Damon left Boston, quite a few think it was after the 2004 season. It's funny how things are remembered or forgotten in some cases. In truth, Damon had one last year on his contract with the Sox for the 2005 season. He came to camp that year newly married and very much a Red Sox. His autobiography, entitled *Idiot*, would soon hit the shelves. Damon remembers the club being nervous about his book tour and all the media appearances he was doing. He also remembers that none of that stuff had any impact on him. In fact, Damon came out blazing in 2005 and had an All-Star season, hitting .316. Unlike in 2004, when he chased cars to burn off some winter weight, Damon arrived in terrific shape in 2005.

"Everyone was worried about me, if I would come to Spring Training in shape. And I was in shape and I felt like I was the only one who was ready to play the next season," Damon said. "When I got to the field, I went off and had a great year and that's when, after the first two months, I remember Theo and I having a small conversation saying I might be having too good of a year to keep me. He knew I was raising my value."

When the 2005 season started, Damon was a bit surprised he was still playing for a contract. With at least some type of verbal nod from ownership that he was probably in the team's long-term plans, Damon bought a house in December 2004 and felt it was only a matter of time before he was re-signed.

"We bought this great house. We were thinking we were going to play out the next four years [in Boston] and maybe more," said Damon. "I was going to live there during the summers and come back home to Florida during the winters. Maybe they wanted me to have a bad year [in '05] so they could sign me for cheaper."

No deal was done with Damon during Spring Training or in the regular season. As time wore on, Damon became resentful that the club seemed to be pushing him aside. And when free agency started, Theo Epstein wasn't working for the Red Sox. After a conflict with Lucchino and ownership on fundamental issues, Epstein abandoned his post as general manager on October 31, 2005. He would return by January 2006, but that was too late to keep Johnny Damon in Boston.

"Well, in September, I pulled a $70,000 insurance policy from Lloyds of London," said Damon. "And after that, I let them know, 'There's no more hometown discount.'"

The insurance policy was for the final two months of the 2005 season. Damon was annoyed that he had to cover his own risk in the event of an injury because the club hadn't granted him the extension he wanted. Damon and the Red Sox were swept out of the Division Series by the Chicago White Sox, who went on to win the World Series. Although Boston hit its way to ninety-five wins in '05—Ortiz and Manny both had monster years—they weren't built to go deep into October that year. After the game, Damon was emotional when asked about his uncertain future. It was starting to hit him hard that he might never be in the home clubhouse at Fenway as an active player again.

"And then, the season is over, maybe October 10 or so that year [it was actually October 7] and they had whole that time until December 20 to talk to me. There was nothing," said Damon.

"I thought I was going to L.A., but they told me they'd messed up, they signed [Rafael] Furcal to three years, $39 million, and they said, 'You deserve more than what he got.' The only team that was left out there was the Yankees, and so, we actually struck the deal with the Yankees before we even got that offer from Boston," said Damon. "I was just waiting."

The Red Sox had made a four-year, $40-million offer to Damon at one point, and they weren't willing to budge from that. So Damon was a New York Yankee, something that felt like poison to the Red Sox followers who had cheered so enthusiastically for their center fielder the previous four years. Damon's move to New York was going to be hard to stomach for Boston fans no matter what the circumstances were. But there is a large portion of fans who took this one more personally because of an article by MLB.com's Alan Eskew published on May 1, 2005, when Damon suggested he wouldn't play for the Yankees and even indicated he'd rather retire than relocate to New York.

"There's no way I can go play for the Yankees, but I know they are going to come after me hard," Damon said. "It's definitely not the most important thing to go out there for the top dollar, which the Yankees are going to offer me. It's not what I need. I want to stay here, but I may walk and go home. I might shut it down in a couple of years."

Damon was one of those players who spoke from the heart, and without filter. He stands by his comments to Eskew, but reasons that it simply represented what he was feeling in that moment. By December

2005, Damon was ticked off at the Red Sox, and was willing to sleep with the enemy, so to speak, to get back at them.

"I was hoping the Red Sox would come and give me that extension they were promising me," Damon said, when asked why he might have said what he said to Eskew. "I fit in perfect here. Why would this team right here let me go? Unfortunately we say a lot of things that, you say it with your heart. When you realize the people that you want to be with [don't feel the same way] . . . And after I heard they didn't believe me, that's when I was like, 'Okay.'"

After things went down in the fashion they did, Damon was ready to get the next plane to New York.

"It wasn't hard to sign it because, at the time, I was just pissed," Damon said.

Because he really wanted to stay in Boston, Damon told Francona and Bronson Arroyo that he had a lucrative deal on the table from another club, much bigger than the four-year, $40-million deal the Red Sox were willing to do.

"I remember reaching out to Bronson and Francona," said Damon. "Bronson later told me that they had a conversation and Tito said to Bronson, 'They think he's lying.' And Bronson goes, 'But Johnny doesn't lie.' "

Johnny cut his hair, shaved his beard, and was a member of the New York Yankees by Christmas. With Epstein back on the job a few weeks later, the Red Sox made a trade with the Indians to get Coco Crisp, a man they had targeted for quite a long time as a potential successor to Damon. "I think they always kind of had Coco Crisp as their backup plan. It wasn't going to cost as much and they saw how much I ran into the walls and [they're] thinking the body is going to start deteriorating," said Damon.

When the Yankees visited Boston on May 1, 2006, the attitude from the fans toward Damon was downright hostile. There were signs all over the park labeling him as a traitor. One memorable sign proclaimed that Damon "Looks like Jesus, acts like Judas, throws like Mary."

It was hurtful for Damon, given how he had helped change the culture in Boston.

"It was tough but I understood," Damon said. "I think they didn't know what the truth was. I don't think they wanted to know. It was just the guy they loved is playing for the enemy now."

The clear nadir of Damon's four-year stint in the Bronx was 2007. Depressed by the death of teammate Cory Lidle, who died in a plane crash shortly after the Yankees were eliminated in the 2006 Division Series, Damon came to camp in subpar shape in 2007. This time, he didn't even make the effort to chase cars.

"When we lost in the playoffs in '06 and a couple of days later Cory Lidle died, I was just saying, 'Why am I really playing?' Cory wanted me to go up on his plane and check out the city and all of that stuff and Michelle was like, 'No, we have to get ready to get home.' Then we were down at our beach place and heard about it. I was just like, 'Do I really want to go back and deal with baseball? What if this happens to me?' I didn't enjoy my life. And then [daughter] Devon was born, so that was great," said Damon. "I started getting ready for the season and you're just not into it. You know you kind of need to do something. Then I show up to Spring Training and I guess Joe Torre looks at one of my baseball cards and it said like 205 pounds. He said, 'What are you weighing now?' I said, 'About 216.' He said, 'I need you to get down to 205.' I was like, 'I haven't been down to 205 since I played for the A's.' He goes, 'I think you can.' So I worked out a lot in Spring Training, got down to like 206 and just felt weak as heck. Sure enough, first game of the season, Elijah Dukes hits a home run over my head and I felt my calf pop. I just didn't feel strong."

Though Damon did hit a big home run for the Yankees to win Game 3 of the 2007 Division Series, his team again got bounced in the first round. And Damon wasn't exactly brimming with excitement when the Red Sox won the World Series that year.

"The Red Sox win and my streak of a hundred runs and thirty doubles [for nine straight seasons] is gone," added Damon.

But he would have a nice bounce-back year in 2008, hitting .303. And in 2009, his last in New York, Damon drilled twenty-four homers to aid a Yankees team that went on to win the World Series against Pedro

Martinez and the Phillies. Damon made perhaps the key play of that Fall Classic. In Game 4, he stole second and third on the same play after wisely noting third base had been vacated due to an overshift. Perhaps he had visions that his signature moment would gain the same type of recognition as his two homers in Game 7 at Yankee Stadium in 2004. But the one thing Damon realized over time is that the ring he won with the Yankees felt a little hollow compared to the one achieved in Boston.

"Well, when we won the World Series with the Yankees, it wasn't about the team," said Damon. "It was kind of empty. You're kind of saying 'Well, we all just won this.' And the only people you're saluting are Jeter, Pettitte, Mariano, and Posada. The rest of us are like . . . especially when they do the autograph stuff after the season, they only asked like eight guys to sign stuff. And with the Red Sox, they asked everybody. It was [family]."

Although the whole Canyon of Heroes thing is always built up as a huge event when the Yankees win the World Series, Damon didn't think it came close to comparing with the joyous duck-boat ride through Boston five years earlier. "Crazy people jumping from the bridge into the Charles River. It was cold. But we brought so much excitement," Damon said of the 2004 parade. "All the signs they had, all the gifts people wanted to give you—it was amazing. I appreciated [the 2004 parade] more when I won the Yankees because we were on this [duck boat] thing for a couple of hours. Then when we did it with the Yankees, it felt like we were only on it for fifteen minutes. You go around in a certain area and that was it. I know [my wife] Michelle and I were kind of wondering if we were actually done with the parade because we had to get to Vegas for her brother's wedding, so we were like, 'The parade is over? That's it?' "

And, as it turned out, that was it for Damon in New York. He spent four seasons with both the Red Sox and Yankees and put up strikingly similar numbers in each city. For the next three years, he would play for three different teams—the Tigers, Rays, and Indians. Perhaps without the New York uniform on, Damon would shed some boos in his return to Fenway. He wanted to find out in his first visit back with the Tigers on July

30, 2010, but his back locked up on him shortly before game time. "I kept having guys step on it so I could play," said Damon. But he was out for the whole weekend. Then, the next season, this time wearing a Rays uniform, Damon heard some cheers when he came to the plate in the top of the first. But those swiftly turned to boos when he ripped a solo homer into the bullpen in right center against Daisuke Matsuzaka.

In 2012, with the Indians, the Red Sox finally gave Damon a peace offering. During a Mother's Day matinee game at Fenway, a video tribute flashed on the screen—a montage of Damon's best moments in a Boston uniform. Then the scoreboard panned to Damon in Cleveland's dugout and the crowd gave him a warm ovation. It was an important moment for Damon, one that seemed to help repair his feelings toward the Red Sox. "Yeah, it did, and then to look over at guys like David Ortiz, it was special," said Damon. "I'm planning on being up around that area quite a bit [in 2014]. I know ten years is a big thing and I think after that ovation last year, I kind of just let go. I was like, 'Okay, it's over.'"

Damon even got annoyed when the final manager of his career, Manny Acta, tried to dampen his moment.

"Manny Acta, he's like, 'Oh, why are you cheering for him? You boo him all the time.' I'm like, 'Manny, this is a pretty important time.' "

And so, too, was Damon's time in Boston, which he is finally able to reflect on and appreciate again.

Epilogue
Coming Full Circle

I f you disappeared from the baseball universe for, say, nine years, and happened to turn on the television in October 2013, you might have thought nothing had changed for the Red Sox since 2004. There was David Ortiz coming up with one huge hit after another, including a game-tying grand slam against the Tigers in Game 2 of the ALCS that might go down as the most clutch hit of his career. And there were the Red Sox, all slovenly, nearly every one of them with beards. In case you were wondering, the Idiots loved the look.

"I like all the beards," Millar said, about a month before the Red Sox would win the 2013 World Series. "They all look alike. I like that they all have their little niche and their shtick and it's working. They're not a bunch of superstars. They're just a bunch of ballplayers and it's someone different every night and you've still got Big Papi in the middle of the lineup."

A quieter and more professional-looking group won the whole thing in 2007, and perhaps that's why they never quite captured the imagination of New England like the team that won three years earlier or six years after. For the second championship, the eight holdovers were Ortiz, Varitek, Youkilis (a bit player in 2004 and a key performer in 2007), Timlin, Ramirez, Mirabelli, Wakefield, and Schilling.

Millar and Mueller followed Damon out of Boston as free agents after the 2005 season. Bronson Arroyo was traded to Cincinnati in 2006 in perhaps the most regrettable trade Theo Epstein made in his time in Boston. Wily Mo Peña, who was released before the playoffs in '07, was the only return in that deal for Arroyo. By the end of the 2013 season, Arroyo had never missed so much as one start in his time with the Reds.

And in 2013, the only active players in baseball left from the "Idiots" were Ortiz, Arroyo, and Youkilis, who was dealt to the White Sox in 2012 and put on Yankee pinstripes in a highly forgettable and injury-plagued 2013 season.

Nixon left for Cleveland in 2007 and actually had a game-winning hit against the Red Sox in Game 2 of the ALCS. But the Sox would break Nixon's heart by coming back from a 3–1 deficit in that series, showing shades of '04. By then, young stars had come through the farm system and played major roles, from Dustin Pedroia to Jon Lester to Jonathan Papelbon to Jacoby Ellsbury. That team had Theo Epstein's fingerprints all over it, from a player development standpoint.

"The '07 team was quieter, but I didn't care about the decibel level in the clubhouse," Francona said. "It was how we played the game. And we played the game the same. I just wanted each team to get their own personality and not try to be the team from the year before or somebody they weren't. Jacoby Ellsbury is quiet. He's not going to be Johnny Damon. He can be him on the field, which is what we're looking for. That's what I cared about."

The Red Sox put up a much better title defense in 2008 than they did three years earlier. This time, they went all the way to Game 7 of the ALCS at Tropicana Field before losing a 3–1 heartbreaker. Another Idiot left town on July 31, 2008. Manny Ramirez all but forced his way out of Boston, taking a swing at Kevin Youkilis in the dugout in early June and then decking revered traveling secretary Jack McCormick over a ticket dispute in Houston later that month.

Millar and Cabrera were no longer around to babysit Ramirez, and the other veterans grew tired of his narcissistic ways. The Red Sox loved

Jason Bay, the power hitter who came over in the three-way deal from the Pirates, while Ramirez went to the Dodgers. And if Boston had won the World Series, Bay would have reached Orlando Cabrera–like status among Red Sox fans for being a huge difference-maker after a deadline deal.

After his departure from Boston, Ramirez's legacy took a huge hit. Early in the 2009 season, he tested positive for performance-enhancing drugs. Ramirez would never again be the same player after returning from a 50-game suspension. Two years later, teamed with Johnny Damon in Tampa Bay, Ramirez again tested positive early in the season. He attempted comebacks with the A's in 2012 and the Rangers in 2013, but never made it past the Minor Leagues. "Yeah, yeah, it's really hard and it's sad," said Pedro Martinez.

But Martinez disputes that what the Red Sox did in 2004 could at all be diminished because of Ramirez's subsequent association with steroids. Whether he was on something in Boston or not, the use of performance-enhancing drugs was rampant throughout the game. "You can't take away what we did based on assumption," Martinez said. "Manny's problems developed afterwards. But at the same time, on the other team we were facing, they had Giambi, A-Rod, and other guys who were mentioned."

After helping the Red Sox win the World Series in 2007, Curt Schilling never pitched in the Majors again. He came back on a one-year deal in '08, but his labrum went out on him before Spring Training even started. The big righty announced his retirement with a blog entry on March 23, 2009. Even though he was born to be a baseball analyst, Schilling chose another, additional career path—creating a gaming company called 38 Studios. After showing some initial promise, Schilling moved his company to Providence, Rhode Island, after getting a $75-million loan from that state. But shortly after 38 Studios created its first game, Schilling's company went bankrupt in 2012. The righty lost close to $50 million of his own money. He even sold his bloody sock from Game 2 of the World Series at an auction for $92,613. Schilling was ridiculed in Rhode Island for the failure of his company.

"Nothing was ever done illegally," Schilling said. "Nothing was ever done with ill will. I never took a dime from that company. I lost almost $50 million of my own money. It happens. The thing I tell people is, 'Every year is not going to be 2004.' Listen, like I said, I've been so blessed. I would love to have that not have happened but it happened. One of the things I tell people is that the measure of a man is what he looks like when he dusts himself off. Get up and find a way, and I'll figure it out."

The Red Sox had their own problems as an organization around the same time Schilling's company went under. Prior to the 2011 season, Epstein got bold during the Hot-Stove season, making a blockbuster trade for Adrian Gonzalez and subsequently signing the first baseman to a seven-year, $154-million contract. There was genuine shock when Carl Crawford came to Boston just three days later on a seven-year, $142-million deal. While the baseball universe was awed by what the Red Sox had done, Kevin Millar, who was working for the Baseball Network, expressed skepticism.

"It's all on paper, everything looks great on paper," Millar said. "Our team in 2003 and 2004 was a bunch of grinders."

By the end of 2011, Millar proved to be prophetic. The Red Sox had the biggest collapse in the history of September baseball, blowing a nine-game lead and failing to make the playoffs. Gonzalez and Crawford didn't seem to have the mentality to thrive in Boston, and former players took notice.

"Some guys will just not flourish in that kind of atmosphere," said Nixon. "No offense, but I never really believed that Carl Crawford was going to be that guy in Boston. I never did. Adrian Gonzalez, I'm sure these guys are all great people, but coming from San Diego, it's different. We used to tell guys, when they come from different places, this is a different animal, guys. This is a completely different animal coming to the Red Sox."

Epstein and Francona both say they never forgot how important chemistry can be to a winning team. But it's also not something you can build with some kind of paint-by-numbers picture.

"It has to be organic . . . you can't really manufacture it," Epstein said. "That's what made that 2004 team so special."

Not only did a trip to the playoffs slip away from the Red Sox when Crawford dropped a line drive in the 2011 season finale at Baltimore, but the fallout was off the charts. Stories came out that Boston's starting pitchers, including Josh Beckett, Jon Lester, and John Lackey, were drinking beer in the clubhouse during games they weren't pitching in. There were silly stories about takeout fried chicken to accompany the beer.

So it was fine to drink Jack Daniels before playoff games in 2004, but the chicken-and-beer crew was reviled? As it turns out, that was just a symbol of the unity that team didn't have. The Jack Daniels toasts were inclusive to anybody who wanted to be a part of it, and they didn't happen during the heat of battle. In 2004, Francona could trust the players to hold each other accountable in the clubhouse.

"The starters, we had our own rules about how many innings you had to be on the bench," said Derek Lowe. "Pedro would not always do it, but I knew if I sat in there for too long and came down, I was disrespecting the other guys and I knew someone was going to say something to me. Again, that's how you police yourself. That's how you make a clubhouse work. That was just . . . we had it down to a T."

Francona's style never wavered, but the group in 2011 took advantage of him. Two days after the 2011 season, Francona and the Red Sox parted ways. It was stunning, considering Francona's accomplishments in his eight years. The Red Sox didn't fire Francona, nor did he quit. The club simply said the sides had agreed not to pick up the two option years on his contract. Despite the carefully worded nature of the divorce between the manager and his team, it seemed clear the Red Sox were looking for a new voice in the dugout.

Francona took accountability, saying he hadn't been able to get through to some players as well as he had in the past. It seemed like the split would be amicable enough until a *Boston Globe* story surfaced a couple of weeks later, citing team sources who believed that the unraveling of Francona's marriage, not to mention the use of painkillers, had distracted him during the 2011 collapse. Francona was livid and still hasn't forgiven the Red Sox for that story coming out.

Francona didn't put on a baseball uniform during the 2012 season and was ESPN's lead baseball analyst for the Sunday night games. He was given universal praise for the job he did in that role. But he felt odd out of uniform, and was hired as manager of the Indians for the 2013 season.

"I think when I got hired in Cleveland, it made the Boston stuff a lot easier," Francona said. "I was so happy where I was that it made it easier to think of the good stuff. I'll never change my opinion on the end. It doesn't mean I wake up bitter. But I'm never going to change my mind."

Theo Epstein, citing a departure not to get stale by staying in one place, left less than a month after Francona to become president of baseball operations for the Chicago Cubs. While he's immersed in trying to build a winner in Chicago, Epstein realizes more every year how special an accomplishment he was part of with the 2004 Red Sox.

"A lot more," said Epstein, when asked how much more he appreciates it now. "In a lot of ways, it's just starting to sink in."

With Epstein and Francona gone at once after 2011, life as the Red Sox knew it for so long was changing drastically. The one cohesive thing that happened was the promotion of Ben Cherington into the general manager's seat. Cherington had been with the Red Sox even before Epstein, and everyone in the organization respected his knowledge and his even-keeled demeanor. But ownership was heavy handed in the pursuit of Francona's successor, and the controversial Bobby Valentine, who hadn't managed in the Majors since 2002, was the choice. It was an unmitigated disaster with Valentine in the middle of one controversy after another en route to a 69-93 season.

The organization took its first step back to prominence on August 25, 2012, when Cherington was able to make a stunning trade in which Crawford, Gonzalez, Beckett, and Nick Punto—and salary obligations equaling $264 million—were shipped to the Dodgers for a group of prospects. It was a fresh start for the Red Sox, one that enabled them to reconstruct their roster for 2013 with gritty players like Mike Napoli, Jonny

Gomes, Shane Victorino, David Ross, and Ryan Dempster. Valentine, not surprisingly, was fired the day after the 2012 season ended. This time, Cherington got the opportunity to be the primary voice in the search for a new manager and he got John Farrell free from his contract with the Blue Jays. Everybody liked Farrell during his four years as pitching coach under Francona from 2007–2010, and the Red Sox rediscovered their way under their new dugout leader. Just like in 2004, players bonded and played for one another, putting personal interests aside.

"These guys seem to love each other," said Mike Timlin. "That's what makes a good team. You can take thirty guys and put them in a room and there's going to be fights, and I'm sure these guys have had arguments and they've had disagreements and pretty much come close to blows. But that makes a family. If you have a family working in the right direction, it's almost unstoppable."

The 2013 Red Sox, picked by many to finish last again in the American League East, instead won the World Series. They were a lovable bunch who made a difference in the community after the tragic Boston Marathon bombings. And in the playoffs, there was one big hit after another, many by Ortiz, but also quite a few from Victorino, Napoli, and others. Adding more symmetry with 2004, the Red Sox again played the Cardinals in the World Series. They were tested a lot more this time, but ultimately won the deciding Game 6 at Fenway Park, marking the first time the Red Sox had won a World Series at home since 1918.

Ortiz, at the age of thirty–seven, hit a ridiculous .688 in the World Series and was named the Most Valuable Player.

His former manager was impressed as anybody.

"He was as locked in as I've ever seen him," said Francona. "He was taking swings that were just . . . if they were throwing it close to the plate, he was taking swings that were unbelievable. That was scary."

Many thought that Farrell would win Manager of the Year, but the award instead went to Francona, who guided the small-market Indians to 92 wins. Cleveland lost a one-game playoff to the Tampa Bay Rays for the Wild Card spot, denying Francona the opportunity to face the Red Sox in the playoffs.

"When you get eliminated, to be blunt, you're envious; you want to be playing," Francona said. "So the biggest thing I wanted was for baseball to be over so nobody is playing. But at the same time, when I saw them show Ben Cherington on TV, and he looked kind of stoic, and I had known Ben for ten years, when he was really young, I was so proud of him. To see John Farrell in the dugout and Petey and David—there were so many people that I'm so close to that it made me feel good."

And Francona was also happy for the city of Boston, which treated him with great affection in his return to Fenway with the Indians.

"The fans there, they are the best fans. You can't ask for better fans," Francona said. "I know every city says they have the best fans and every city can't have the best fans. But, I mean, there wasn't a game that I managed there that wasn't sold out. There's interest out the ying-yang. You can't have all that interest without having some fallout. And I think I understood that. I think that's why I survived for as long as I did. That's just the nature of the beast there sometimes. It wears on you sometimes. But also, you have a chance to always win and that was a good feeling."

During the 2013 postseason, Millar, Schilling, and Wakefield were among those on the scene as analysts. Varitek was there working for the Red Sox. They were watching a familiar story unfold in front of them. Instead of snapping an eighty-six-year championship drought, this group was going from worst to World Series champions, and winning back the heart of the city in the process.

"I was watching this team this year and obviously with my job at ESPN, I'm watching baseball a lot more than I might otherwise watch it," said Schilling. "And part of me was, I don't want to say jealous, but part of me was saying, 'If they win it, it might make what we did less.' And then at the end of the day, when they won it, I was so excited for them because of friends like John Farrell and Jon Lester and all the things that they did. But then I also realized nothing will ever change what we did. Nothing will ever take away from it. There will never be another '04."

Acknowledgments

Growing up, I was one of those die-hard Red Sox fans who hoped against hope to see them win it all one day. My parents indulged my obsession with baseball and the Sox, taking me to games while I was young and listening to me talk about sports all day and all night. In fourth grade, I had tickets to a game at Fenway Park on the same night as my end-of-year band concert. My mother, sensing I wasn't much of a trumpet player while realizing I had a pretty good feel for baseball, allowed me to go to the game and skip the concert. Ms. Fox kicked me out of the band. I glowed as the Red Sox won on Gary Allenson's double off the Green Monster in the bottom of the twelfth inning against the Mariners.

The next year, my mom let me skip school so I could go to Fenway Park with my older sister to watch the decidedly mediocre Red Sox get pounded by the Twins in their 1983 opener. The next day, my teacher Mr. Levine announced to the class that "Mr. Browne wasn't in class yesterday so he could watch his beloved Red Sox lose."

I would discover girls at some point, but sports was my first love. I started watching the Red Sox in 1980, when my dad took me to the Marathon Monday game at Fenway. I took to the game right away while watching the Red Sox outslug the White Sox, 10–9, on an eighty-degree day. My face was beet red from the sun by the time I got home, yet my mother noticed the gleam in my eyes; she noted later that my life changed forever that day.

The first time the Red Sox broke my heart was Game 7 of the 1986 World Series. I was so naïve at the time that I thought they could simply shake off the Bill Buckner error in Game 6.

By the time the Red Sox finally did win the World Series, I was a journalist, entrusted with my dream job of covering the Red Sox for MLB.com. And in that capacity, you don't root for the team you cover. Instead, you remain as passionate about the game as you were as a kid. But instead of cheering for a team, you root for the big story. Chronicling the Red Sox in October 2004 was the ultimate "big story."

Instead of writing about it in book form 10 years ago, I let the story age like a fine wine, and waited for the players to gain more perspective on all they had accomplished.

The start of any book project is nerve-racking. Fortunately, I had the perfect leadoff hitter. Derek Lowe invited me to his home in Fort Myers, Florida, in June 2013, a few hours before the Red Sox would play the Rays in St. Petersburg. Lowe was always easy to get along with and fun to talk to, and he gave me confidence right away with his candid recollections that this was going to be a process worth pursuing.

I hadn't seen Keith Foulke in seven years when we sat down in June in the player's family room at Fenway Park. The former closer—an avid hockey fan—was nice enough to give me some time on a night he was in a rush to get across town and watch the Bruins play a Stanley Cup game.

Dave Roberts is the ultimate good guy, and he took me into a small room in the cramped visitors' clubhouse at Fenway on the morning of July 4 and relived practically every moment of his memorable stolen base in vivid detail. Roberts, who was the Padres' first-base coach at the time of our interview and later promoted to bench coach, sounded as animated nine years later as he was the night he stole the base.

ACKNOWLEDGMENTS { 221 }

Gabe Kapler had me meet him at a coffee shop in Malibu, California, a few hours before the Red Sox would face the Angels in Anaheim. His strong feel for the personalities of his teammates was a big help in constructing this book.

I had completely lost track of Orlando Cabrera since his retirement. But Spanish radio broadcaster Uri Berenguer, a close friend of Cabrera's, was nice enough to help me track him down. After Uri put in a good word for me, Cabrera and I had a long phone conversation, which helped me gain a sense of the type of energizing force he was on and off the field for the Red Sox in 2004.

One of the thrills of the 2013 season was sitting in the box seats along the first-base line in the early afternoon at a near-empty Fenway Park with the great Pedro Martinez for over an hour, as he recollected his final season with the Red Sox.

Nobody is more enthusiastic with 2004 Red Sox stories than Kevin Millar, so he took time out from his busy schedule to tell some more one September morning over the phone.

After trying to track down Bill Mueller for a couple of months, the stars aligned just right when the Dodgers assigned their advance scout to study the Red Sox for the final couple of weeks of the 2013 season. In the media dining room at Coors Field, I asked Red Sox PR Director Kevin Gregg, "Have you seen Bill Mueller around?" Kevin said he hadn't. And right at that moment, Mueller walked up next to me. We connected for an interview a couple of days later in the stands at Camden Yards during batting practice and he remains as self-effacing about his accomplishments these days as he was during his playing days.

Mike Timlin filled in as a NESN broadcaster during the final road trip of the season and caught up with me just outside the dugout at Camden Yards on the last day of the regular season. The spiritual leader of the bullpen back in 2004 is the proud owner of four World Series rings, including two with Boston.

Trot Nixon woke me up out of a sound sleep one morning just before the 2013 playoffs, and it was certainly worth it. The gritty right fielder spent over 90 minutes talking about his trying regular season and satisfying postseason and loved talking about all of his teammates.

Johnny Damon remains one of my favorite players that I've covered. He was always quotable, always cordial, and always appreciative that sportswriters had a job to do. When the Red Sox were in St. Petersburg for the Division Series, Johnny had me meet him at a golf club near his home in Orlando. By the way, my good friend Evan Drellich was nice enough to let me borrow his rental car that day. The Mustang ran great, Evan. At any rate, we sat on an outdoor patio for more than an hour, and Damon talked about the highs of playing for the Red Sox, the lows of leaving, and the clear realization that his championship in Boston was more meaningful than the one he got with the Yankees.

The most shocking return call I received during this whole process was from Mark Bellhorn. Hardly anyone had heard from the quiet second baseman since his playing days concluded. But when he called one night from his home in Phoenix, I scrambled for my notes and my tape recorder and enjoyed listening to his recollections of coming up big when it counted most.

Tim Wakefield spoke with me on the phone from Florida while he waited to meet his kids at the circus. The veteran knuckleballer continues to be amazed—and almost overwhelmed—at the phone call he received from Joe Torre the night the Red Sox beat the Yankees in Game 7.

Terry Francona was a treat to cover during his eight seasons as the manager of the Red Sox, and we've kept in touch since he left Boston. Francona did three phone interviews with me for this book, the lengthiest of which took place hours before he would win the 2013 Manager of the Year Award for the job he did in his first year with Cleveland.

There are few athletes in the history of Boston sports who were more equipped to play in the sports-crazed city as Curt Schilling. In a phone conversation that lasted more than an hour, Schilling still got a charge talking about the lift he got playing in Boston. He also shared some terrific recollections from that city. I especially enjoyed listening to Schilling talk about all he absorbed while watching Pedro Martinez from their one season together.

Though Nomar Garciaparra wasn't with the Red Sox anymore when they won the World Series, he felt connected to it, given that he started the year with the team and had been one of the finest players in club history. Garciaparra was heartfelt during our 45-minute chat, speaking openly about the emotions he felt during the spring, summer, and fall of 2004.

Theo Epstein is immersed in the ultimate challenge of trying to turn the Chicago Cubs into a winner. But he took some time out of his busy Hot-Stove season to provide his best remembrances of '04 in a descriptive e-mail that had several great anecdotes.

Certain things had to happen for this book to become a reality. Someone needed to believe in it, and that someone was Tris Coburn of Tilbury House.

MLB.com, my employer since 2001, needed to approve this project. And I want to thank Dinn Mann and Carlton Thompson for giving me the green light to make this book a reality. And also to Dinn and MLB.com for putting their trust in me to do a job a lot of people would love to have, covering the Boston Red Sox. The writers at MLB.com are like family to me. So rather than listing all of them, I'll just simply say thanks to all of them for their friendship and support through the years.

My good friend Pam Kenn, who does a terrific job making former players feel like they are part of the Red Sox family, was a big help in coordinating some of the key interviews for this book.

Thanks to everyone on the Red Sox beat for their support over the years. Rob Bradford deserves special mention, since we've eaten sushi and/or seafood in nearly every Major League city. Thanks to John Tomase for indulging my Larry Bird obsession, which often includes late-night YouTube links to some highlights hopefully one of us hasn't seen before. Alex Speier started on the beat the same year I did, and he's a great friend and an incredible talent. The current beat, which also includes Scott Lauber, Michael Silverman, Gordon Edes, Joe McDonald, Nick Cafardo, Peter Abraham, Sean McAdam, Tim Britton, Brian MacPherson, and Jonny Miller, is full of competitors and good people. And special thanks to up-and-comers Evan Drellich and Jason Mastrodonato, who have made me feel like a worthwhile mentor.

More thanks to writers who inspired me during my youth and still do to this day, including Peter Gammons, Bob Ryan, Dan Shaughnessy, Steve Fainaru, and Jackie MacMullan. The late, great Will McDonough was the best, treating me like gold when I was answering phones and taking high-school scores at the *Boston Globe.*

Also, I owe a debt of gratitude to Bill Chastain and Louise Cornetta, two people who continually expressed faith that this book would be a winning project, lifting me up when I had some self-doubt.

The biggest thanks of all goes to my family, particularly the four people who live with me. My wife Amy is the best. I try to make sure she always knows that. My oldest son Tyler has a better handle on baseball history than almost anyone I know and would have helped me write this book if not for the fact he was busy trying to keep his good standing at Boston Latin Academy. My middle guy Ryan stayed enthusiastic about the book, even when his all-time favorite player Jason Varitek declined to be interviewed. And my youngest son Casey kept me company during marathon transcription sessions, sitting next to me and doing his homework while I typed away.